THE AMERICAN DRAMA SINCE 1918

An Informal History

THE AMERICAN DRAMA

SINCE 1918

An Informal History

by

JOSEPH WOOD KRUTCH
Professor of English · Columbia University

1957   GEORGE BRAZILLER, INC.   NEW YORK

T O

RAYMOND WEAVER

3.4

CONTENTS

FOREWORD

THE purpose of this book is to offer both a connected account and some critical evaluation of playwriting in America since the World War. It is by no means a complete record of theatrical production. Such a record for most of the period covered may be found in Mr. Burns Mantle's annual volumes. It does not always mention all the plays written by even highly successful or important authors. In certain cases the plays seem to me to have little or no significance. On the other hand the intention is to provide what the subtitle promises—an informal history—rather than an essay on this or that aspect of the contemporary American drama. A great many plays are discussed and the attempt is made to provide a continuous account of the course of playwriting in the United States during the two decades ending with the present. I cannot, of course, hope that anyone will be entirely satisfied with either my inclusions or my omissions. For the task which I have undertaken I can claim at least one qualification: I have seen performed on the stage nearly all of the plays mentioned.

The dates in parentheses refer to the first productions in New York.

I am deeply indebted to Professor Dorothy Brewster who read the proofs. She does not necessarily share my opinions.

J. W. K.

FOREWORD TO THE
REVISED EDITION

JUST before the First World War the American drama came suddenly to life. During the immediate postwar years our new plays began for the first time to be widely and successfully produced in the major European countries and for a time, indeed, they all but dominated the European stage. Since 1918 we have had a succession of playwrights who deserve to be called "serious" in a sense that few of their predecessors do, and we are still part of the tradition which was established then.

This book is an attempt to describe them as a group, to define differences and to trace trends. Its method is selective rather than inclusive but it aims to omit no playwrights who seem to the author of more than very temporary significance.

The major part of it was written and published just before the outbreak of the Second World War, but a section has been added to continue the story up to the end of 1956. No changes have been made in the portion dealing with the earlier period. The playwrights and plays are presented as they seemed to the author at the time he wrote, but in general the judgments are those he would want to stand except, perhaps, that, as is almost inevitable, the absolute importance of any striking work is likely to seem greater at the time of its first impact than it does later. It has also not been thought necessary to make corrections where a playwright who has since died is referred to as still living or where a play is called his latest though other plays have been written since. The contemporary point of view makes such anachronisms understandable.

J. W. K.

CHAPTER I

THE NEW AMERICAN DRAMA
AND
THE EUROPEAN TRADITION

IN FEBRUARY, 1915, an enthusiastic group of young amateurs calling themselves the Washington Square Players waved a solemn manifesto in the face of New York drama critics and opened the Bandbox Theater near the corner of 57th Street and Third Avenue. Just a year and a half later another group, equally young and equally enthusiastic, came home from a summer on Cape Cod to take possession of a stable in MacDougal Street to be known thereafter as the Provincetown Theater. Eugene O'Neill acted a role in *Bound East for Cardiff*, the first playlet on its first bill, and thus the New American Theater, which had been born once on Third Avenue, was born again in MacDougal Street. The Neighborhood Playhouse, established in Grand Street just before the opening of the Bandbox, presented European plays almost exclusively. For reasons we shall presently come to, the starting point provided by any of these events is more than a little arbitrary, but a more suitable one would be difficult to discover.

By this time the "modern drama" was already an old story in several of the capitals of Europe. Ibsen was already a classic and more than twenty years had passed since Bernard Shaw, tired of scolding the English managers for their neglect of a non-existent new English drama, had decided to create it for himself. America was far behind the times, and our stage knew Ibsen, Shaw, and the rest chiefly in so far as certain isolated plays had succeeded in establishing themselves commercially on Broadway. Indeed, these foreign masters were beginning to be almost passé as literature without having exerted a very profound influence on the native stage, and the fact had consequences not wholly unfortunate. By 1915 new thought was no longer so very new.

The original manifesto of the Washington Square Players was a pastiche of now familiar phrases— "the future of the American theater—experiment and initiative—commercial managers—not organized for purposes of profit—if you are in sympathy with our aims . . ." Its program was vague and there was no hint of commitment to any social or political program, not even of an enthusiastic concern with the particular variety of moral radicalism associated with the "free theater" in England, Germany, and France. As subsequent productions showed, the new group was nothing if not eclectic in its taste and it was rather more precious than earnest. Its first offering consisted of four short pieces of which one was Maeterlinck's vaguely mystical *Interior*. The other three were Lawrence Langner's *Licensed*, Edward Goodman's *Eugenically Speaking* and a pantomime called *Another Interior*, supposed to take place in a human stomach and having Gastric Juice for its hero.

All three playlets were more impudently than seriously satiric, mildly shocking rather than grim, and the product of authors obviously quite as much under the influence of the newly fashionable Havelock Ellis as impressed by the gloom of Ibsen or the puritanism of Shaw. During the four years of its existence the Washington Square group produced sixty-two one-act plays and six long dramas including *Ghosts* and Andreyev's *The Life of Man*. But its most characteristic achievements were playlets like Susan Glaspell's youthfully brutal *Trifles*, or prankish satires like Philip Moeller's *Helena's Husband*. The atmosphere was predominantly bohemian and the rebelliousness of the group was something which it took a great deal more lightheartedly than rebelliousness had ever been taken by the Ibsenites or the Shavians.

The early productions at the Provincetown Theater were almost as varied as those of the Washington Square Players but its first guiding spirit, George Cram Cook, was of the stuff of which cult

leaders are made and from the beginning its writers
were more earnestly conscious of their mission. With
the exception of O'Neill, none attained great fame
as a playwright but several—John Reed, Floyd Dell,
Maxwell Bodenheim and Mike Gold—either were
or were about to become prominent literary radicals.
It is significant, perhaps, that whereas the Washington Square Players disbanded in the spring of
1918 because America's entry into the War had
produced an atmosphere unfavorable to their activities, the Provincetown Theater continued under various directors to house productions straight through
the War years and offered its stage to O'Neill's
early plays one after another.

Inevitably a discussion of the development of the
contemporary American drama begins with some
reference to these two groups. They made the first
successful attempts to provide a local habitation for
the unconventional American playwright. When
the Washington Square Players were reorganized
after the Armistice as the Theatre Guild, they presently built the only "art theater" which has ever
succeeded in competing directly with the commercial manager in New York. It would, on the other
hand, be easy to create a false impression by suggesting that the development of the American playwright was more closely associated than it actually
was with the activities of these groups. Under various leaderships, the Provincetown group continued

for a number of years and the Guild is still an important institution, but neither has ever had any monopoly of important American plays and the serious American drama very soon ceased to find the doors of the commercial manager closed against it. Broadway learned much from the Provincetown Theater and from the Washington Square Players; but it learned quickly, and the history of the American drama during the past twenty years is almost as much a part of the history of regular commercial productions as it is the history of any art theater.

This fact raises a question. To what extent may we speak of the modern American drama as of something which began at a definite time and which has exhibited characteristics marked enough to furnish the basis for a satisfactory definition? Certainly the playwrights who created it form no school and are the common disciples of no acknowledged master, either native or foreign. Indeed, until the recent rise of the little company of devoted Marxians, none proclaimed himself, as Shaw for example had done, the protagonist of a set of definitely formulated ideas. If individuals occasionally drew up manifestoes there was never any general agreement upon any set of propositions.

It is plain that even the Washington Square Players were clearer concerning what they did not want than what they did. They wanted whatever the established theater would have none of; and in the beginning that included a great deal—the esoteric, the radical, the intellectual, and the merely shocking. The influence of Ibsen and Shaw was plain in some of their productions, but they were not committed to the aims or methods of either. Maeterlinck was just as welcome because, if Maeterlinck resembled Shaw and Ibsen in no other respect, he resembled them in having little appeal for the Broadway manager. For a similar reason Susan Glaspell was an equally "advanced" playwright, whether she was composing the determinedly grim *Trifles* or the naughtily Freudian *Suppressed Desires*. Even the Provincetown group, somewhat more earnest though it was, took O'Neill because he happened to be there, rather than because O'Neill's then only half-declared mysticism fitted any program upon which the various writers and actors were agreed.

The new American playwright wrote at first for the new American theater. And the new American theater was, in the beginning, merely a theater which hoped to find an audience for various kinds of plays, native or foreign, which the more conventional Broadway managers believed to be unacceptable to their public. But the little theater did not keep its monopoly of the new drama for the simple reason that a larger audience awaited it than any except the most enthusiastic had ever supposed. Very soon any sharp distinction between the writer for the new theater and the writer for the general public ceased to exist. The ideals of Arthur Hopkins, Kenneth MacGowan and Winthrop Ames, though they operated in established theaters, were not essentially different from those of the Theatre Guild. Maxwell Anderson's first play was produced by Brock Pemberton in 1923, but Maxwell Anderson is as much a new playwright as if he had begun with the Provincetown Theater. Few plays produced in recent years by the Guild might not have found a "commercial manager" willing to undertake them.

Between 1915 and the present day, various other "insurgent" groups have undertaken to perform plays which, for one reason or another, even the enlarged commercial theater could find no place for. The Neighborhood Playhouse continued to do interesting work in connection with the Henry Street Settlement. The New Playwrights Group, operating for a time uptown and then in Cherry Lane, bewildered a diminishing public with imitations of Russian expressionism. The Theatre Union struggled for a few years with aggressively left-wing dramas, but there was, apparently, no considerable audience for the wares of either the New Playwrights or the Theatre Union, and the influence of neither is demonstrably important.

To say all this is not, however, to say that the new American drama is non-existent as a body of dramatic writing at least loosely definable, or that it has no separate history. Neither is it to say that the various little theaters were not of great service in developing it or that the service was less important merely because the theaters ceased very soon to have any monopoly upon the kind of plays for which they helped to find an audience.

It might, indeed, be possible to define the new drama in terms of intellectual attitudes and artistic creeds. In nearly every case the playwrights who contributed to it were to some extent familiar with playwriting since Ibsen, and their attitudes were determined by the literature of the twentieth century rather than by that of any previous time. Most of them would have aggressively proclaimed themselves "modern," whether or not they could have agreed upon what the adjective meant, and at least a considerable number regarded themselves as in some degree iconoclastic—intellectually, morally and aesthetically. That alone would set them apart from most of the earlier playwrights who tended to be much more conventional and conservative than the novelists or the essay writers contemporary with them. On the whole, the theater had been a last refuge for attitudes and sentiments not only long demoded in serious fiction but the subject of satiric comment in intellectual circles.

To attempt to define the modern American drama in intellectual terms is, however, to be brought face to face with the fact that its intellectual heritage was contemporary literature as a whole, and that individual playwrights often had in common nothing more definite than some sort of participation in characteristically contemporary intellectual life. For that reason it is better to think of them simply as a group homogeneous only in so far as each member looked upon playwriting as an art which need not accept limitations any more severe than those imposed upon the novelist or the poet and might aspire to interpret contemporary life as freely, as imaginatively and with as much originality as contemporary writing in any other form had succeeded in interpreting it. It was not that they all wanted to write any particular kind of play but that they all wanted to create a serious American drama which could take its place as part of American literature.

However vague and however mildly revolutionary that objective may seem at first sight, it did actually mean something and does serve to set apart the playwrights who cherished it, not only from their immediate predecessors, but from most of those who had written in the English language during the nineteenth century.

Most plays produced on the stage during that period were not literature and only a relatively small proportion of them aspired to be. The history of English playwriting is a part of the history of English literature only during brief, long-separated intervals, and the history of American playwriting was never a very important part of the history of

American literature until after the twentieth century had well begun. Between Sheridan and Oscar Wilde there were few successful plays in the English language by men of letters. Disraeli and Sheridan Knowles in England and George Henry Boker in America are dramatists as distinguished as either country can offer for that period.

If occasional playwrights like those just mentioned took themselves with a certain seriousness, the vast majority did not. Plays were commonly written either to exploit the talents of popular performers or as entertainments quite frankly upon a level below that of artistic pretension. In a generous mood Bernard Shaw can find words of praise for Tom Robertson, and historians of the American stage praise the work of James A. Hearn or Clyde Fitch. But whatever merits any of them had those merits are purely relative. All are praised for a certain degree of sincerity and a certain measure of realism but these qualities are remarkable only if their work is compared with that of other playwrights, not if compared with the fiction written at about the same time. It is not merely that they seem conventional, unreal, timid, and old-fashioned by the "smart" standards of today; they seem almost equally conventional, unreal, timid, and old-fashioned if they are read with the best novels of the time in mind. Through Victorian fiction ran the strong current of Victorian thought; but a generation which read Meredith and James and Howells, and which was ready to accept Tolstoi and Dostoievski and Zola in translation, could find on the stage no contemporary work better than that of Robertson or Clyde Fitch.

That it tolerated them at all is proof merely that it expected little, that the theater had almost been given up as a medium for serious expression and that its puerilities were accepted in much the same spirit that intelligent people today accept as inevitable the puerilities of the motion picture. With only a few exceptions, the American playwright of the late nineteenth and early twentieth centuries tended to think of himself, not as an artist, but as an artisan practicing an absurdly specialized trade. His favorite maxim and the favorite maxim of his admirers was the oft-quoted dictum, "plays are not written but rewritten"; by which it was meant to imply simply that the best play was the one which most painstakingly exploited the tricks of the trade. Bronson Howard's famous essay on the art of playwriting is concerned almost exclusively, not with truth to life, sincerity of feeling, or with any aesthetic consideration, but with what are assumed to be the prejudices of a contemporary audience and the devices by means of which those prejudices may be satisfied. He does not assume that the playwright has any serious concern with the truth that is in him, and it is this fact rather than any change

which may have taken place since his time in intellectual convictions or standards of taste which sets
him apart from dramatists who regard themselves
rather as artists than as artisans.

In England and Germany the theater had re-
emerged as an institution to which a man of serious ambitions might devote himself chiefly because
Henrik Ibsen happened to write for the stage. The
backwardness of the drama had been nowhere more
conspicuous than on the intellectual side and here,
by a curious accident, was an arresting thinker who
wrote in the dramatic form. He was read not so
much because people were interested in plays, as because they were interested in ideas. The fact that
ideas were to be found in works intended for acting
furnished the startling suggestion that the theater
might be used, not as a refuge for concoctions sub-
literary in form and childish in thought and sentiment, but as a platform for the dissemination of advanced ideas.

For that reason the beginnings of the modern
drama in both England and Germany were somewhat more closely bound up than they were in
America with "advanced thinkers" whose primary
aim it was to change ideas and, if possible, remake
society. By 1915 there was already a considerable
body of serious foreign playwriting, and ambitious
American playwrights had as models not only Ibsen
and Hauptmann and Strindberg and Shaw, but also

the folk drama of Synge, the rapt mysticism of
Maeterlinck and the impudence of Schnitzler. They
knew that audiences had been found for playwrights
who demanded that they be listened to with at least
as much intelligence as the novelist had always expected. But they knew also that the serious play was
not, as Shaw seemed to think, inevitably a play
which preached explicitly some moral or social doctrine. They came to playwriting, not as a group
united by adherence to a set of ideas, but as a group
in which some members had little in common with
certain other members except the assumption that
the drama could be a branch of contemporary literature and concern itself primarily with sincere expression rather than with the tricks of a trade. Thus,
while the new American playwrights were segre-
gated from most of their immediate predecessors by
their serious literary ambition, they were also somewhat set apart from the European founders of the
modern drama by their less intimate concern with
radically novel ideas.

The fundamental premises of their thinking were
not, indeed, very different from those of their potential audience. They were compelled to overcome
that inertia which resists all artistic innovation, but
the majority of them never faced the kind of hostil-
ity which greeted Ibsen and Shaw. As a matter of
fact, many of the best American plays of the last
two decades were immediately successful. The pio-

neers of the new drama in Europe often attacked
their audiences because, like Shaw, they professed
to believe that attacking audiences was the only useful occupation for a playwright, or because, like Ibsen, the stories they had to tell were meaningless
unless interpreted in connection with a set of ideas
foreign to the public before which they were presented. Indeed the peculiarities of Ibsen's technique
arise from this difficulty and its special excellence
consists in part in the fact that he solves better than
any other dramatist has succeeded in solving the
problem created when it is necessary, not only to
tell a story, but to expound at the same time the
moral background against which it has meaning.

The new American dramatists, on the other hand,
faced no such problem or, at worst, faced it in no
such inclusive a form. Such radical social and moral
ideas as appear, for example, in the earlier plays of
O'Neill were only relatively new and relatively
unpopular; he shocked no audience as Ibsen had
shocked his public and O'Neill was more forcefully
disturbing than most of his successful fellows. New
thought was, as has already been remarked, no
longer new. A good deal of the talk which lingered,
even during the twenties, about "daring ideas" was
no more than cant since it had long ceased to require any particular courage to question either the
social or the moral code. Attacks upon "puritanism"
were almost as safe as attacks upon "snobbery" had
been during the Victorian era, and even the most

conservative were no longer startled to hear con-
servatism denounced. New ideas may have had a
certain novelty in the theater but they were new
nowhere else and the new playwrights were at their
worst when they whipped dead dogs with self-con-
scious courage. They were at their best when they
ceased expounding their philosophy and turned to
the task of writing plays which assumed in the audiences for which they were intended the convictions and attitudes which familiarity with modern
literature had established.

In very recent years the aims and position of the
Marxian dramatists has been somewhat analogous
to that of Shaw and Ibsen. The Messrs. Lawson and
Sklar and Odets are convinced, that is to say, that
the meaning of such stories as they have to tell cannot be understood without a radical revision of the
convictions of the theater-going public. But of the
important dramatists who emerged between 1916
and 1930 few were intellectually at outs with a potential public to the extent that Ibsen had been or
that Mr. Odets was to be again, and the fact must be
borne in mind if the nature of such excellence as
they actually possess is to be understood. They were
pioneers in so far as they were the first Americans
to exploit the dramatic possibilities of certain aspects of modern life and of modern attitudes, but
they were not intellectually pioneers as Ibsen and
Shaw had been.

The distinction is probably one which they them-

selves did not always clearly recognize. Sidney Howard, having written in *They Knew What They
Wanted* a brilliantly effective theatrical piece which
took for granted moral judgments which previous
generations would have found it impossible to make,
turned, in *The Silver Cord*, to the diagramming of
a Freudian case history which owed such interest as
it possessed almost exclusively to an abstract problem in psychology. So, too, O'Neill argued the case
for racial equality in *All God's Chillun Got Wings*
and hesitated between sociological preachment and
tragedy in *The Hairy Ape* before he came to the
final realization that his talents lay in that region
which is the furthest removed from argumentation.
It is also a distinction which critics have sometimes
overlooked when, for example, they have tried to
praise O'Neill as a social thinker—which he is not
—and when, failing to find in *Mourning Becomes
Electra* a novel social or moral thesis, they have con-
cluded that it was insignificant as drama.

The difference is nevertheless real between the
play which exploits the emotional consequences of
an attitude whose existence is taken for granted and
the play which undertakes to define or to win acceptance for the attitudes which alone can give its
story the meaning which the author intended. It is
a difference not too clearly perceived but responsible for much confused wrangling about "propaganda" versus "art" and one which can best be dis-

cussed, not as a question of the right way versus the wrong way to write a play, but as a question concerning both the nature of the talents of an individual author and the intellectual atmosphere in which he happens to be working. Ideas are born and ideas are propagated. They are also explored, assimilated, and lived with. Shaw and Ibsen happen to be dramatists concerned with the propagation of ideas. So, for example, was Mr. Odets—at least at the beginning of his career. Shakespeare was a dramatist who explored the emotional consequences of the fundamental attitudes which he borrowed from the Elizabethan man in the street. And most of the best American dramatists of the past two decades have been, in that one respect, more like Shakespeare than like Shaw.

It would not be, as it is, necessary thus to labor a point had not Shaw himself thrown the weight of his eloquence and his fame behind the opinion that an effort to change conditions or ideas is the sole legitimate concern, not only of the artist, but of every decent man. He was prepared to scorn even a Shakespeare if Shakespeare could be convicted of the crime of "borrowing his morality." But Shaw failed—or perhaps only pretended to fail—to distinguish between what happened to be true of himself in the situation in which he found himself and what was necessarily true of any artist at any time. The plays which Shaw had to write could not be written except upon the basis of a morality which he at one time boasts of having invented, at another freely attributes to Samuel Butler, and at still another more correctly credits to Ibsen, Nietzsche and Karl Marx. It is not that the accepted traditions of no theater and of no civilization can be made the basis of genuine literature. It is merely that Shaw happened to possess a certain kind of mind and also, perhaps more importantly, found the theater in a peculiar situation. That theater was behind the times, and the times themselves were at one of the cultural crises which are a recurrent phenomenon in all cultures. It is not that the ideas of the man in the street can never furnish the basis of any drama. The ideas of the Elizabethan man in the street had done so. It is, first, that the ideas of the English man in the street were due for a change about 1890 and, second, that the morality of the conventional English drama was not even the morality of the contemporary man in the street. It was the morality which the Victorian had tried in his most sentimental moments to convince himself that he believed in. The ideas of even so "advanced" a playwright as Pinero, whatever reputation for daring he may have acquired in the theater, can hardly have been other than absurdly stuffy to that part of the public which had read George Eliot—to say nothing of more recent novelists, native or foreign.

Such a situation provides the playwright with a

great opportunity of one particular kind since it permits him to become an intellectual force brought
directly to bear upon the thinking, even possibly the
legislation, of his time. It makes it possible for him
to become a prophet, not only in the large sense that
all great poets are prophets, but in the more limited sense that he wins a body of earnest disciples
who eagerly scan his successive works for obiter
dicta, who cite him as an authority on social or
moral questions, and who even come to him as to an
oracle with a demand for an answer to some specific
problem. Shaw, indeed, carefully stage-managed his
appearance in such a role and loved to emphasize
the contention that his choice of the dramatic form
as the vehicle for his messages was mere accident.
Ibsen, on the other hand, took refuge from eager
"seekers" in the gruff proclamation that his business
was to ask questions rather than to answer them
and, late in life, protested sadly that he had been
more of a poet and less of a social philosopher than
was generally supposed.

On the other hand, such a situation creates limitations and difficulties also. Though written for the
stage, the plays of Ibsen and Shaw have been more
often read than acted and have exerted a far wider
influence in the study than in the theater. Nor can
there be much doubt that in the case of Shaw, whose
gifts as a "poet" are far less than those of Ibsen, the
plays will be acted less and less. The burden of dis-

quisition which they carry is far too heavy, and they sink under the weight of expositions and arguments too familiar to be longer interesting. Except for two or three of the very best, even Ibsen's comedies and tragedies are clogged with explanations or pronouncements which now impede an action they are no longer necessary to render meaningful even though they may have seemed at one time both indispensable and, actually, the most interesting passages in the play.

Modern audiences take for granted what it was once necessary to establish. The more successful the author is in his efforts to change either a condition or an attitude, the less intrinsically interesting he soon becomes. Nothing is duller than a social problem which has been solved, and nothing is duller than an epigram which has become a platitude. Many of Shaw's paradoxes fall flat for the simple reason that they now appear as truisms. That he is often as much responsible as any other one man for making them just that does nothing to render the plays more interesting, however much it may contribute to our respect for him as a figure historically important. Nor are the solemner theses of Ibsen's *raisonneurs* always exempt from the effects of the process by which the startling becomes the commonplace. When Mrs. Alving, caught by Parson Manders in the possession of certain unspecified books of a "dangerous" character, is asked if she feels any

"better" for having read them, and when she replies, "Not better, perhaps, but safer," the effect is
no longer that of a brilliant thrust. We blush as we
blush when we hear a "serious thinker" proclaim
with an air of defiance his opinion that the problems of sex ought to be discussed with frankness.
The pamphlet is the least enduring form of literature, and the more successfully a pamphlet achieves
its purpose the deader it becomes.

No American playwright of the last two decades
either found or created an opportunity to become a
prophet in the sense that Ibsen and Shaw were
prophets. At least two, Eugene O'Neill and Maxwell Anderson, aspired to be poets in a sense that no
successful American playwright had aspired to be a
poet since the days when William Vaughn Moody
seemed about to succeed. But in so far as even these
two introduced into the theater specific ideas and intellectual or moral attitudes challenging those then
current, these ideas and attitudes were largely borrowed from the literature of the recent past and addressed to an audience already pretty well prepared
to accept them.

To whatever extent this fact may have detracted
from the importance of the new playwrights, it also
conferred upon them certain advantages. They were
compelled to be primarily playwrights in the sense
that whatever relative interest or novelty or power
they may have possessed was largely dependent upon

their ability to carry on from the point where the exponent of new ideas leaves off, upon their ability to vivify such ideas in terms of situation and character, to explore their meaning in terms of specific human lives. And one result of this fact is that though most of them have been published and a few rather widely read, their plays have almost without exception had an even more effective life in the playhouse itself.

Another result is that whatever the *degree* of such excellence as they may have, its *kind* is of the kind which has distinguished most of the great playwrights of the great epochs. It is true that most of the individual plays which achieved success with public and commentators alike will probably never be revived on Broadway or live beyond the few seasons which gave them scattered production by provincial stock companies or amateur groups. It is, moreover, by no means certain that a single one of their works will continue to be regarded as having permanent value. But the question will be decided on the basis of their excellence in their kind, and if they fail to survive it will be exclusively because they were not good enough, because they did not succeed well enough in what they tried to do, not because their ideas have grown stale. And that indicates the way in which they differ from those plays of which Shaw's are the most conspicuous example in English and the *raison d'être* of which is the at-

tempt to introduce new premises and new conclusions of an abstractly intellectual sort. No matter
how good *Widowers' Houses* may be, its interest is
of a kind inevitably temporary and if any of its author's other plays should survive, as they probably
will, it will be, not because of anything which is
part of their declared intention, but because they
happen to possess incidental wit enough to keep
them sweet. Shaw himself seemed to recognize, at
least, the distinction when he dismissed O'Neill with
what is, coming from him, a double insult—when
he called him a "banshee Shakespeare." Probably
he did not at the moment recall that Voltaire had
described Shakespeare himself as a "barbarian genius" and if the fact is cited here it is by no means
with the intention of suggesting that O'Neill is of
Shakespearean proportions. The point is simply that
he, like most of the best of his contemporaries, resembles Shakespeare and the majority of other per-
manently interesting dramatists in resting his claim
to attention, not on the basis of any new morality
which he had invented, but upon his success in cre-
ating characters and arousing passions. For that reason a critical discussion of the recent American
drama is most fruitful when it is a discussion, not
in terms of "ideas," but in terms of imagination
and literary form.

CHAPTER II

THREE NEW REALISTS

IN 1923 the Theatre Guild produced Elmer Rice's first serious independent play, *The Adding Machine*. Up to that time neither the Provincetown group, the Washington Square Players, nor the Guild itself had introduced any new American playwright except O'Neill who was destined to achieve lasting prominence. A considerable number of persons later to be heard of in various connections had had contact with the Provincetown, and the Guild had popularized a number of ambitious foreign plays including *Heartbreak House* and *Back to Methuselah*. But none of the "art theaters" had been able to obtain any American works except those of O'Neill which were of more than transitory interest.

Meanwhile, however, there had begun to appear in the commercial theater various plays whose tone was not quite that which had been most familiar on our stage. Jesse Lynch Williams's *Why Marry?* (1917) had unmistakable Shavian touches a little startling in a theater accustomed to think of comedy in terms of Winchell Smith's mechanically expert mixtures of homely sentiment and the gospel of material success. Several of Clare Kummer's polite farces, beginning in 1916 with *Good Gracious Annabelle*, had been marked by a kind of sophistication which probably owed as much to *The Importance of Being Earnest* as to any other source of inspiration but were "smart" in a sense that most popular plays were not, and in 1921 *Wake Up, Jonathan*, by Hatcher Hughes and Elmer Rice, had sought to give intellectual body to comedy. In 1920, a dramatization of Zona Gale's *Miss Lulu Bett* brought into the theater a kind of realism which had for some years been making its way in the novel, and in the following year *Dulcy*, by George Kaufman and Marc Connelly, pointed satire in a direction more familiar to readers of H. L. Mencken than to frequenters of Broadway.

It was, however, during the years 1923 and 1924 that the emergence of a new tendency became most clearly evident in the commercial theater and during the same years that several dramatists who were to remain prominent for some time to come first attracted conspicuous notice. Besides *The Adding Machine*, 1923 saw also *Icebound*, a determinedly grim study of frustration by Owen Davis, and *The White Desert*, Maxwell Anderson's first produced play. With 1924 came the sensational success of *What Price Glory*, by Laurence Stallings and Maxwell Anderson, and the almost equal success of Sidney Howard's *They Knew What They Wanted*. The

same year brought also George Kelly's *The Show-
Off* and Hatcher Hughes's prize-winning *Hell Bent
fer Heaven*. Shortly after and during the same season (January, 1925), the Guild produced *Processional*, certainly the best of the plays by John Howard Lawson, a writer who had been introduced to
New York with the adolescent but interesting *Roger
Bloomer* in 1923 and whose subsequent career as a
theatrical rebel kept his name before the public.

Meanwhile the fortunes of O'Neill, the earliest
as well as much the most prolific of those who were
to figure largely in the history of the contemporary
drama, continued commercially precarious. In addition to the short plays of the sea and several other
one-act pieces now almost totally forgotten, he produced some seventeen plays before 1928, but until
the Guild gave *Marco Millions* in that year he had
got no firm foothold on Broadway, though two of
his plays, *Beyond the Horizon* (1920) and *Anna
Christie* (1921), had attracted some attention there
and the last had enjoyed a considerable success. Two
other very inferior efforts, *Gold* (1921) and *Welded*
(1924), had been failures. Nevertheless, his best
work up to that time—*The Emperor Jones*, *The
Hairy Ape*, *Desire Under the Elms* and *The Great
God Brown*—as well as a number of his other plays,
had been compelled to see the light either at the
Provincetown or Neighborhood Playhouses or at
the Greenwich Village Theater on lower Seventh

Avenue. If, however, the commercial theater was still dubiously hospitable to O'Neill, it had by this time found a definite place for plays which were generally regarded as in some way experimental, unconventional, or daring.

To several of the dramatists whose names have just been mentioned we shall later return in different connections, but we may choose now for examination two plays, *What Price Glory* and *They Knew What They Wanted*, significant for more than one reason. Both were extremely successful and both illustrate the extent to which certain new tendencies were compatible with an appeal not precisely popular in the broadest sense of the term but broad enough to keep both many months on Broadway. Neither illustrates, as certain other plays of our generation do, the probably inevitable tendency of any drama to crystallize into formal comedy or tragedy as soon as it reaches a certain level of excellence. Nor does either exhibit markedly what is probably an equally inevitable tendency of any drama approaching the same level to attempt the creation of a language either more rhythmical, more eloquent, or more polished than that which serves the playwright whose avowed intention is to produce the illusion of everyday speech. Indeed, both Mr. Howard and Mr. Stallings (though perhaps not Mr. Anderson even then) would probably have avowed at least as great a respect for the successful crafts-

man of the theater as for the consciously experimental drama. And yet both plays were based upon attitudes rather new to the theater and both are not
only excellent theatrical pieces but also well above
the usual level of popular contemporary literature.

Despite the Briticism which serves as its title,
What Price Glory is thoroughly American in the
only way in which the British will consent to define
the term—it is, that is to say, robust, colloquial,
bustling, and violent. The chief characters are Captain Flagg, a tough professional soldier, and certain
of his amateur companions who have been long
enough at war to adopt his cynical attitude toward
the business of saving democracy in the mud of
northern France. Whatever noble aims may moti-
vate those remote authorities responsible for the
conduct of the enterprise as a whole, these members
of the rank and file are as little concerned with such
aims as they are with the comprehensive strategic
plan which requires them to take part in what must
appear random movements and meaningless skir-
mishes. Fighting has become a mere professional
routine and filth, no less than bloodshed, a normal
concomitant of daily life. Such an existence is toler-
able neither because they are sacrificing themselves
in a great crusade nor because they any longer look
forward to a return to what would seem, by now,
the abnormality of a peaceful existence. It is toler-
able only because they have learned to compensate

for the loss of all usual human independence and security with ribald indulgence in certain licenses respecting language and conduct which the conditions of a soldier's life enormously enlarge. As men who have lost all dignity as individuals and all right to any ultimate control over their lives or destinies, they turn naturally to those satisfactions which can be snatched hastily in brief moments of independence. They get methodically drunk and they fornicate semi-publicly because reticence is not a virtue likely to be cultivated where the right to no sort of privacy is recognized. Their talk is almost exclusively profane or bawdy because they labor under the necessity of convincing themselves that so ribald a life is the only one a realist would care to live.

The plot concerns a quarrel, half-earnest, half-contentiously sportive, over the favors of a farmer's daughter whom neither of the rivals regards in a romantic light, and the solution is reached when both automatically drop the affair to hurry off together in response to a summons to action. This plot is developed through a series of not unfamiliar melodramatic devices, but the conclusion enforces the point—which is simply that, for all their ribald recklessness, the combatants are so disciplined as to respond automatically to the call of "duty." And the effectiveness of the play depends primarily, not upon the conventional melodramatic incidents, but upon the convincing robustness of the language and the originality of the implied study of the war-time psychology of the seasoned soldier.

Reviewing it in *The Nation* on the occasion of its original performance—and it is worth while for the sake of the discussion to remember what sort of impression it created at the moment for which it was intended—I wrote:

> "Maxwell Anderson and Laurence Stallings have seized the perfect moment. During the five years which have passed since the Armistice, nerves have regained their tone but memory has not been dimmed, and thus they have managed to set down without a suspicion of hysteria and without a suspicion of sentimentality their vision of that strange and terrible phenomenon, modern war. They have described its brutality without rancor and pictured the inhuman verve and endurance of its heroes without blinking the ugly uselessness of the circumstances which called those virtues forth, so that they have written unquestionably the finest play of the war which America has seen. Moreover, they have imbued it with so robust a spirit that we are treated to the strange spectacle of a tragedy which is played to the accompaniment of a continual ripple of laughter without once ceasing to be powerful and moving.
>
> "*What Price Glory* is written, not out of thought, but out of experience. The terrible impartiality of its verisimilitude, which none of the

opposing camps of thought can deny, comes from
its authors' realization that whatever their own
thoughts may be, what they have seen is more
tremendous than their theories. Thus, though
they have described, not argued, admirable judgment has played its part. Keen intelligence, sweeping the field of memory, has seized upon the
significant fact that, dramatically, the most important thing about war is not death and destruction
but the way of life which it develops, that the
great conflict just passed lasted long enough and
drew into itself a sufficient number of men to develop a civilization or anti-civilization of its own,
with a language, a philosophy, and a whole *kultur* as different from that of normal life as the
kultur and philosophy of the Stone Age were different, and yet perfectly adapted to the conditions of life as it was lived. Upon the description
of this way of life they have concentrated their
attention.

"It was Mr. Stallings, it seems, who actually
participated in this new and tremendous mode of
life, and he possessed a spiritual robustness sufficient to grasp and understand it. He has caught
the Rabelaisian rhythm of its speech in which
mouth-filling oaths are an appropriate element
contributing to the epic vigor of expression, and
also the rhythm of a strange life dominated by
simple values and inexorable demands. Captain
Flagg, professional soldier, is the perfect type
which such conditions require and strive to pro-

duce. Brutal to his men, because he knows that
brutality alone can fit them to endure the life
they need, foul-mouthed because only so can he
give vent to his emotions, and heroically faithful
to his job for no reason at all except that men
must have something, however irrational, to believe in and serve, he cultivates, unashamed,
drunkenness and lust in every leisure moment,
not because of any innate depravity, but because
they alone are anodynes powerful and simple
enough to drug such an existence. His men, from
the top sergeant down, imitate as closely as their
capacities will permit his adjustment to monstrous conditions; drinking like him, swearing like
him, and, like him, reckless in all things, they
nevertheless have come to accept hardship and
death as normal and unescapable. They have forgotten the desires, the beliefs, and the habits of a
former life, and developed new, hardy souls fit
for the new life which they lead.

"Perhaps the concluding incident will best
convey the spirit of the piece. Just back from the
lines, the captain and his sergeant have failed to
conclude a duel to the death over an innkeeper's
daughter who is too generous with her favors.
Then word comes to move forward again. 'Good
God!' ejaculates the captain, almost dead from
exhaustion, 'it's the first time in months that I
have had a real reason for fighting and now I
can't fight. Tell 'em I won't go.' But he does go,
and his sergeant with him, both quite willing, if

both should return, to take up at the earliest moment of leisure their little private tragedy of
lust."

The play, produced it is worth noting by Arthur
Hopkins and hence at least technically in the "commercial" theater, was tremendously successful and
widely discussed. But it was not always discussed in
terms relevant to its most significant aspects. It is, for
one thing, necessary to remember that the American intellectual's somewhat ill-defined revolt against
puritanism, optimism, sentiment, and the genteel
tradition, still furnished the most familiar topic for
current literary discussion and that the "daring" of
the language no less than the ribaldry of certain of
the incidents in *What Price Glory* were often cited
either in condemnation or as though they were the
most important elements of the play's generally recognized excellence. A current anecdote related that
a gentle grandmother, who was observed searching
the floor after the performance, replied to a query
from the young man who had brought her to the
performance by remarking with absent-minded
mildness, "I've lost my god-damn spectacles."

A more significant because a more subtle misconception was implied in much of the discussion over
the question whether the play was to be regarded as
a pacifist tract or as a justification of war in terms
of a kind of ribald romanticism. Heywood Broun,

for example, proclaimed the excellence of the play while at the same time he shook his head gravely over what he regarded as its plain implication that war was, after all, fun. There were, perhaps, as many who agreed with him as there were those who held that it was, on the contrary, a bitter exposé of the ugly truth behind the heroic legend of the war for democracy. In a sense, both were right and both were wrong. So far as the dramatis personae are concerned, their attitude is as far from the rationalized anti-militarism of, for instance, John Dos Passos' already well-known novel, *Three Soldiers*, as it is from the *dulce et decorum est* of official patriotism. And whatever may have been the formal intellectual convictions of the authors, the attitude which controlled the creative workings of their imagination was an attitude not far removed from that of their characters.

Mr. Stallings, as subsequent events in his life have indicated, is a man by temperament not unin- clined to adventure approached in sanguine, robust, and probably not too analytic a temper. Doubtless actual participation in war had turned out to be a good deal less romantic than at a distance it ap- peared likely to be. But he was not as wholly in- capable as men like Dos Passos or Remarque were of participating, to some extent at least, in an enter- prise for which the temperaments of the two latter rendered them totally unfit. In the play he is interested rather in dealing with the nature of the adjustments which ordinary men made and the kind of experience which resulted from such adjustments than he is in formulating a moral or sociological thesis. He and his collaborator carried their purely intellectual processes as far as was necessary to give form and consistent tone to their play, but they did not carry them to the point where a doctrine crystallizes out of an imaginatively recreated experience. For that reason their work has a vividness and a warmth not easy to maintain in any play less close to an actual experience even though embodying a judgment upon such an experience further evolved in the direction of abstract statement.

What effect, if any, the piece may have had as propaganda against war is not a question necessary to ask as part of the present discussion. The authors were not inventing a new morality calculated to shock and outrage a public unaware that any new morality was called for. They hardly carried the *thinking* of their audience further than the audience itself, already cynical on the subject of military glory, had already carried it. What they did do was take advantage of the fact that a play which had never been written—which until about that time could not have been written—was now possible: a play which assumed that the psychology of the soldier could be interpreted in terms such as those they chose and still remain immediately comprehensible. The great and instantaneous success of the play is itself proof of the fact that its moral assumptions were those which a large public was ready to accept even if it had never before accepted them so explicitly.

Of course the play could never have been written if the new drama of Europe, as well as the disrupting moral experience of the War, had not prepared the way for it. In the first place, the ribald frankness of the language would not have been endured by an audience which had not been gradually accustomed to plain speaking by the more solemn audacities of the earlier playwrights. But that is by no means all. Only an audience which had achieved a far more inclusive repudiation of the ideal of respectability could accept as heroes such thoroughly unrespectable characters; only an audience for whom long-established ideological complexes involving patriotism, courage, and honor had completely disintegrated could have comprehended, much less accepted, the attitudes taken by the authors toward persons or events. But the important thing is that the play was not primarily concerned with persuading the audience into a position which would have made the drama understandable. It took for granted the fact that this audience was already prepared to understand. The moral ideas of Messrs. Stallings and Anderson were almost as nearly those of the man in the street as the ideas of Shakespeare had

ever been. But of course the ideas of the American
man in the street *circa* 1924 differed from those of
the Elizabethan by, among other things, just the
results of that revolution in which Ibsen and Shaw
had played so large a part. And, in any event, the
dramatic author was no longer at war with his
audience.

In other words, the purpose of the play was to
discover how the experiences of two uncultivated
but emancipated individuals who found themselves
committed to a conflict which they were unable to
idealize could be arranged into a satisfactory pattern. In another age their experiences would have
taken shape around the ideas of patriotism, heroism, and honor. Their exaltations and their suffer-
ings would have acquired a meaning by reference
to these fixed points. But for these particular heroes
these particular fixed points no longer existed. They
could no more reconcile themselves to their adventures by conceiving themselves as heroic defenders
of a mystic fatherland than they could dignify their
interlude with the farmer's buxom daughter by at-
tributing to it the traditional values of romantic
love. When life becomes as painful and as precarious as theirs was, then the human need to make life
justify itself becomes desperately acute, and, in
their case, the justification had to be made in terms
of that witty animality which alone had been left
them.

The play was immediately and enormously popular because in its essence it was closely relevant to the needs of its audience. Some part of that audience had recently emerged from literally similar adventures. Most of the rest of it had been participating in them vicariously at least. Emotionally the War had not been assimilated. Desperate efforts had been made to achieve that assimilation by interpreting it in terms of conventional patriotism and conventional conceptions of martial glory. But so far at least as the more intellectual section of the public was concerned, those efforts had been unsuccessful. Its emotional response to events had been too full of conflicts to achieve clear form. But by choosing as the heroes of their melodrama two scamps who had unconsciously but completely repudiated any effort to attribute conventional dignity to their roles, the authors were able to illustrate a perfectly consistent attitude toward events and a perfectly consistent emotional response to them. What is more, this emotional response, or rather this set of emotional responses, could be made to yield a certain desperate exultation not wholly unjoyous, and the result was to achieve for the audience a clarification and a release. A channel had been provided for the discharge of confused emotions. Here was a pattern into which, without recourse to dead ideas, hitherto confused reactions could be arranged, a channel through which pent-up emotions could flow.

Most recent discussions of the modern drama tend to employ various quasi-technical terms unknown to earlier criticism. The classification of plays as "comedies," "tragedies," or "dramas" had gradually come to seem of minor importance and those regarded as possessing the highest interest were labeled "new" or "advanced" on the assumption that those adjectives had a special and commonly understood meaning. The term "thesis play" was invented to describe a certain dramatic form and, in fact, serves well enough to identify the sort of play represented by Shaw's *Widowers' Houses* or Brieux's *Damaged Goods*, though it is less satisfactory as applied to much of Ibsen as well as some of Shaw for the simple reason that it implies a more exclusive concern with a single narrowly defined proposition that is characteristic of, let us say, *Hedda Gabler* or even *Man and Superman*. Still more recently the designation "revolutionary drama" has come into use, often accompanied by the assumption that all literature worthy of the name may be seen to have been revolutionary at least in relation to its age. The term now plays so prominent a part in contemporary discussion that in the analysis of such a play as we are now examining it becomes interesting, even necessary, to ask what the phrase "revolutionary play" really implies and to what extent it is here applicable.

Unless the term means, as it occasionally does, simply a play which preaches the desirability of a political revolution, a "revolutionary play" can be only a play whose moral, intellectual, or social implications involve a revolution in the attitude of author or audience toward moral, intellectual or social questions. And if that definition be accepted I suggest "classical play" as a convenient designation for such plays as proceed on a contrary assumption, on the assumption that is to say, that the story which its author is about to tell has meaning in relation to the convictions and attitudes current in the society for which he writes. In other words, a revolutionary play is one which "invents its morality," a "classical play" one which, in Shaw's contemptuous phrase, "borrows" it.

In terms of such a classification *Ghosts* was a "revolutionary play" and so, as we shall see, Clifford Odets's *Paradise Lost* or *Golden Boy* may be. But *What Price Glory* appears to be "revolutionary" only if we think of it in connection with the morality then most familiar on the stage rather than with that already at least developing in the minds of a potential public large enough to make the play a conspicuous financial success. Indeed such a play is one which is again establishing with the ideas of an audience the relationship characteristic of the "classic" drama. It was, in other words, not concerned so much with changing ideas as with exploring the emotional possibilities of life in a culture based upon the acceptance of certain newly established moral and intellectual convictions.

And to many, among whom I include myself, it seems that the means which literature has at its disposal make it peculiarly fitted for that task rather than for any other. It begins where abstract thinkers leave off, not in the sense that it is concerned either with advocating or revolutionizing their ideas, but in the sense that it reveals the significance of these ideas in relation to the more complex and intangible, as well as more intimate, experiences of living. Shakespeare, as Shaw charges, did not undertake to modify very importantly the ideas of the Elizabethan man in the street. What he did do was to illustrate what life could be made to yield when judged and interpreted in terms of these ideas. And what can be said of Shakespeare can be said also of Racine or Molière or almost any other of the great dramatists, whose business has usually been primarily with what eludes the direct statement of the philosopher, the moralist, or the statesman.

The crisis in sentiment of which *What Price Glory* took advantage and which, no doubt, it helped to develop was, after all, one specifically concerned with a particular set of attitudes grouped about a single phenomenon—the World War. But a similar crisis had long existed in the public attitude toward many aspects of contemporary life. The novel had already done much to exploit it and the impulse to exploit it in the theater was finding expression in other dramatists. During the season 1924–25 the enthusiasm of dramatic critics and of the public alike was divided between *What Price Glory* and three other plays of some literary pretension—*The Show-Off, Hell Bent fer Heaven*, and *They Knew What They Wanted*—of which the last, especially, is both continuingly interesting as a play and significant of the trend under discussion.

They Knew What They Wanted was Mr. Howard's third play. He had come from California and the University of California to spend one year in Professor Baker's class at Harvard. After that he had served in the ambulance corps on the Western Front during the early days of the War and as a captain in the flying service after the United States became involved. He had also collaborated on a book of reporting, *The Labor Spy*, and produced the play *Swords* (1921) and *Bewitched* (1924)—the latter in collaboration with Edward Sheldon. The first of these plays was a romantic melodrama with more than a suggestion of pastiche; the second a romance rather poetic than realistic. Both achieved a certain *succès d'estime* without attracting any large audience, and both were apprentice work for a man who found himself as a dramatist in *They Knew What They Wanted.*

He had had no connection with any of the little theaters of New York and the extent to which he combined a certain unconventionality of outlook with an unusually acute sense of what were the technical requirements of a commercially successful play made the Guild—now established as an "art theater" through its production of numerous "advanced" foreign plays—a natural choice from among those who might have undertaken the production. Unlike *What Price Glory* the play is not topical; it deals with no specific or recurrent social problem; and in so far as it may be said to have any thesis at all that thesis is a highly generalized one.

The story is concerned with a gentle, lonely, uneducated and somewhat bewildered girl working as a waitress on the West Coast. She receives by mail a proposal of marriage and from the address of the sender (a vineyard some distance away) she leaps to the conclusion that he is the young man whose name she does not know but whom she has liked as a patron of the restaurant where she works. She accepts the proposal, and goes to the vineyard only to realize shortly after her arrival that she has committed herself, not to the young man who is staying there, but to the proprietor—a genial Italian of middle age anxious to have a head for his establishment and, above all, the mother of an heir. In what is perhaps the finest scene of the play she conceals her mistake and her dismay with exquisite natural tact, and rapidly concludes that, in her loneliness and helplessness, she is willing to accept the respectable security now offered, especially since, as is obvious, the young man has no thought of marrying her.

The intended bridegroom suffers an accident which necessitates a postponement of the wedding. A love affair develops between the girl and the young man who are thrown together in the house; they yield once, but once only, to the temptation and presently the girl realizes that she is pregnant. When the guilty pair, appalled by their treachery, confess to the Italian, he is at first thunderstruck. But the young man, half a vagrant, has no means of supporting a wife even if he were inclined to undertake the obligation, and a solution is finally reached. The young man will depart and the marriage will take place as planned. Both the Italian and his prospective bride knew what they wanted— she a protector and a home, he a child to call his own—and if neither is getting it in exactly the way he wished both are getting rather more than human beings can always be sure of.

The situation here presented is one which could obviously be developed either as comedy or as tragedy. As tragedy it might end either in suicide or death, or in some other less definitive calamity. As it is, the triumph of common sense brings it closer to comedy. But it is not quite either. The mood of the conclusion suggests rather a sober, slightly wistful, acquiescence in the fact that life, even when it spares us fundamental catastrophe, often disappoints our rosier expectations.

The effectiveness of the play was greatly enhanced by very skillful direction and unusually telling performances—especially by Richard Bennett as the Italian bridegroom and, more especially still, by Pauline Lord, who was exactly suited to her role by virtue of her peculiar power to suggest the pathos of essential goodness struggling to meet a situation which the intellect has not been able to think through. It is this essential goodness, coupled with a native generosity in the girl herself, which make it possible for the three simple persons involved to face a problem apparently too difficult for their uncultivated intelligences and yet to succeed, in a measure, in solving it by means of native virtues vigorous enough to make them perceive how by giving up much they can still salvage something from the wreck which circumstance has brought about. The impression created by Miss Lord—especially in the scene at her first arrival when she is trying to hide the fact that the situation gradually forcing itself upon her understanding is not the one she expected —was so powerful that it is difficult for anyone who ever saw her not to attach the impression in-

separably to the scene itself and difficult for that
reason to be sure how much of its effect is due to
what she contributed. But whatever the enduring
merits of the play may be, it was evidence, quite as
striking as *What Price Glory*, that vigorous new
and native tendencies were establishing themselves
in the theater.

For one thing there was a certain significance in
the mere fact that the tone of the play was neither
mechanically cheery nor determinedly "stark"—to
use a word then much in favor among literary radicals. The simple faith usually professed by the old-
fashioned playwright, whether he actually held it
or not, had been that life proposes no problems not
completely solvable by those who are willing in
purity of heart "to do the right thing." It was, on
the other hand, often the dominant thesis of the
realistic drama which swept down from the north
to play an important role in revolutionizing popular
ethical thought, that life's favorite game is the devising of dilemmas from which neither good will
nor intelligence provided any possible escape, and
there was some tendency on the part of English or
American members of the cult of Ibsen and Strindberg to assume that the adoption of some such pessimism was prerequisite for any author whose
pretensions to literary merit were at all serious. The
Theatre Guild had been producing such "grim"
dramas as Strindberg's *The Dance of Death*, An

dreyev's *He Who Gets Slapped*, and Lenormand's *The Failures*. Certain recent American plays of artistic pretension, notably Owen Davis's *Icebound* and Arthur Richman's *Ambush* as well as O'Neill's *Beyond the Horizon*, had been marked by a sort of deliberate despair and there was some danger that the American playwright might escape a convention of unmeaning optimism only to fall into another of almost equally factitious gloom. Between the two, the one so comfortable and so false, the other so dark and so ready to assume the inevitability of unrelieved tragedy, lies the view of those to whom man seems most often balked of his dearest desires and forced into compromises which his spirit does not willingly make, yet capable of finding some *modus vivendi* for his soul in a world to which he need not wholly surrender.

Such an estimate of man's fate, unless it is accompanied by comedy's complete and satisfied acquiescence in it, is not likely to favor the production of drama at its strongest for the simple reason that it cannot reach the emotional heights of fully evolved tragedy. But in the particular case of Howard's *They Knew What They Wanted* his taking up a kind of philosophical middle ground and his evocation of a mood midway between tragedy and comedy had the effect of suggesting sincerity. It suggested that he had approached the problem of treating American life in dramatic form directly and afresh rather than by means of formulae derived from other dramatists. His qualified optimism seemed native and original rather than imitative and as independent of the influence of foreign plays fashionable among intellectuals as it was of the glib conventions of the nineteenth-century theater.

At the same time *They Knew What They Wanted* revealed, quite as clearly as *What Price Glory* had done, the fact that native dramatists were coming to assume the possibility of taking for granted in their audience moral attitudes which were still being described as "advanced." *They Knew What They Wanted* is in no sense a thesis play though it involves moral assumptions which might well have been argued in a thesis play only a decade before. What an opportunity is here presented—and neglected by Mr. Howard—to expound a paradoxical morality, to define love, to explain The Case for the Unmarried Mother, and in general to *"epater les bourgeois!"* Mr. Howard, however, does nothing of the sort. He is not consciously engaged in forwarding a revolution either for its own sake or because he feels that the meaning of his play can be comprehensible only in so far as he is able to produce a revolution in the attitudes of his auditors. But he does assume that such a revolution has already taken place.

What and how much the "revolution" implies can perhaps best be suggested by thinking of the

popular success of *They Knew What They Wanted*
in connection with certain remarks made by Bronson Howard, the leading American dramatist of his
day, in a lecture called "Autobiography of a Play"
delivered at Harvard in 1886. The play in question
was *The Banker's Daughter* and the lecture was
concerned with an account of the author's manipu-
lation of its incidents in order to render it "satisfactory" to its audience, even though, as he says,
"this word [satisfactory] has a meaning which
varies in different countries, and even in different
parts of the same country." There follow some cate-
gorical statements concerning what New York finds
"satisfactory" and though all of them are instructive only two can be quoted. At one time Bronson
Howard remarks: "There are axioms among the
laws of dramatic construction, as in mathematics.
One of them is this—three hearts cannot beat as
one. The world is not large enough, from an artistic
point of view, for three good human hearts to continue to exist, if two of them love a third. If one
of the two hearts is a bad one, art assigns it to the
hell on earth of disappointed love; but if it is good
and tender and gentle, art is merciful to it, and puts
it out of its misery by death." At another he states
as a simple fact of audience psychology: "The wife
who has once taken the step from purity to im-
purity can never reinstate herself in the world of
art this side of the grave."

Now in *They Knew What They Wanted* the
heroine is the mother of an illegitimate child conceived on the eve of her marriage to a kindly old
man; the hero is this kindly old man who discovers
the wrong which has been done him but who ends
by adopting the child because a child was what he
really wanted; and not only these two but the lover
as well are unmistakably "reinstated this side of the
grave." There is no primary intention to challenge
or even shock the spectator but it is plain that audiences even considerably later than those which
Bronson Howard had in mind would have been, not
only shocked, but so bewildered by the difference
between their preconceptions and the preconceptions
of the author that the play would have completely
failed of its effect and the audience would not even
have known in what direction its sympathy was
supposed to go out. It would, indeed, have had the
same sort of difficulty which a modern audience
would have in trying to see Shylock as the comic
character he is supposed to have been taken by the
Elizabethans to be. Writing of Ibsen in 1913 William Winter, once the most distinguished drama
critic of New York, called his plays "flaccid, insipid,
tainted, obfuscated and nauseous." Probably he
would have thought much the same of *They Knew
What They Wanted.*

But the fact that the moral revolution can be
taken for granted makes the play almost as differ-

ent from *Ghosts*, in both method and spirit, as it is
from *The Banker's Daughter*. It means that the author can concern himself, not with intellectual problems, but with character and situation. Since the
intellectual premises are assumed, he can go on to
make the action understandable and acceptable. It
becomes understandable and satisfactory considered
only as a series of concrete situations which work
themselves out in a certain way. The play, in other
words, is not a play about ideas but a play about
men and women, and the same may be said of all
the best of the author's subsequent work. Behind it
may lie a point of view and a philosophy; but the
personages and the situation always come first. They
are not invented to illustrate the thesis. The thesis,
if any, is discovered by the audience—and sometimes, I suspect, by the author as well—after con-
templating them.

Neither Mr. Stallings nor Mr. Howard has ever
surpassed the work which brought first one and then
the other conspicuously into notice. Continuing
with Maxwell Anderson as a collaborator, Stallings
produced two other romantic melodramas, *First
Flight* (1925) and *The Buccaneer* (1925), neither
of which was successful and then, after writing
alone the libretto for an opera, *Deep River*, which
was produced, also without success, in 1926, he
turned to other occupations. Maxwell Anderson was

soon busy with a new career as playwright—a career which was to lead in a direction very different
from that taken up in *What Price Glory*. Possibly
neither Mr. Stallings nor Mr. Anderson ever entirely understood why *First Flight* and *The Buccaneer* failed to repeat the success of *What Price
Glory* but it is easy, on looking back, to see that the
similarity between the earliest play and the two last
is confined to superficialities in tone and method.
All have a certain romantic dash and a hearty air
of robustious delight in daring adventure, but only
the first touches any complex of vivid contemporary
emotions. Neither the story of Andrew Jackson's
youth told in *First Flight* nor the story of the Pirate
Morgan told in *The Buccaneer* becomes more than
cloak and sword melodrama. *What Price Glory* had
romantic dash and robustious adventurousness. But
it happened also to deal with incidents which the
audience itself was ready to clothe with emotion.

Even though, as it seems to me, Mr. Howard has
never quite equaled *They Knew What They
Wanted* he has remained a conspicuous contributor
to the contemporary stage. Since the play was produced he has had (including adaptions and collaborations) some eighteen others on Broadway. The
themes show a variety which would probably be impossible for a playwright who did not, like him, find
his inspiration in the concrete situation, and they
have met a variety of fates—ranging all the way

from flat failure like that which attended *Half Gods* (1929), to the triumphant success won by *Ned McCobb's Daughter* (1926), *The Silver Cord* (1926), and *The Late Christopher Bean* (1932). In the meanwhile he has also found time for a very successful career as a writer in Hollywood, and, as an active member of the Willard Straight Post of the American Legion, to help that post be a thorn in the side of the national organization.

All this suggests the energy and vigor which are so characteristic of his work. Being enthusiastic and impulsive rather than primarily reflective, he is both prolific and not the best judge of his own work. Indeed, the public has been more often right than he, and his finest plays since his first success have been the ones mentioned above. Moreover, each of these is, despite the variety of moods and materials, like *They Knew What They Wanted* in that the author has devoted himself in each to the task of presenting concrete situations and concrete characters. He has, to be sure, a conspicuous gift for achieving a clear, straightforward dramatic construction; he has also been lucky in having a series of excellent actors—Pauline Lord, Richard Bennett, Alfred Lunt, Laura Hope Crewes, and Walter Connolly—for his best pieces. But essentially their effectiveness has been due to the fact that they were less comments on contemporary life than presentations of it. One never knows what Mr. Howard is going to say. With him, one sometimes feels, a conviction is an enthusiasm and, like any other enthusiasm, likely to disappear as soon as it has emerged. But one is always sure that the situations will be dramatic, the characters vivid, and the motives understandable.

The Silver Cord is the only one of his plays which develops in accordance with a rationalistic formula. It deals quite explicitly with a "mother complex," and the most dogmatic Freudian would find little to disagree with. Yet Mr. Howard is known to have quarreled violently with the Theatre Guild because its directors insisted upon discussing it in Freudian terms, and the fact is significant of his temperamental antipathy to intellectual formulas, of his impatience with anybody's ideas even though they happen to be also his own. In 1932 he was one of those writers who signed the manifesto in favor of William Z. Foster. Put that fact alongside the further facts that he rushed into the War as soon as possible and then, once it was over, helped organize the obstreperous Willard Straight Post of the American Legion. Together they give you the picture of a man who loves a row, or, rather, who loves a joyous participation in dramatic events. That also is the man who writes the plays. In them the clash of creeds and temperaments interests him for its own sake. He can take sides enthusiastically but he can also change them. He is, whether he knows

it or not, pretty certain to be on the side most likely
to precipitate a dramatic crisis and pretty likely, in
his plays, to see to it that one takes place. Being
also a man of intelligence, his attitude is usually
intelligible and his crises significant. But it is the
happening which interests him and the happening
which interests his audience.

His most recent plays are *Yellow Jack* (1934),
which recounts with much enthusiasm and in an
effective if rather bare manner the story of the con-
quest of yellow fever in the Canal Zone; and *The
Ghost of Yankee Doodle* (1937), a not very successful attempt to make a play out of the question : "What
would happen if America really tried to keep out
of a great European war?"

Under the circumstances it would obviously be
useless to inquire what Mr. Howard's leading ideas
are. He is not, like George Kelly, primarily a
moralist. Neither is he, like O'Neill, a writer of
tragedy, nor, like S. N. Behrman, a consistent writer
of comedy. He can expound Freudianism in *The
Silver Cord*, approach tragedy in *They Knew What
They Wanted*, declaim rather intemperately in *Half
Gods*, and achieve a serene comedy in *The Late
Christopher Bean*. But none is more characteristic
of him than the rest. Neither is there anything common to them all except the vigor of the characterization plus a certain robust delight in the conflict for
its own sake. Their unity, therefore, is only the

unity of a temperament, and the only way to describe what kind of plays Mr. Howard writes is to
describe what sort of man he reveals himself to be.

To witness one of his plays is to experience the
same sort of exhilarating pleasure one gets from the
society of an active man with quick and vigorous
perceptions. One is plunged at once into a series of
happenings and made to share the wholehearted
interest of a writer who throws himself into everything with an unreserved enthusiasm. The characters are observed with extraordinary intentness and
set down in sharp bold strokes. Something of the
author's own decisiveness is communicated to them,
and the dialogue has something of the crisp clarity
of his own speech. Subtlety of a kind is by no means
absent and poetry of a kind is also present. But the
subtlety does not exhibit itself as hair-splitting and
the poetry is neither rhapsodical nor dreamy. The
men and women are plain people with their feet on
the ground; the scene, some very definite corner of
our particular America. Obviously Mr. Howard
hates any sort of artistic pretentiousness as much as
he hates intellectual dogmas. He is determined to
exercise his subtlety in the accurate observation of
familiar things, to find his poetry in the loves and
hates of people who may be distinguished by the
strength and the clarity of their passions but who
remain, nevertheless, essentially familiar types.

His is, therefore, a daylight world, in which com-

mon sense is still the standard by which everything
is judged. An epigram may flash forth here and
there, but in no other way does he ever permit himself to approach a conventionally literary style.
There are no Orphic utterances, no purple patches,
no evocation of what the more esoteric devotees of
the drama call "moods." Nothing ever eludes the
spectator, nothing ever seems vaguely to mean more
than it says. But what it does unmistakably say is
enough for anyone capable of sharing Mr. Howard's very active pleasure in straightforward passions and straightforward events. His plays are not
"highbrow" plays because their author is not a
highbrow, and they teach no doctrine because he is
not a doctrinaire. Essentially tough-minded, he is
interested in facts and out of them he builds his
plays. It is for that reason, no doubt, that the captain
of aviation never wrote a patriotic play nor the
supporter of Mr. Foster a communistic one. He took
part in a war and some day he may, conceivably,
help along a revolution. But it would be safe to
wager that he will never either preach loyalty to
the flag or write a treatise on dialectic materialism.

Writers who are intelligent without being "intellectual," and artistic without being in any sense
"arty," frequently get from critics somewhat less
consideration than they deserve. They are too clear
to require explaining and too popular to need defense. The critic, accordingly, all too frequently

prefers to discourse at more length upon the merits
of those persons whose excellences are less evident.
But the fact remains that Mr. Howard's plays are
among the best ever written in America. They have,
in addition, probably had more influence upon dramatic writing than can ever be directly measured.
Mr. Howard stands very near to the head of the list
of those who rescued the popular drama from that
sentimentality which for some reason continued to
be considered indispensable in plays long after it
had disappeared from most serious writing in other
forms.

That he figures somewhat less conspicuously in
current discussions of the theater than he did a few
years ago may be due in part to the fact that he has
not developed in any of the new directions recently
taken by various other playwrights. Despite a lively
interest in contemporary events he has, on the one
hand, held aloof from the Marxians who proclaim
themselves creators of a new and aggressive "revolutionary drama" and, on the other hand, he has
not, like Eugene O'Neill and Maxwell Anderson,
tried to evolve formal tragedy, or like S. N. Behrman to create formal comedy. Instead he has continued to write plays dominated by the spirit of
thoughtful but straightforward realism.

A somewhat similar reason might be assigned for
the diminuendo which marks the career of George

Kelly, another dramatist of very substantial merits who seemed to have established himself at about the same time that Howard and Stallings came into prominence, but who has produced no successful play since 1925. Mr. Kelly began as an actor and presently turned to the vaudeville theaters where his elder brother, Walter Kelly, was extremely popular in the character of "The Virginia Judge." This seems a rather odd beginning for a man whose most recent plays have been conspicuously austere. But Mr. Kelly wrote vaudeville playlets before he wrote for the legitimate stage and the second of his full length plays was expanded from a skit.

In 1922 he had achieved a certain *succès d'estime* with *The Torchbearers*, a farce satirizing the artistic pretensions of amateur "little theater" groups, but his first large commercial success came with the production of *The Show-Off* in 1924. This farce comedy, despite certain overtones of bitterness, hit the taste of a large public. In the first place its central character, the brazen, and back-slapping bluff, Aubrey Piper, represented a type which recent satire on rotary clubs and the gospel of success had made familiar. In the second place the play was not only effectively written but subtly calculated to appeal to a public wider than that which would have been ready to accept a really logical development of the theme. The hero's last bluff really works to the tune of fifty thousand dollars and makes possible a

sentimental blurring of the conclusion which renders
the play as a whole so ambiguous that it might almost
be taken as a "success story" after the manner of
Winchell Smith.

In the following year Mr. Kelly won the Pulitzer
Prize with *Craig's Wife*, a more simple, direct and
serious play which adheres almost fanatically to the
single theme developed in the story of a "good
housekeeper" who coldly sacrifices her husband's
love as well as everything else to her mania for
maintaining impeccable order in a house which she
mistakes for a home. Interest is maintained through
the skillful use of almost obviously simple dramatic
devices. The final revolt of the husband is objecti-
fied by the deliberate smashing of a cherished piece
of bric-a-brac and the final curtain goes down upon
the heroine standing alone in the midst of the perfect drawing-room which has now lost all meaning,
even for her.

Probably neither of these two very successful
plays is as close to the author's heart as others which
the public has classed as failures. Both *The Show-
Off* and *Craig's Wife* were soundly constructed and
both were based upon shrewd and honest observation, but each had, in addition, the advantage of
belonging to a familiar and popular genre. The
first, with a blustering Babbitt for a hero, was a
recognizable addition to the growing literature of
native satire. The second, which drew at full length

the portrait of a hard woman in whom the virtue
of being a good housekeeper had become a vice, was
typically "modern" in a slightly different way. It
illustrated admirably that tendency to "transvaluate
values," which Ibsen had introduced into the theater and which, in a somewhat popularized form,
one will discover in such typical plays of the recent
past as *The Silver Cord* and *Rain*. No wonder that
Mr. Kelly was set down as a dramatist working in
a current tradition and sufficiently of Broadway to
find ready acceptance. No wonder, also, that his
public was somewhat *froissé* by the increasing bitterness of *Daisy Mayme* (1926) or that it should
have been frankly bewildered by the almost mystical tone of *Behold the Bridegroom* (1927). Mr.
Kelly refused to stay put and was determined to
accentuate those aspects of his attitude which were
the least familiar and the least acceptable to his
audience.

With his latest work in mind it is easy to look
back over the earlier plays and to catch in their text
ominous hints of this more stern and acrid tone.
Even in *The Show-Off* there are moments when a
certain unexpected bitterness rises momentarily to
the surface, as when, for example, the harassed
mother hears the remark that her daughter must
lie on the bed she has made and replies quite simply:
"It's often not the people who make the beds who
have to lie on them. It's someone else." A few mo-

ments later the observation has been forgotten in
the flow of pure fun, but for an instant there had
found expression something in the author which
would be cynicism if it were not too sternly moral-
istic to be quite that. Indeed, the whole character
of this mother adds to the play an element quite
foreign to its dominant tone, for she is a sort of
chorus supplying disillusioned comment, prophesy-
ing woe, and refusing to enter fully into the easy
joy of the rest when good fortune solves all their
difficulties.

Even more significant is the one-act play,
Smarty's Party, written long before, during the
five years when Mr. Kelly was appearing in vaudeville in playlets of his own composition. Here the
story is that of a vulgar adventuress who entangles
a young man supposed to be very wealthy, who
comes to his supposed mother to enjoy her moment
of triumph, and who then is crushed with the information that her victim is not really the woman's
son at all. Here Mr. Kelly first delineates with cruel
expertness the vulgarity of the adventuress and
then, with a kind of savage delight, destroys her
utterly. Thus the pattern of the play is exactly the
same as the pattern of *Craig's Wife*, where another
evil woman is analyzed at full length before the
author, with an almost sadistic fury, plunges her
into a special circle of hell so arranged that her vice
will constitute the means by which she is tortured.

The heroine of *Smarty's Party* wanted money and got poverty; Craig's wife loved her home so much that she found herself homeless at last.

One cannot help observing that Mr. Kelly's three most bitterly excoriated characters—namely the two just mentioned and one to be discussed later—are all women. There is in him, therefore, a strain of what one is tempted to call misogamy, but it is not certain that the term would be exactly accurate. He does not seem to be saying that women as a sex are worse than men. He is only saying instead, "Lilies that fester smell far worse than weeds," and the key to his temperament is a particular kind of austerity which goes commonly under the name of puritanism. Vulgarity offends him, not only aesthetically but morally as well, and the kind of meanness which he finds most common in men and women strikes him always as a sort of vulgarity of the soul. He despises it with a certain cold fury, and his desire is the puritanical desire to see a crushing justice meted out to it. Others may feel that to understand all is to pardon all, but to the puritan that saying is incomprehensible nonsense. To understand all is to hate all—if that "all" be hateful. Each of his most striking heroine-victims is understood with a cruel clarity, but none is pardoned and none, be it noted also, is reformed and then rewarded. All three are cast instead into outer —and utter—darkness.

Behold the Bridegroom (1927) represents Mr. Kelly's most determined and most nearly successful effort to break completely away from the themes and methods of the contemporary stage in order to give full expression to his underlying attitude. All his other plays are richly overlaid with local color. The immediate effectiveness of all the preceding ones depends in large part upon skillful mimicry and upon the literal realism with which he pictures middle-class American life. Here, however, he departs from his accustomed milieu. Manners are more elegant, characters more self-consciously analytic, and the whole style is more formally literary. But the effect is only to disengage more completely the essential moral problem and to make the discussion of it quite clearly the only *raison d'être* of the play. Again the hero—if she can be called that —is a woman, but this time her sin is that vulgarity which results from the indulgence of a too facile and too shallow emotional nature. She is smart, sophisticated, and charming. She has moved gracefully from one love affair to another and thinks that she has demonstrated by her success how completely the intelligence may dispense with those simple rules of puritan morality which are never far from Mr. Kelly's mind. But the moment comes when she realizes that she really loves for the first time in her life. And her creator seizes the opportunity to destroy her as he had destroyed Craig's wife. She looks into the bridegroom's eyes, reads there his contempt, and then dies, not so much because of that contempt as because she has realized at last her own emptiness.

Probably most persons were made a little uncomfortable by the mercilessness with which justice was visited upon Mr. Kelly's earlier heroines. Some have even suggested that a more knowing playwright would not have pushed retribution so far as to swing the sympathy of the audience around in the direction of its victim. But it is no mere dramaturgic mistake which is responsible for Mr. Kelly's relentlessness either in the case of *Craig's Wife* or in the case of *Behold the Bridegroom*. He must have known very well that the public would not judge the heroine of the latter play so harshly as he did; that there is, as a matter of fact, no sin which this public is more ready to forgive—in fiction at least—than the sin of light love. Indeed, the romantic-sentimental tradition makes it almost the necessary prelude to a grand passion. But Mr. Kelly would not compromise here with his puritan conscience or make any effort to hide his contempt for contemporary morality. His heroine had wasted her capacities on cheap loves. She was not ready when the bridegroom came, and she had forfeited all right to the thing whose value she had come to understand only when it was too late. Hence she awakes, not to be saved, but only in order that she may realize what she has lost. Only thus can the puritan sense of justice be served, for the damned must be given one glimpse of paradise before they are plunged into hell forever.

No other play by Mr. Kelly—indeed, few contemporary plays by any author whatsoever—has, in certain respects, a finer literary quality than this one has. There is a passionate sincerity in the conception and a beautiful clarity in the dialogue which raise it far above the level of merely successful dramatic writing. The author seems to be struggling to free himself from the limitations of mere naturalism, and very nearly succeeds, by his passion and his coherence, in raising the play to the level of quasi-poetic tragedy. Yet the fact remains that it was commercially a failure and, what is more important, that all the respect which one feels for it does not prevent certain objections from arising in the mind of either the spectator or the reader.

One is, to put it briefly, neither quite convinced nor quite sure that one ought to be. "Men have died from time to time and worms have eaten them, but not for love." This we have upon the authority of one of Shakespeare's heroines, and it may be urged against the conclusion which Mr. Kelly has given to his play, but the most serious of my doubts are not of this naturalistic kind. I can accept the physical features of his conclusion and I can respect the moral sincerity which has enabled him to develop an almost pietistic thesis without falling into mere priggishness on the one hand or into rant on the other, but I honestly doubt that nature is constructed upon any plan so in accord with a puritan sense of moral fitness. Perhaps a spoiled and empty woman should die of self-contempt when she sees herself; perhaps she should feel herself forever unworthy of love if she chances at last to meet it; but I doubt that she would actually feel so or that there is anything to be gained by trying to make her. We forgive ourselves more easily and it is as well that we should. Artists and moralists both love to contemplate the irreparable—it helps the one to be dramatic and it helps the other to satisfy his sense of justice. But nature is more compliant. Time cannot be called back, and what has been physically destroyed cannot be found again, but nothing else is irretrievably lost and there are no sins that ought not and cannot be forgiven.

In *Maggie the Magnificent* (1929) Mr. Kelly returned to the middle-class milieu and the more realistic manner. But here again he is concerned with integrity of character as it is brought out in the contrast between the orderly soul of an uncultivated mother and the efficient determination of a daughter who lifts herself by her own efforts above the vulgarity amidst which she grew up. But Mr. Kelly seems incapable of making either men or women as likable as they ought to be. There is in

the characters whom he admires something stiff
and prim and priggish which chills the beholder
and seems to suggest that the author hates what
is cheap and common with such an all-absorbing
fury that he has become incapable of exercising his
critical judgment upon anyone who escapes the one
vice he cannot forgive. The "bridegroom" in the
previous play was not intended to be repellently
self-righteous; but there was a suggestion of repel-
lent self-righteousness in him. Similarly, the Maggie of this piece is actually a good deal less than
magnificent. She is neat, orderly, assured, decent,
and correct, but only Mr. Kelly would admire her
with warmth. We are expected to feel in her an
austere nobility, but we actually feel a kind of
spinsterish frigidity, and we cannot rejoice as we
should in her triumph because we cannot sympa-
thize warmly enough with her essentially negative
aspirations. *Maggie the Magnificent* was followed
by *Top o' the Hill* (1927) and in 1931 by *Philip
Goes Forth* in which the vulgarity of a would-be
playwright is excoriated. But these works also were
failures and Mr. Kelly has not since been represented on Broadway.

The key to the mystery surrounding the fact that
Mr. Kelly's most characteristic and most seriously
meant plays do not quite achieve the success that
they seem at times about to reach is suggested, I
think, by the touch of coldness in his nature, by a

certain stubborn negativeness in his moral attitude which lays a blight upon his plays. Essentially they are rather dour and frost-bitten, rather bleak at the very moments when a grave beauty ought to emerge. He wants, like Milton, to express the grandeur of puritanism, but he is somewhat earthbound and cannot entirely escape from a certain unlovely rigidity. There is too much realism, too much prose, where a kind of ecstasy is called for. When a puritan is also a poet, the result can be magnificent, but Mr. Kelly is not quite poet enough. He commands respect but he cannot quite inspire a genuine enthusiasm.

Answering some queries from Burns Mantle in 1929, Mr. Kelly expressed his distaste for personal publicity and refused to be drawn into any discussion of the state of the drama, the future of the theater, etc. On an earlier occasion he declared, somewhat unconvincingly, that he had no ambition to write for "artistic success" and that he was interested only in the box office. If one is willing to accept that statement as the truth and the whole truth then no explanation for his eight-year-long silence is necessary beyond that afforded by the very limited popularity of his last five plays. But there is obviously some conflict between the themes which seem to concern him most and the willingness as well as the ability to calculate popular taste exhibited both in *The Show-Off* and, to a lesser extent, in *Craig's Wife. Behold the Bridegroom* is an attempt at tragedy which fails in part because the form, while not really that of straight realistic drama, does not quite succeed in becoming something else. Mr. Kelly, I suspect, has found himself somehow blocked in mid-process of evolving a dramatic form suitable to what he most wants to say. The relatively successful completion of such a process constitutes the most important achievement of several currently prominent playwrights—notably O'Neill, Anderson and Behrman.

CHAPTER III

TRAGEDY: EUGENE O'NEILL

IN MOST instances the new playwright had little
interest in the classical theory of tragedy. It was
associated in his mind with that "closet drama"
which, with reason, he distrusted, and in general
he regarded all the fixed traditional forms as im-
pediments to the expression of a fresh or sincere
feeling. He sometimes spoke of "Greek inevitability" but that was hardly more than a cant phrase
and had only the most remote reference to Aeschylus or Sophocles.

If, however, he had little interest in the tragic
tradition he had, on the other hand, an almost su-
perstitious respect for something quite different,
namely, "the unhappy end," which was associated
in his mind with a defiance of all vulgar theatrical
prejudice. Ibsen, as well as many of his followers,
had cultivated it assiduously and it seemed, among
other things, to guarantee that the author was making no compromise with his audience. One could
never be sure whether cheerfulness and optimism
were genuine or merely put on for the purpose of
pleasing a shallow-pated public. But no one, it was

assumed, would be gloomy from any unworthy motive and the pessimist was, at the very least, testifying to the truth that was in him. Indeed, if it had not been for the example of "the laughing Ibsen," Bernard Shaw, the modern drama would probably have had even more difficulty than it actually did in escaping from the conviction that some sort of unrelieved frustration must be the subject of every worthy play. No matter how hard Shaw tried to be a philosopher, "cheerfulness kept breaking through."

Even when not part of the exultant sweep of genuine tragedy, "unhappy ends" may be of various sorts and may produce various effects. Sometimes they may even be, like the end of *Craig's Wife*, related more closely to the traditional end of a melodrama than to the end of a tragedy because they represent poetic justice administered to a villain or quasi-villain rather than a calamity overwhelming a hero and are, for that reason, more satisfying than disturbing to an ordinary audience. Without being genuinely tragic, the unhappy end may, on the other hand, create a mood of sentimental pathos quite as acceptable to the movie-going youth of today as it was to the vast international public which delighted in *Camille*. Sentimental pathos of that sort has always found a place on the stage.

The particular type of unhappy ending for which

admirers of the new drama had the greatest respect was, however, neither of those just described. It was more unrelieved than either and it usually presented a picture of utter frustration which resulted in a dissonance not even by implication resolved. Modern "tragedy," it was sometimes said, differed from classical tragedy in that it dealt, not with something which comes to an end, but with something which goes on. And Mrs. Alving, who must continue to live after she has administered the fatal dose to Oswald, or Hauptmann's Rose Bernd, furnish typical examples. The fate of such personages is not fully tragic nor is it given a sentimental pathetic value, and when this aspect of Ibsen's formula is imitated by a lesser hand the result is likely to be a play from which the more ordinary theater-goer flees muttering that there is, after all, enough tragedy in real life.

Some of the playlets presented by the Provincetown group and the Washington Square Players represent American attempts to achieve this complete sunlessness, though perhaps the only ones likely to be remembered are Susan Glaspell's *Trifles* and Sherwood Anderson's *The Triumph of the Egg*. Broadway, also, saw a little group of much-discussed plays, praised chiefly for the "starkness" of their realism, unmistakably in the newer "defeatist" manner, with the emphasis upon catastrophes without hope, without grandeur and without poetry.

Thus in *The Detour* (1921) Owen Davis told the story of a farmer's wife who for years saves money to enable her daughter to study art in the city and then discovers, not only that her husband has taken the money, but that the daughter is devoid of talent. In *Icebound* (1923) the same author told the almost equally depressing saga of another frustrated New England family. Arthur Richman's *Ambush*, produced by the Guild in 1921, was concerned with the inescapable trap which life had set for the hardworking head of a lower middle-class family who loses in the end even the respectability he had clung to. But perhaps the ultimate in tragedy without dignity was reached in Patrick Kearney's *A Man's Man* (1925). Mr. Kearney, who later dramatized Theodore Dreiser's *An American Tragedy* and died by suicide, was a writer of some real talent and *A Man's Man* has a certain undeniable power. It is, however, not only concerned with the complete failure and utter humiliation of its hero, but so designed as to make it clear that the failure and the humiliation are the inevitable consequence of a well meaning but contemptible littleness of mind assumed to be characteristic of the average man.

Perhaps these plays, as well as others like them, performed a certain function by accustoming the audience to the contemplation of the more distressing aspects of existence and by freeing the playwright from an oppressive sense of the necessity

for what he then regarded as the falsifications traditionally demanded in the theater. But it is doubtful
if any body of dramatic literature can be long interesting unless it can discover in human life more
meaning than these plays revealed. The serious
playwright needed both to free himself from a
prejudice in favor of the unhappy ending as such
and to discover ways in which such an ending, when
logically demanded, could be made to serve a purpose beyond that of merely affirming a blind pessimism.

We have already seen how such a dramatist as
Sidney Howard wrote dramas which might arrive
at no completely happy end but which neither aspired to be true tragedies nor strove to emphasize
frustration. We shall later discuss the meaning
which playwrights with strong sociological interests strove to give the unhappy terminations sometimes characteristic of their works. But it would be
best now to consider a playwright who came to concern himself more and more with the problem of
writing plays essentially modern yet striving
toward an effect analogous to that of tragedy in
traditional forms.

In more than one respect Eugene O'Neill is
unique among serious contemporary playwrights.
No other has written so much or remained so persistently in the forefront of discussion; no other

has devoted himself with such dogged insistence to the single task of writing plays. While many of his contemporaries have engaged in various activities— translating, adapting, collaborating, or producing; while others have taken a fling at the movies or dabbled in public affairs, he has, in late years, lived almost as a hermit far from New York, not even attending his own first nights, and externally exhibiting no interest in anything except the play he happens at the moment to be engaged upon. At the same time the work of no other important contemporary has been more uneven. In the long list of his works are a number which were flat failures on the stage and at least a few which seem unfortunate from any standpoint. With the possible exception of one or two, even his best works nearly always suggest that they intend more than they succeed in embodying and that—possibly because the aim is so high—they are, in certain respects, less adequate to their purpose than the plays of lesser men. For all that he is so prolific, he has no facility; there is a continual, seldom wholly successful struggle, not only with the central conception but even with the language itself, so that one often gets the impression of positive clumsiness, as though neither the imagination nor the tongue was quite articulate enough to achieve full or clear expression.

His themes have, at the same time, been extraordinarily varied. But neither the variety of themes nor the restless, sometimes extravagant experimentation with forms and unusual technical devices is the result of the exuberance of a skillful craftsman trying everything because he has discovered in himself a kind of universal competence. Neither do the varied subject matters suggest that vivacious type of mind which, having no center of its own, exhibits an eager concern with everything suggested to it. On the contrary, an intense, almost pathologically introverted personality obsessed with what is really a single idea, seems to be seizing, one after another, upon themes or forms of expression and then dropping them after more or less prolonged experimentation because each is discovered to be less closely related to a central concern than it seemed at first sight to be.

O'Neill has been chary of public attempts to explain his intentions or his theories and though one or two phrases dropped in conversation are extremely illuminating, such an extended attempt at clarification as the communication which he wrote at the time when *The Great God Brown* was puzzling his admirers is not particularly illuminating, for O'Neill is not a man who thinks incisively in abstract terms and, for all his introversion, not a man whose self-analyses are of a sort very clearly communicable. It seems plain, however, that the history of his development is the history of a persistent, sometimes fumbling attempt to objectify his emotions, accompanied by a persistent hope that this or that opening suggested by some current intellectual fashion would provide the opportunity for which he felt the need. Radical sociological theorizing, Freudian psychology, and Roman Catholicism have successively concerned him. At other times rather dubiously Greek masks and long novelistic soliloquies have been adopted as devices thought of for the moment as almost magically significant, and in form his plays have varied from that of direct sociological preachment, through the German expressionism of *The Hairy Ape*, to the vague symbolism of *The Fountain*. The man who was to say rather recently that he was not interested in the relation of man to man but only in the relation of man to God once made in *Welded* a disastrous attempt to discuss incompatibility in a modern marriage, and though no contemporary playwright has touched current interests superficially at more different points, none has been at bottom less satisfied with current answers. That mysticism which is, perhaps, the most fundamental of his characteristics is the one which, for a long time, was permitted to reveal itself only in the background. *Anna Christie*, commercially the most successful of his early plays—partly no doubt because it is the one closest to a reigning tradition of slightly romantic realism—is cherished so little by him that he refused the publisher's request to include it in a volume of nine of his representative plays published in 1932. Obviously he can be understood only if his career is followed step by step.

Part of O'Neill's childhood was spent on tour with his father, the romantic actor James O'Neill, who for years went up and down the country performing in *The Count of Monte Cristo.* Doubtless this fact influenced him in the direction of the theater and doubtless early familiarity with popular drama has had something to do with his revolt against theatrical convention and his shrewd theatrical sense of how even his most eccentric technical innovations will work out on the stage. But a brooding temperament is even more fundamental in him than any specific predilection for the drama, and the history of his development as a writer begins as significantly with his discovery of that temperament as it does with his early familiarity with dressing rooms. The restlessness which made him something of a problem child and which sent him, after a brief career at Princeton and an unhappy period as secretary in a mail-order house, wandering to South America and to Africa aboard tramp steamers, has its significance, and so have the drinking bouts which somewhat later made him a legend in Greenwich Village. Possibly the attack of tuberculosis which confined him for some time to a sanitarium first brought the realization that one cannot leave one's self behind when sailing to Africa and that one is likely to find one's self quietly waiting when one

sobers up after a debauch. Certainly the accident of
his meeting with an enthusiastic group of amateurs
at Provincetown was of crucial importance. That
group produced his already written playlet *Bound
East for Cardiff* and when the group moved to New
York offered it on the first bill presented at the Mac-
Dougal Street home.

Bound East for Cardiff and the other short plays
of the sea which the Provincetown group was also
to produce, reveal not only O'Neill's penchant for
"strong" incidents and his preference for primitive,
not wholly articulate characters, but also his persistent sense that pure rationality cannot exhaust
the meaning of any really important situation. It
is significant that the dying hero of his first produced play should be chiefly concerned with what
God will think and significant also that the hero of
Ile (1917) should be a fanatical whaling captain
whose wife goes mad when a sudden opening of the
ice makes him break his promise to head south.
Many of O'Neill's characters were to be obsessed
by something stronger than themselves and it is
that obsession, that relation to something good or
evil bigger than their conscious minds, which makes
them interesting to their creator. They, to use the
words of one of them, "belong" to something, and
the most tortured of his characters are those who,
like Dion in *The Great God Brown*, have lost all
sense either that they "belong" to anything or that

there is anything in the universe to which it is possible to belong. At its lowest the obsession may be, as in *Gold* (1921), hardly distinguishable from mere greed and at his most rational O'Neill may try to discover in Freudian psychology a rational explanation of what seems super-rational; but whatever the form it may take and in whatever terms the character himself may rationalize his obsession it is always the fact that men are moved by forces whose influence reason cannot justify which O'Neill finds interesting.

Before the end of 1918 he had written a number of one-act plays, and the five dealing with the sea are characterized by a compactness and clarity not to be discovered in many of his later works. The very fact that they are short prevents over-complication or confusions and it is noticeable that as O'Neill turned to longer plays he showed a tendency, not only to lose himself in the uncertainty of his own emotions, but also to allow the intrusion of themes which did not concern him as deeply as he perhaps at the moment supposed. Both *Beyond the Horizon* (1920) and *Anna Christie* (1921) were produced "up town." The first won the Pulitzer Prize, and both might be taken as essentially "realistic plays." Indeed the first, with its story of two brothers so trapped by fate that the one who wanted adventure stays at home while the one who wanted to stay at home is driven to find wealth in far places, suggests the tragedy of mere bleak frustration already referred to as characteristic of certain new playwrights; while the second, the story of a waterfront prostitute redeemed by the love of a sailor, might be mistaken for no more than a piece of slightly romantic realism. But *Beyond the Horizon* is also the story of a mystical force, that of the possessive female, destroying another mystical force embodied in the young man whose desire for adventure was a desire to find the meaning of life, and *Anna Christie* is also the story of the old sailor, retired to a barge and resentful of the sea, who realizes that when his daughter Anna is married to a sailor, the sea, to which he and his "belong," will have claimed its own.

Between these two plays, close as they came together, O'Neill had produced, besides the unsuccessful *Gold* which appeared briefly on Broadway in June, 1921, two others at the Provincetown: *The Emperor Jones* (November, 1920) and *Diff'rent* (December, 1920). The former, which concerns a Pullman porter who flees from the police to a small island in the West Indies and there, by the practice of wiles learned in a white civilization, makes himself emperor, is still regarded by many as one of O'Neill's best works. The use of the persistent beat of a tomtom to communicate to the audience the irrational terror of the Emperor fleeing through the jungle from his rebellious subjects is the first of the unusual devices for which O'Neill became famous and the piece is effective as sheer melodrama quite aside from the characteristic theme. Its hero's lust for power and his contempt for the fellow-blacks he has dominated spring from his desire to prove to himself that he has escaped from the black universe. When he falls in the jungle cowering under fears which he had despised and terrorized by the atavistic force of superstition, he is another proof that one cannot escape from that to which one "belongs."

In *Diff'rent* we see a New England maiden, unreasonably proud of her purity, dismiss her lover when she learns that he, like other sailors, has participated in the idyllic free life of a South Sea island. It is not, she thinks, that she cannot understand or forgive; he is pardonable by ordinary human standards and good enough for an ordinary mortal. But she is "diff'rent" and only purity equal to hers is worthy of her. In the last act we see her again years later. She had sacrificed her chance of happiness to pride and she is presented, quite brutally, as merely a sex-starved old maid now bidding in vain for the love of a crude and cruel youth who frankly despises her.

Some have found in the play a certain crassness unworthy of the author and have dismissed it as merely "unpleasant;" but it furnishes a striking illustration of a fact to be observed in connection with several of O'Neill's plays—the fact, that is to say, that they are subject to a double interpretation, that they mean something in terms of current popular thought and also something—perhaps not clearly separated from the less esoteric meaning even in the author's own mind—in terms of O'Neill's deeper, more private concerns. On the surface *Diff'-rent* is a fable for Freudians and was undoubtedly interpreted by many spectators as merely a warning, almost ribald in tone, against the then much feared evil of "suppression." But I doubt that any such interpretation exhausts the meaning which it had for O'Neill even though his meaning is more deeply obscured here than it is in other related plays. In the first place, the sin of the heroine is not simply prudery but something much grander— the sin of Pride. Pride is connected, as it is in many of his other proud characters, with the sense of "belonging" to something, and he never forgets that Pride, even when a sin, is the sin of the angels. The heroine of this play is reduced to smallness before it is over but she is not, whatever else she may be, merely small in its first act. She "belongs" to an austere ideal of herself.

O'Neill seems to waver somewhat in the judgment which he passes upon the imperatives outside themselves which men obey. Sometimes—most often perhaps—they enslave. But he never loses the sense that those who recognize them gain some sort of stature, attain some sort of eminence—either good or evil. As he came later to attempt more clearly defined tragedies, he realized that what the catastrophes of the mere unhappy play most obviously lacked was magnitude, and that the first step in the creation of a tragic effect must consist in giving that magnitude to catastrophe by relating it to something real or illusory outside of man's mere rationality as well as outside his mere animal desires.

In *The Hairy Ape* (1922) the mystical overtones become so pronounced as hardly to remain mere overtones any longer. Yank, the primitive and inarticulate stoker on a luxury liner, is, to be sure, a member of the oppressed proletariat. The scene in which he and the elegant young lady on a tour of inspection come face to face in the boiler room takes its point from the fact that each is aghast to see in the other a human being more different from himself than he had ever imagined any creature could be while still remaining human, and it serves, like the scenes on Fifth Avenue, to draw in violent terms the contrast between the enfeebled luxury of the parasites and the laborious lives of the poor. But Yank's tragedy does not spring from any resentment at his discovery that he is a member of the class materially dispossessed. He had been content with his lot as long as he believed that it was he, in the bowels of the ship, who was indispensable— who made things go, who, as he put it, "belonged."

His faith is first shaken by the fellow seaman who talks of the good old days when sailors could really "belong" because sailing ships were part of the sea, and his nightmarish exploration of the unfamiliar world of a metropolis is a series of discoveries which leave him crushed by the realization that he does not "belong" to anything.

As the play develops it grows more and more fantastic, leaving realism behind and adopting the devices which German expressionism had made familiar. Everything is presented, not as it is, but as it would seem to the by now disordered mind of Yank. Fifth Avenue, a region of shops displaying articles of fantastic luxury bearing price cards marked with astronomical figures, is inhabited by a race of frock-coated robots incapable of becoming aware of even his physical existence. Somewhat later he is ejected from a radical meeting in which, now that he has grown violent, he believed he must certainly belong, and, finally, he wanders to the zoo where he beholds in a cage the great ape. At last he has found a creature who seems more like himself than any he has seen since he left the stoke-hole and, by implication, he has found where he "belongs." As he advances toward the cage the ape stretches out his arms. But it is not, as he supposes, to welcome him as a brother. It is to crush him to death and furnish the final proof that one variety of hairy ape does not "belong" even in a zoo.

The moral of the play does not involve merely an attack upon capitalism. The world which it presents is a world disordered because its inhabitants have lost touch with things larger than themselves at the very moment when they thought they had not so much lost touch with as conquered them. Here those things are symbolized, rather vaguely perhaps, by the sea. Ships have rendered themselves independent of it but the result is that the seaman is brutalized while the passenger has become trivial. If the pessimism of a play like *Beyond the Horizon* suggests Hardy and his merely capricious Destiny, much in *The Hairy Ape* and certain of O'Neill's other plays suggests the less clearly defined despair of D. H. Lawrence and his search for the "dark Gods" who may be terrible but with whom, nevertheless, man cannot dispense. The theme concerned with "belonging" occurs specifically again and again. It appears in *Dynamo* (1929), whose insane hero electrocutes himself on the Dynamo which has come to seem the altar of the god Electricity and again, as late as 1934, in *Days Without End* where the hero can find peace only by "belonging" to the God of Roman Catholicism.

The Hairy Ape was followed by several plays of which none achieved more than moderate success until *Desire Under the Elms* was produced at the Greenwich Village Theater in November, 1924, where it attracted so much attention that it was moved to Broadway. The success of this play marks a stage in the widening of O'Neill's public as well as in the clarification of his method. But it can best be discussed in connection with later works and after an analysis of *The Great God Brown*, produced again at the Greenwich Village, a little over a year later (January, 1926). This last mentioned play is important, less because of the elaborate and much discussed technical device which allows the chief personages to wear masks representing their public selves and to remove them when they soliloquize their secret thoughts, than because it represents the author's most direct attempt to expose in terms already more or less familiar in current literature the ultimate source of his tragic dilemma.

The story is the story of two boyhood friends, William Brown and Dion Anthony, who represent respectively commonplace success and the tortured failure of genius. Brown prospers as a plodding architect. Anthony, having married the girl they both love, takes to drink, seeks consolation for his dissatisfaction with the prim though deep love of his wife in the arms of a mystically "understanding" prostitute, and finally dies miserable—though not before, as an underling in Brown's office, he has drawn the plan for a magnificent building for which Brown will take the credit.

On the surface the play is a sneer at poor old "respectability" and a bitter satire upon the popular subject of material success and its over-evaluation. But even when O'Neill touches current themes he is never content to treat them merely according to current formulae. Dion is, as his name suggests, also Dionysus, and Cybil, the prostitute, "Mother Earth." But Dionysus is a tragic figure because that portion of his spirit now incarnate in a modern American boy finds nothing in modern life to nourish or satisfy. Even the best of the boy's companions are too concerned with their small safe aims to be aware, even, that they are related to something larger than themselves. Even Margaret, his future wife, is so alarmed by the vehemence of his declaration of love and by the sight of his real face that he resumes his mask and vows that she will never again see him as he really is. He is alone with desires and fears which no one else can understand and he cannot turn to the pretended religion of his age because it is as dead to him as the worship of that god from whom he takes his name.

He is blasphemous and cynical because neither his companions nor his own intellectual convictions leave him any choice except that between blasphemy on the one hand and, on the other, a hypocritical formalism in which he will not acquiesce. When, in the prologue, he turns to his parents for love, he finds that the love which they have for him can find expression only in sound, sensible, apparently condescending advice about the choice of a career, and his disappointment breaks out in the cynical exclamation: "This Mr. Anthony is my father, but he only imagines he is God the Father." And later: "Why am I afraid to dance, I who love music and rhythm and grace and song and laughter? Why am I afraid to live, I who love life and the beauty of flesh and the living colors of earth and sky and sea? Why am I afraid of love, I who love love? Why am I afraid, I who am not afraid? Why must I pretend to scorn in order to pity? Why must I be so ashamed of my strength, so proud of my weakness? Why must I live in a cage like a criminal, defying and hating, I who love peace and friendship? *(clasping his hands above in supplication)* Why was I born without a skin, O God, that I must wear armor in order to touch or to be touched? *(A second's pause of waiting silence—then he suddenly claps his mask over his face again, with a gesture of despair and his voice becomes bitter and sardonic.)* Or rather, Old Graybeard, why the devil was I ever born at all?" Dion is sensitivity and genius but he is sensitivity and genius which feel themselves alone, not only in the world, but in the universe; for the universe itself is now empty and the God to which his emotions bid him turn has become only the Old Graybeard of a dead mythology.

To George Jean Nathan, O'Neill once wrote: "The playwright of today must dig at the roots of

the sickness of today as he feels it—the death of the
old God and the failure of science and materialism
to give any satisfactory new one for the surviving
primitive religious instinct to find a meaning for
life in, and to comfort its fears of death with. It
seems to me that anyone trying to do big work now-
adays must have this big subject behind all the little subjects of his plays or novels, or he is scrib-
bling around the surface of things." This is surely
not only explicit enough but stated in terms so familiar as to be commonplace, and O'Neill's distinction can hardly consist in the fact that he has arrived at such a conclusion. It does, however, consist
in part in the fact that he has found original symbols through which to present the conviction and
told exciting stories which take on meaning in the
light of it. "I've loved, lusted, won and lost, sung
and wept!" cries Dion. But to have done those things
is not enough. The crude and obvious fact that life
is vivid and restless, exciting and terrible must be
turned by tragedy into some peace-giving beauty.
O'Neill is not concerned simply with saying that it
is. As a writer of tragedy he is attempting to get beyond the mere fact. Hence the tragedy of Dion is
fundamentally the incomplete tragedy of frustration, not the complete tragedy of fulfillment.

The Great God Brown is subjective, almost a personal confession. *Lazarus Laughed*, written in 1926
but never acted in New York, is a lyrical, wholly

symbolic drama in the Greek form which concerns itself with the effect produced by a man who, having penetrated the secret of death, can communicate nothing except his free and joyous laughter. O'Neill had, however, in *Desire Under the Elms* (1924), already discovered how the problem of writing tragedy significant for him could be approached in a different way: objectively not subjectively, and through the interpretation to be put upon a series of realistically imagined events rather than in terms of symbols invented directly for the purpose. The life of early New England had always appealed to him even as mere history or romance and to it he turned for a fable in which the conflict of violent passions leads to violent deeds.

Outwardly the play is a realistic, if heightened, study of the manners, morals, and psychological processes of a definite society—that of puritan New England in the middle of the last century. But it is impossible not to realize that the author is interested in New England as such no more, at least, than he is interested in an aspect of the eternal tragedy of man and his passions. He chose this particular time and particular place, partly because he knew something about them; partly because the stern repressions of puritan customs make the kind of explosion with which he proposed to deal particularly picturesque and particularly violent; but chiefly because it is necessary to give every dramatic story *some* local habitation and name. Questions concerning the historical accuracy of any detail are not strictly relevant. Realistic in manner though the presentation is, this puritan society is treated as already half fabulous, and the events, though feigned to occur in New England, also happen out of place and out of time.

The chief characters are Ephraim Cabot, a hard and self-righteous patriarch; Eben, a son by his second wife; and Abbie Putnam, a proud and ambitious young woman who has married Ephraim in his old age. There is a three-cornered struggle for power. The patriarch will yield nothing; Abbie schemes to secure for herself and her children the farm on which they all live; Eben is determined to escape the domination of the patriarch and also to retain the rights of an eldest son now threatened by Abbie. She realizes that an heir of her own would be the surest road to her purpose and undertakes to seduce Eben by whom she hopes to bear a son to be foisted upon the patriarch as his own. Eben resents her as the usurper of his own mother's place but he succumbs, not so much merely to lust, as to the feeling that he will revenge his mother and establish his own spiritual independence if he steals Ephraim's wife. Presently the son is born. Ephraim is now beside himself with triumph, quarrels with Eben whom he tells that Abbie has always despised him, and gloats over the fact her son will inherit the farm. Feeling now that Abbie has merely used him, Eben rejects her protestations that it is now he whom she loves, and Abbie, taking the only way to prove that she no longer cares chiefly for her claim on the farm, kills the child. Eben, horrified and furious, goes off to call the sheriff but when the sheriff comes he declares himself a partner in the crime and wins the grudging admiration even of Ephraim.

Eben, thinks his father, is at least hard—not soft like the other sons who have left the farm to seek gold in California. "God's hard, not easy! Mebbe they's easy gold in the West but it hain't God's gold. It hain't for me. I kin hear his voice warnin' me agen t'be hard and stay on my farm. I kin see his hand usin' Eben t' steal t' keep me from weakness. I kin feel I be in the palm o' His hand, His fingers guidin' me. *(A pause—then he mutters sadly)* It's a-goin' t'be lonesomer now than ever it was afore—an' I'm gittin' old, Lord—ripe on the bow—*(Then stiffening)* Waal—what d'ye want? God's lonesome, haint He? God's hard an' lonesome." As the sheriff is about to lead the two murderers away Abbie turns to say, "I love ye, Eben" and he replies, "I love ye, Abbie." Then the sheriff looks enviously about and remarks to a companion "It's a jim-dandy farm, no denyin'. Wished I owned it." And the curtain goes down.

The success of *Desire Under the Elms* was in part a success of scandal. Many saw it either to giggle at

the scene in which Eben is seduced or to raise right-
eous hands in indignation that such obscenity should
be permitted. Still others, fashionably intellectual,
took it as an attack upon puritanism, a bold muck-
raking exposé of what really went on in the prim
houses of our revered forebears. But what the prud-
ish and the advanced, as well as the merely ribald,
failed to perceive is the fact that the themes of *Desire Under the Elms* are the themes of the oldest and
the most eternally interesting tragic legends here
freshly embodied in a tale native to the American
soil. The intense, almost religious possessiveness felt
by Ephraim and Eben and Abbie for the soil of
New England is set off sharply from the mere im-
personal greed of the sheriff. But this is not all or
even the most important thing. The struggle of the
son against the father, the son's resentment of the
intruding woman, canonical incest itself, are part of
the story whose interest is deeper than any local
creed or any temporary society, whether of our own
time or of another. It is one of the great achievements of the play that it makes us feel them not
merely as violent events but as mysteriously fundamental in the human story and hence raises the actors in them somehow above the level of mere characters in a single play, giving them something which
suggests the kind of undefined meaning which we
feel in an Oedipus or a Hamlet.

O'Neill's fondness for violent situation has al-

ways offended some. Others who had accepted it in
The Hairy Ape or *All God's Chillun Got Wings*
because it seemed there to enforce a moral relevant
to contemporary society, found it merely gratuitous
in a play like *Desire Under the Elms* whose plot
seemed invented for no purpose beyond that of providing blood and horror. "What's Hecuba to him or
he to Hecuba?" they asked. The tragedy of mere
lust and blood belongs, they argued, to a more primitive age, and incest is not one of the crimes by
which contemporary society finds itself seriously
threatened. But sensible as such criticisms may at
first sight appear, it is worth remembering that they
might have been made with almost equal pertinence
against Aeschylus or Sophocles. The adventures of
Oedipus or Jason do not suggest the home life of a
Greek in the Periclean age. Their legends were already remote, archaic, and monstrous. The horror
of the plays was for the Greeks as it is for us, nightmarish rather than immediately pertinent, and the
singular hold which they continue to have upon the
imagination is somehow connected with the fact.
Nor is it necessary to agree upon any explanation
of that fact in order to agree upon recognizing it.
Perhaps archaic desires and fears lead even in us a
more vivid subterranean life than we know. Perhaps tragedy seems grandest when the soul is purged
of just such terrors for the very reason that, being
so buried and so cut off from conscious life, they can

be reached in no other way and find in stories
concerned with the ancient themes the only chan-
nels through which they may be discharged. That
O'Neill should be led back to them as the result, not
of academic imitations of older literature, but of the
independent exercise of his imagination, is one more
indication of the power of that imagination. There
is, to say the very least, no *a priori* objection to such
themes. He has a right to be judged according to his
success in making something of them, and not pre-
judged merely because he has discovered for himself situations akin to those which have occupied
some of the greatest tragic writers.

Not until he came some years later to *Mourning
Becomes Electra*, probably the finest of his plays, did
O'Neill find another story so well suited to development in a spirit fundamentally related to that of
classical tragedy. It is not only that the personages
of *Desire Under the Elms* are involved in a story
which suggests their kinship with the enduring legends of the race. They are also personages who, in
the sense so important to their creator, "belong" to
something. They "belong" both to their soil and to
the traditions of their culture; to both of these they
feel an obligation which, when it comes into conflict with individual desires, is the source of conflicts
which shake them to the bottom of their souls. And
old Ephraim at least belongs also to God. That God
may be, as he says, hard and lonesome. Rationally

there may be something absurd in his thorough-
going identification of himself and his will with the
personality and the will of God. But that identification gives him stature. It gives him strength of passion in his struggle with the son whom he feels it
necessary to subdue and with the young wife in
whose arms he hopes to defy time. It also gives dignity and elevation and a kind of grandeur to the
end where he is spiritually triumphant in defeat.
Neither Oswald Alving nor his mother, to take familiar examples, makes any such appeal to the tragic
imagination.

Between this play and *Mourning Becomes Electra* came not only *The Great God Brown* and such
relatively unimportant works as the romantically
mystical *The Fountain* (produced in 1925 though
written somewhat earlier) and *Marco Millions*
(1928), a romantic satire rather lacking in crisp-
ness, but also *Strange Interlude* (1928) and *Dynamo* (1929). This last was announced as the first
of three plays dealing with modern man in search
of a god and the Theatre Guild's production was
notable for one of Lee Simonson's finest stage set-
tings, the power house in which the crazed hero
immolates himself upon the altar of Electricity.
Dynamo was not, however, either popular or well
received by most of the critics and O'Neill who is,
despite his long struggle with popular prejudices,
remarkably sensitive to criticism from sources he

respects, dropped the plan which called for two more plays. *Dynamo* may therefore be dismissed. *Strange Interlude*, on the other-hand, was the first of his experiments with a play very much longer than is conventional; it attracted wide interest; and it is of considerable significance even though it will probably suffer more and more by comparison with the later trilogy on *Electra*.

In *Strange Interlude* we again have themes which suggest the ancient ones and motivations which the chief characters only half recognize as somehow related to impulses too deep lying to be rationalized in terms of their public selves. But the setting is contemporary and the stress is laid upon attempts at self-analysis made possible by long soliloquies which represent a much more extensive use of the device than the masks had provided for in *The Great God Brown*. Instead of the crisply defined characters and motives of *Desire Under the Elms* where the definite religious and moral code of the personages provides a background against which the significance of their deeds is, in one sense, clear enough to them, we have modern characters so completely *déracinè* that they can only fumble in the effort to understand themselves.

Nina Leeds is mourning the death of a lover whom the objections of her father prevented her from marrying before he went away to the World War. Both she and her father at least half realize

that his efforts had been at bottom due to a jealousy
which is interpreted in Freudian terms. Nina, feeling that a certain failure of firmness in herself as
well as the treachery of her father has deprived her
of the normal fulfillment of life, finally agrees to
marry a pleasant unimaginative suitor. But it is
soon evident that he is no substitute for the now
completely idealized lost lover and when she learns
from her husband's mother that insanity in the
mother's family makes it prudent that she should
abort the child which she is carrying, Nina rebels
against what she regards as a second frustration
and defeat. And after a time she takes Ned Darrell
as a lover, only to attempt to dismiss him after he
has become the father of a son whom her husband
believes his.

Nina has come to feel that the loss of her first
love in the War meant the loss of all possibility of
real happiness, and whether this is actually true or
whether that loss has become merely the symbolic
excuse for a spiritual sterility which would have existed under any conditions, she now attempts to
compensate for the feeling of emptiness by refusing to let go of what she does not deeply want. She
absorbs the lives, not only of her lover and her husband, but also of "poor old Charlie," the timid bach-
elor "uncle" who has renounced all life of his own
in favor of genteel literature and the ambiguous
avuncular affection which he lavishes on Nina. To

this stalemate there is no real solution. In time, the husband dies; all passion in the relation between Nina and her lover, Darrell, subsides; and her son, named Gordon after her first love, flies away to a life of his own. Nina, all passion spent, sinks resignedly back upon what tepid affection she can continue to receive from her former lover and from "poor old Charlie."

The central situation of the play is powerfully imagined and, despite a certain inconclusiveness, it is continuously absorbing—at least up to the last section, after the beginning of which it becomes more and more apparent that the piece will end without ever achieving any satisfactory clarification of all that has been suggested. But the interest is rather interest in a static situation than in a developing drama. What we feel most powerfully is the mood generated by the spectacle of this group of people, each caught between the horns of his particular psychological dilemma, and each foredoomed from the beginning to struggles which are bound to be ineffectual. Perhaps the most impressive scenes in the play are the first in which Charlie, surrounded by his books, analyzes his renunciation of life, and that in which Nina, seated with her husband, her lover, and "poor old Charlie," contemplates "my three men." But both of these scenes are static; they are concerned with being rather than becoming; and the actual events of the play seem usually of

secondary interest, sometimes even arbitrary or for-
tuitous. Because the characters themselves do not
believe anything, they cannot really want anything.
The life of each is over before the play begins and
they fight sham battles over issues which might be
decided either one way or the other without changing the fact that all concerned are already damned.

It is impossible to say just how conscious O'Neill
may have gradually become of all he had learned of
his own aims, powers, and limitations in the course
of writing more than a score of plays. Unconsciously, at least, much clarification had taken place
by the time he came to compose *Mourning Becomes
Electra*. Some time before he had come to realize
clearly that he was concerned with "the relation of
man to God"—with, that is to say, the relation of
man to something, whether that something is the
universe itself or merely the enduring laws of his
own being, which is independent of local or temporary conditions. Now he realized also that tragedy
is essentially a story of some calamity growing out of
that relationship and that it differs from the story
of any failure, however calamitous, involving merely
human relationships by virtue of two facts: On the
one hand it involves a great deal more; on the other,
the protagonists take on a dignity they cannot otherwise have. But the would-be writer of tragedy to-

day labors under an almost insuperable difficulty. He lives in a society most of whose members are either confused and uncertain or explicitly deny that any such relationship between man and God exists; that there are any problems to solve except problems to be faced by men so entirely the product of temporary conditions, that even their past is no more than a ghost which it is their business to lay as promptly as possible.

This almost insuperable difficulty he has tried to elude in several ways. In *The Great God Brown* he treated subjectively the problem created in his own soul by the absence of any ability to define in satisfactory terms the something outside with which he felt the need to establish a relationship. In *Desire Under the Elms* he had written a tragedy which could be satisfactory as tragedy because it dealt with personages clearly related to both eternal human nature and their conception of God but which was "modern" only in the sense that it was made comprehensible to modern understanding, not in the sense that it represented modern life. Finally, in *Strange Interlude*, he had tried to tell an objective story dealing with the relation of recognizable contemporaries "with God." But *Strange Interlude* is vague and inconclusive like the characters' conception of that relationship. It lacks passionate directness in its action because they lack passionate direct-

ness in their own souls. And for this reason the
personages lack grandeur no less than the action
itself lacks tragic elevation.

No radical solution of the difficulty seems possible and perhaps none is. To ask for a tragedy
"modern" in every sense is to ask for a play whose
characters must have toward the universe as a whole
an attitude which would render them no longer typically modern. Hence the choice seems to be inevitably a choice between genuine tragedies about
people more or less remote from us and mere demi-
tragedies like *Strange Interlude* about ourselves.
Nor can it be said that O'Neill has ever completely
solved the perhaps insoluble difficulty though he
has, I think, come nearer to doing so in *Mourning
Becomes Electra* than in any of his other plays.

Here the story itself—considered merely as a se-
quence of events as distinguished from the interpretation which its personages put upon it—is almost
identical with the classical story of Electra and Clytemnestra while the characters are men and women
essentially like ourselves. The action is, to be sure,
set back to the time of the American Civil War and
hence, in years, almost as remote from us as that of
Desire Under the Elms. But the characters belong
to a different culture and the world of their consciousness is almost as far removed from that of
old Ephraim or his son as it is from that of the
Greeks. These personages no longer feel the eye of

God closely upon them and they no longer instinctively interpret life in terms of theology. Indeed, they differ from us less because of what they believe about their relation to the universe than merely because they are not, like us, quite aware either how much they no longer believe or what the implications of their non-belief are. Hence, though their situation is not complicated like that of Dion Anthony by the conscious agonies of lost faith, their story unfolds in a nearly godless universe. A play about them is necessarily a play which can borrow no grandeur from any sense they themselves may have of a relation to the universe more intimate or more clearly realized than ours.

Closely as the action follows the action of the legend and direct as is the correspondence of its characters, the modernization of characters and motives is carried through to the end. O'Neill's Clytemnestra murders Agamemnon and his Electra persuades his Orestes to bring about the death of their mother. But each is also a figure who belongs unmistakably in the historical setting which has been given the play and the motives of each are comprehensible in our terms. No anachronisms of thought or feeling remain; the story is meaningful and completely comprehensible without reference to the older form in which it was told. And yet the effect is also less different from the effect of the classical story than one would have supposed inevitable.

Such changes as are of necessity made in the mo-
tivation of the characters do not so much modify
the effect of the story as merely restore the force of
as much of it as can be made significant for us by a
translation into terms which we can still feel are
valid. It is true that the characters are no longer
the victims of fate so much as the victims of psychological processes presented in a manner which
reveals unmistakably the influence of Freud. It is
true, that is to say, that Electra loves her father and
that Orestes loves Electra in a fashion which the
Greeks did not understand, or perhaps, that they
merely did not specify. In addition, even that conflict between "puritanism" and earthy love which
O'Neill had suggested in other plays here enters
again. But such interpretations of such events represent merely the ways in which we understand
these situations, and the interpretations are not argued or insisted upon. They are there because they
are, given our own intellectual world, inevitable,
and they serve merely, as the intellectual background of a classical play should serve, to render
the action intelligible in current terms.

Obviously *Mourning Becomes Electra* is something of a tour de force. But it would be very wrong
to think of it as primarily a stunt or to assume that
it is interesting chiefly as such. The author certainly did not intend merely to play a trick, and
though he doubtless did not formulate his intention

for himself in any such analytic terms as are here to
be used, one may interpret the play as an attempt to
discover how much of the effect of a great tragic
story like that of "Electra" can survive the death of
the particular culture out of which it arose.

Considered merely as a series of events it hardly
belongs more in one time or place than in another.
In all ages women have murdered their husbands
for the sake of their lovers and it must have happened innumerable times that their children re-
venged the deed with the shedding of more blood.
What changes is the emotional meaning of this recurrent series of events and, consequently, what the
story-teller can make of it. To the Greeks it presented itself as something suitable for tragedy in its
highest form. We, on the other hand, are most familiar with the tale in terms of a criminal report.
We would not be surprised to find it told in a tabloid newspaper, for it seems, indeed, precisely the
sort of thing which sensational journalists find most
congenial. But we are surprised to find it the subject of an ambitious play for the simple reason that
in our culture it seems to have lost all values except
those which are crudely sensational.

But what is the meaning of that fact? Does it
mean that the story can have real significance only
when told against the background of the Greek religion and that it has been inevitably reduced to the
level of cheap journalism by the decay of everything

which could confer dignity upon it? Obviously
O'Neill is moved by the conviction that this debase-
ment of a story of passion and crime to the police
court level is not inevitable; that there remain to us
depths and dignities which could lift it into a different realm if they were properly exploited. And
Mourning Becomes Electra is precisely an effort to
exploit them. At least for the purposes of this play
it is not only assumed that we can no longer think
of man's relation to the universe in Greek terms,
but also that the puritan consciousness of man's importance in a universal drama of good and evil has
been lost as a possible source for either a sense of
the weightiness of human actions or a sense of "belonging" to something. Hence the play must attempt, by means of the sheer intensity with which
it presents strength of character and high passion,
to make these things seem sufficient in themselves
and to demonstrate that the possibility of emotional
greatness has not departed from us. It is, in effect,
the tragic poet's answer to a charge which he himself had previously seemed to make, to the charge
that both the sense of sin and the sense of greatness
have disappeared from the human consciousness
along with the religious sanctions which supported
them.

Perhaps the difference between Aeschylus and
O'Neill is to some degree a measure of the extent to
which the weakening of the sanctions has weakened

the emotions which they supported, if they did not create. But the difference between what the Greeks could feel and what we can feel is not as immeasurably great as it may sometimes have seemed when we were in the presence of tale-tellers who accepted too readily the police-court view of human nature. And in that fact lies a measure of the importance of the play. In no other of O'Neill's major works do the characters make with equal success the attempt to lift themselves by their own bootstraps, to gain stature, less by relating themselves to something outside, than merely by virtue of the strength that is in them. It is far less mystical than even *Strange Interlude*; it accepts without protest the validity upon its own level of a purely rational psychology. But it also manages somehow to reassert human dignity and to prove by the emotional elevation it manages to maintain that to explain human conduct even in Freudian terms is not necessarily the same thing as to explain it away.

Keats believed that science would be fatal to imagination, and since his time the fear has been repeatedly expressed in connection with various specific sciences or pseudo-sciences which threatened to render imagination irrelevant to the interpretation of human nature. Perhaps, however, there is nothing inimical to literature in either Freudian psychology or the economic interpretation of history. Perhaps the danger lies in failing to realize the difference between believing that Electra "had a father complex" and believing that her story is "nothing but" the story of such a complex. O'Neill seems to accept the current psychology as an account of behavior, but he seems to have realized that our emotional life is bound to remain something qualitatively different from any account of its determinates however adequate we may believe the account to be, and it is his success in recreating the quality of an emotional experience which makes the success of the play.

Much modern literature has been concerned with the defense of its own intellectual or moral background. It has been written to demonstrate that one may legitimately understand or judge men in the new ways characteristic of our time. But in *Mourning Becomes Electra* a reversal of emphasis has been effected. Because its thesis is taken for granted it has no thesis. It is no more an exposition or defense of a modern psychological conception than Aeschylus is an exposition or defense of the tenets of the Greek religion. It is, on the other hand, like all great literature, primarily about the passions and addressed primarily to our interest in them. It does not mean anything in the sense that most of the plays of Ibsen or Shaw or Galsworthy mean something but it does, on the other hand, mean the same thing as *Oedipus* or *Macbeth*—namely that human beings are great and terrible creatures when they are in the grip of great passions and that they afford a spectacle not only absorbing but also and at once horrible and cleansing. Once such stories have been adequately reclaimed for us in the only way in which it is possible to reclaim them; once they have been retold in terms we can understand, we cease to be concerned chiefly with the terms and again lose ourselves in amazement at the height and depth of human passions, the grandeur and meanness of human deeds. No one has ever explained exactly what it means to be "purged by pity and terror" but we return to the phrase because it describes, if it does not analyze, the effect of tragic art.

Since *Mourning Becomes Electra* O'Neill has produced two other plays, neither of which is of major importance but both of which must be considered in any estimate of his work as a whole. The first was *Ah, Wilderness!* a pleasant sentimental comedy (1933), very popular indeed, partly because of its own virtues and partly because the easy minor works of difficult writers have a special appeal to that large public which likes to pay its tribute to fame on occasions which make few demands upon its intelligence or imagination. But it is useless to pretend that O'Neill's peculiar powers are anywhere exhibited in this agreeable tale of a typical American family exhibiting the virtues William Dean Howells might have seen in it and no vices he would have thought it improper to mention. The kindly, rather futile mother, the wise if uncultivated father, the uncle with a weakness for strong drink, and the callow son who discovers love and literature together are recalled, as it were, with a tender nostalgic affection. The boy comes through and the play ends with the two parents standing in the moonlight, happily remembering their own springtime and concluding that autumn also has its joys. Is this—can this be— the work of an author who has so often brushed sentiment aside, assaulted heaven itself, and cursed God for giving His creatures thirsts which no earthly liquor can quench and passions which can consume nothing except themselves?

It is not merely that Mr. O'Neill has here dispensed with those murders and rapes, those incests, and those insanities which furnish the material for most of his tragedies—as well, let his flippant critics remember, as the material for most of the great tragedies of the world by any authors whatsoever. The really striking fact is that for the purposes of this play he has also dispensed with the whole of that attitude toward human life which had served in the past to distinguish him from dramatists content to deal with life in terms of its local manifestations and current standards of value. All his other recent work and, to a lesser extent, even all his earlier work dealt with ultimates. The characters had, of course, their local habitations and names; some of them—the Anna Christies and the Ephraim Cabots—were rooted in a time and place to an extent to which the Hairy Apes and the William A. Browns obviously were not. But even the most concrete of his personages were only secondarily, and for the sake of convenience, men and women specifically of a yesterday or a today and dressed in the mental or physical costumes of their period. Essentially they were all naked souls; forked radishes trying to be gods; helpless Lears exposed to the thunder of high heaven and the pitiless rain of God. The houses they lived in, the clothes they wore, the words with which they tried in vain to conceal from themselves and others the real nature of their predicament, were all so little substantial that they were only by convention treated as real at all. The sky of eternity was the only roof above them, and when they talked they could actually communicate with no one except themselves and God. Something of this sort is what O'Neill's symbolism has always been intended to convey, and it is everything of this sort which *Ah, Wilderness!* quite deliberately refrains from suggesting at any moment.

In conversation the explanation was given simply by O'Neill himself. He found his imagination haunted by the recollection of a youthful experience and he dramatized it in order that a ghost might be laid. That the play was, however, merely a strange interlude and not the result of any fundamental change in the character of his imagination

is clearly enough indicated by *Days Without End*
which was begun before *Ah, Wilderness!* was written and produced without success in 1934. Here the
theme is again the necessity of "belonging," but
here, for the first and only time, the hero finds
peace through the acceptance of a traditional religious creed. Like Dion Anthony in *The Great God
Brown* he is at war with his own nature. One half
of his personality demands love and faith, the other
half is cynically convinced that neither is possible.
Through the interposition of a Catholic priest he is
reconciled with himself and finally lies prostrate literally at the foot of a cross.

O'Neill himself later insisted that the events in
this play had meaning only as drama and that it
was not to be taken as a statement of his personal
belief. Not unnaturally, however, the public inclined to suspect the contrary and Roman Catholics
tended to assume that they might soon, if not already, claim the most famous American playwright
as their own. The truth probably is that *Days Without End* meant rather more than its author was willing to grant though rather less than Roman Catholics had some reason to hope. It could hardly have
been written by a man to whom the formula "In
Thy will we find peace" did not make a profound
appeal, but the disavowal could hardly have come
from one who had not already drawn back from the
step he seemed about to take.

In 1935 Richard Dana Skinner, formerly drama critic of *The Commonweal*, published a volume entitled *Eugene O'Neill: A Poet's Quest*, in which he not only assumed the playwright's conversion as an obvious fact but proceeded to analyze the entire body of his work upon the assumption, likening his development to that of a saint who passes through his periods of despair, suffers regressions from those states of peace which he is able to achieve, and finally wins through to faith. In many respects the result is the most illuminating account yet written of O'Neill's work as a whole and it owes its virtues to the fact that the central concern of the plays actually is very closely related to the central concern of the Catholic faith. But to follow Mr. Skinner all the way is to be led into judgments concerning the relative importance of individual plays which are patently perverse. Something is obviously wrong with a critique which seems to pronounce *Days Without End* the most successful of O'Neill's works and elevates so feeble a play as *The Straw* to a position of great importance while it treats *Desire Under the Elms*, *Strange Interlude* and *Mourning Becomes Electra* under the head of "Regression." O'Neill is most impressive as a playwright at the very moments when, according to Mr. Skinner's thesis, he ought to flounder most hopelessly and the fact can mean only that he draws strength from his resist-

ance to the solutions which a traditional religion
has to offer.

It is true that he is a mystic and that to him the
essential fact about human life is not that manners
and creeds vary from place to place and from time
to time but that two phenomena—the conflict between good and evil and man's desire to feel himself in harmony with something outside himself—
eternally re-appear. It is likewise true that the persistence of these phenomena is also a chief concern
of the Catholic Church, and if one assumes as correct and final the Church's attitude toward them,
then it is natural that its standards of truth should
be regarded as highly relevant to the judgment of
any man's work. But if, on the contrary, one assumes that Catholic teaching represents only one of
the attempts to formulate and solve problems more
universal than even Catholic theology itself, then
one may assume, not only that its terms are not necessarily the most appropriate to O'Neill, but also
that his most significant treatment of his themes
may have been those in which he seemed to be either
solving or failing to solve problems in a highly original way rather than in that single play where he
seemed to bring himself at last to the acceptance of
a ready-made solution which he had rejected many
times before.

To whatever extent it may finally appear that the
best of O'Neill's work falls short of absolute great-

ness, it is not likely that his failure will be found to consist in a failure to accept soon enough or fully enough any intellectual formula. Both as an intellectual and as an emotional conception *Mourning Becomes Electra* at least is in the true grand manner. To find in it any lack one must compare it with the very greatest works of dramatic literature, and to do that is to realize that the one thing conspicuously missing is language—words as thrilling as the action which accompanies them. Take, for example, the scene in which Orin (Orestes) stands beside the bier of his father and apostrophizes the body laid there. No one can deny that the speech is good and, indeed, one of the best in the play; but what one longs for with an almost agonized longing is something not merely good but incredibly magnificent, something like "Tomorrow and tomorrow and tomorrow" or "I could a tale unfold whose lightest word . . ." If by some miracle such words could come the situation would be not unworthy of them. Here is a scenario to which the most soaring eloquence and the most profound poetry are appropriate. Here also is a treatment of that situation imaginative enough to prepare the spectator to accept language as elevated and as moving as any a dramatic poet ever found. If the language came, we should be swept aloft as no Anglo-Saxon audience since Shakespeare's time has had an opportunity to be. But no such language does come and *Mourning*

Becomes Electra remains, therefore, only the best tragedy in English which the present century has produced. That is the penalty we pay for living in an age whose most powerful dramatist cannot rise above prose.

Mr. O'Neill is not, of course, our only playwright to attempt tragedy or near-tragedy. He is, however, the only one who has devoted himself consistently to the single task and hence the only one whom one thinks of as primarily a tragic writer. Certain plays whose conclusion is catastrophic will be discussed in the chapter on social criticism in the drama, certain others—notably those by Maxwell Anderson—in connection with the recent attempts to use verse on the stage. There remain to be mentioned here only a few isolated plays and the work of one man whose style it would be difficult to classify but who has demonstrated abilities of an extraordinary sort.

Two attempts, neither conspicuously successful, were made to dramatize Theodore Dreiser's *An American Tragedy*. On the other hand, *Ethan Frome* (1936) succeeded to an extraordinary degree both in catching the spirit of Mrs. Wharton's novel and in rearranging the material into genuinely dramatic form. Paul Green's *The House of Connolly* (1931) and *The Field God* (1927) are, on the other hand, consciously intended as "folk dramas." Like Miss Lulu Volmer's *Sun-Up* which had attracted much attention in 1923 their appeal is based primarily upon our interest in the picturesque customs of simple peoples, and one may summon the authority of Aristotle to support the contention that in genuine tragedy the delineation of manners exists for the sake of the action, not the action for the sake of the manners which may be exhibited.

Two plays dramatized from novels by Erskine Caldwell deserve more extended comment. *Journeyman*, the more recent of the two, was commercially a complete failure; the other, *Tobacco Road*, has at the present moment already enjoyed a continuous run longer than that of any other play in theatrical history except Miss Anne Nichols' *Abie's Irish Rose*. Mr. Caldwell has allowed himself to be claimed by the group which insists that social criticism is the be-all and end-all of the drama. He has himself been associated with various efforts to draw public attention to conditions among the economically depressed class in the South, and his novels deal ostensibly with life as it is lived by members of this same class. It would, however, be difficult to find any works whose tone or effect is less that of the simple sociological preachment than these novels and the plays which have been made from them. Instead of earnestness one discovers a brilliant but grotesque imagination and a strange humor which ranges from the Rabelaisian to the macabre. It is, indeed, only out of deference to public opinion that even the first and grimmest of the two plays is treated here rather than in the chapter on comedy where it really belongs.

Tobacco Road was produced in December, 1933. The dramatization was made skillfully by Jack Kirkland but the quality is so precisely the quality of the novel from which it was taken that it may be treated as though by Mr. Caldwell alone. And of Mr. Caldwell one may say that the rank flavor of his work is as nearly unique as anything in contemporary literature. One may, to be sure, assign him his special place in a rather vague tradition. He is, let us grant, as "hard-boiled" as Hemingway and as brutal as Faulkner. Like the latter he loves to contemplate the crimes and perversions of degenerate rustics; like both, his peculiar effects are made possible only by the assumption of an exaggerated detachment from all the ordinary prejudices of either morality or taste and a consequent tendency to present the most violent and repulsive scenes with the elaborate casualness of a careful pseudo-naïveté. Yet Mr. Caldwell is not, for all that, really like either Hemingway or Faulkner. Hemingway has something of the dogged, repetitious gravity of one of his own drunks; the second sometimes suggests the imbecile earnestness of his favorite half-wits; but when Caldwell is being most characteristically himself the mood which dominates his writing is the mood of a grotesque and horrible humor. The element of which he is most aware and that which he seems most determined to make us perceive is the element of an almost pure macabre. His starveling remnant of the Georgia poor-white trash is not only beyond all morality and all sense of dignity or shame, it is almost beyond all hope and fear as well. As ramshackle and as decayed as the moldy cabins in which it lives, it is scarcely more than a parody on humanity, and when some hidden spark of anger flashes briefly forth, or when lust—the most nearly inextinguishable of human impulses—motivates a casual and public seduction or rape, one is bound to regard these crimes almost as one regards the deeds of that traditional embodiment of moral imbecility, Mr. Punch. Perhaps it is difficult to believe that a play which centers about the determination of an old man to return a twelve-year-old child to her husband, which involves the almost continuous presence of a rutting female monstrosity with a hare lip, and which ends with the death of an old woman beneath the wheels of an automobile, can be funny. Yet funny it was, to me at least, and funny—though perhaps ambiguously so—it was also, I believe, intended to be.

That the material would fall most easily into a tragic or quasi-tragic pattern is obvious enough. Mr. Caldwell does violence to all our expectations when he treats it as comedy, but he succeeds because he manages to prevent us from feeling at any

moment any real kinship with the nominally human creatures of the play. All comedy of whatever
sort has as a necessary condition the fact that the
spectator maintains his sense of separateness from
the personages involved, that he is not inside and
feeling with them but outside and judging by standards different from theirs. Once we participate in
the life of any character, he immediately becomes
heroic or tragic, pathetic or romantic or sentimental. Once we succeed in detaching ourselves from
him, he must remain in some sense comic if he continues to be anything at all, and Mr. Caldwell puts
this law to its severest test by endeavoring to maintain a comic detachment in the face of characters so
depraved that mere revulsion, if nothing else, would
seem to make detachment impossible. It would be
interesting to inquire how one may account for the
fact that this detachment is, to a considerable extent, maintained, and one obvious answer would be
that the characters themselves are represented as
creatures so nearly sub-human that their actions are
almost without human meaning and that one does
not feel with them because they themselves obviously feel so little.

When *Tobacco Road* was first produced reviewers
were almost unanimous in finding it devoid of merit
and the success which it has enjoyed is probably due
far more to the atmosphere of scandal which has
surrounded it than to its very real power. *Journey-*

man, produced in 1938, was, on the other hand,
quickly withdrawn after it had been greeted by an
outburst in which certain of the critics of the daily
press seemed determined to outdo one another in
their effort to say that it was, without any exception, the worst play ever produced on Broadway.
That it should have created strong feeling is not in
itself surprising. Even if it be judged by the broad
standards of the present moment it is a violent and
bawdy piece which makes no apologies, either sentimental or otherwise, for its violence and bawdi-
ness. Anyone who denounced it as lewd and perverted would be taking a position understandable
enough if not necessarily justified. But to treat the
play as it was treated, to speak as if it were the mere
meanderings of an illiterate, is to exhibit a blind-
ness difficult to comprehend in view of the fact that
its imaginative force is the one thing which no one,
it would seem, could possibly miss.

Mr. Caldwell, it has already been remarked, is
said to think of himself as a realist with a sociological message to deliver. If that message exists it
would be even more difficult to find in *Journeyman*
than it was in *Tobacco Road* and one might maintain in addition that the chief characters, far from
being realistic portraits of real human beings, are
absolute monsters. But there is no use discussing
what a work of art means or whether or not it is
"true to life" unless one is convinced that the work

"exists"—that it has the power to attract and hold attention, to create either that belief or that suspension of disbelief without which its "message" cannot be heard and without which the question of its factual truth is of no importance. And to me the one incontrovertible fact is that both Mr. Caldwell's novels and the plays made from them do in this sense "exist" with uncommon solidity, that his race of curiously depraved and yet curiously juicy human grotesques are alive in his plays whether they, or things like them, were ever alive anywhere else or not. And if they seem, when abstractly considered, highly improbable, that only strengthens the tribute one is, in simple fairness, bound to pay to the imagination of a man who can make them credible. Perhaps this imagination is corrupt and perverted. Perhaps—though I don't think this is true—the world would be better off without Mr. Caldwell's vision of its corruption. But that is not the point. The point is that his imagination is creative in the most direct sense of the term. His creatures live, and no attempts at analysis can deprive them of their life.

Journeyman is concerned with the adventures of a fabulous traveling preacher who descends upon a remote Georgia community to drink its whisky, seduce its women, arouse it to orgy in a revival meeting, and then disappear one morning in an automobile acquired by the aid of a beneficent Provi-

dence working through the instrumentality of a
crap game. I have already remarked that the bawdi-
ness of the play is bare enough to shock even a
Broadway audience. I might add that I am inclined
to doubt the literal truth of the play as a picture of
rural Georgia for the simple reason that I find it
hard to believe a people physically so depressed could
be endowed with so much lusty life. But neither,
for that matter, do I find it easy to believe in the existence of Falstaff outside Shakespeare's plays, and
the important fact is that in Mr. Caldwell is some
power of story-telling by virtue of which I at least
cannot choose but hear. Nor do I see how any attack upon him, whether upon moral or any other
grounds, can hope to be effective if it does not begin by recognizing the primary fact that he has, to
an extraordinary degree, the power to imagine. It
is said that John Ruskin once refused to write an
article against the "poisonous honey" of the young
Swinburne. I am, he said, righter than he, just as
the lamb is righter than the tiger. But I am no
match for him. That was sound sense. Moral fervor
usually ends by seeming absurd when it refuses to
recognize the power of anything which has been
solidly imagined.

It is quite possible that Mr. Caldwell has no desire to be defended in such terms as these. It may be
that creative imagination is the last thing he wishes
to be praised for and "truth to life"—whatever that

may be—the only virtue for which he has any respect. But creative imagination is one of the rarest things in the world and probably rather rarer now than it usually is. Accuracy, right-thinking, goodwill—even, perhaps, virtue itself—are commoner. And Mr. Caldwell has creative imagination.

If, however, neither critics nor the public seem prepared to recognize in the theater those merits which novel readers have recognized in Mr. Caldwell's work, both critics and public have, on the other hand, given rather more than its due to another dramatization—that of Mr. John Steinbeck's *Of Mice and Men* which was produced in 1937 and awarded the Critics Prize. Mr. Steinbeck, also, deals with the lives of the lowly and he owes an obvious debt to the style of Hemingway, but for all the effectiveness of his writing and the equal effectiveness of the dramatization it is difficult, on sober consideration, to find in either novel or play the high imagination, stunning reality, and almost ineffable tenderness which many profess to find there.

The story—difficult to tell without seeming to do it an intentional injustice—is concerned with a strange friendship between two migratory harvest workers, one of whom is a witless but amiable giant given to fondling all soft and helpless things with a hand so unintentionally heavy that, sooner or later, he infallibly breaks their necks. The theme is tenderness taking strange forms in a brutal environment, and the dramatic tension arises out of our foreknowledge of the fact that at some time and for some reason the heavy hand will be laid with fatal results upon the camp's only member of the female sex—a pathetic little nymphomaniac married to the boss's cruel son. All the grotesqueness inherent in the tale is emphasized rather than concealed (we first meet the strange pair when the giant is being unwillingly deprived of a dead mouse he has been keeping too long in his pocket), but the skill of the writing is such that the whole is carried off far better than one could well imagine and that success is absolute in so far as it consists merely in forcing the spectator to take the whole with perfect seriousness. The only question is whether he is right so to take it, whether what we are presented with is really a tale of eerie power and tenderness, or whether, as it seems to me, everything from beginning to end is completely "literary" in the bad sense and as shamelessly cooked up as, let us say, the death of Little Nell.

After all, Dickens, as well as thousands of his readers, sincerely believed that Little Nell was the real thing. A fascinating but largely unexplored field lies ready for any psychologist-critic who wishes to examine the reasons behind the demand of every age that sentiment be served up according to some formula, the peculiar charm of which no previous age would have recognized and which every succeeding age finds patently ridiculous. Your Victorian was ready to weep over the fate of any sentimental monster if that monster could be described in sufficiently convincing terms as "innocent." Today nothing arouses the suspicions of any audience more infallibly than either that word or that thing, but a tough Little Nell, thoroughly familiar with four-letter words, would be a sensation on any stage, and the moronic giant of Mr. Steinbeck seems real because all the accidents of his character and surroundings are violent and brutal. Mr. Steinbeck, as I have already suggested, writes with great technical adroitness. But neither that adroitness nor all the equal expertness of staging and acting exhibited in the performance of his play would avail if the whole were not concocted according to a formula which happens to be at the moment infallible. Sentiment flavored with a *soupçon* of social criticism and labeled "Ruthless Realism" is well nigh certain to be applauded by thousands quite unaware that they are responding to an appeal as old—not as the theater itself—but as the rise of the middle-class public. Mr. Steinbeck's most recent novel, *The Grapes of Wrath*, is written in quite a different style and may possibly indicate that he himself realizes the extent to which *Of Mice and Men* was meretricious.

Neither Lillian Hellman's *The Children's Hour*

(1934) nor her more recent play *The Little Foxes* (1938) can be called genuine tragedy if that term is assumed to imply some resolution of the emotional tension which tragedy sets up. Indeed, the somewhat unusual effect of both plays depends in part upon the dissonances upon which they conclude and both might, in view of the violence of the actions, be called melodramas which end with the triumph of villainy. Both are, nevertheless, striking plays which have earned for their author a considerable reputation in the current theater and seem to imply the existence of a talent which has not completely realized itself.

The Children's Hour is the story of a fiendish child who threatens and cajoles her way from one despicable triumph to another until she has crowned her slighter achievements in making other children wretched by the wreck of four adult lives. It is a study in malice as disinterested as that of Iago, and it proved powerful enough on the stage to enjoy a run of almost seven hundred performances despite the fact that its cruelty seemed singularly gratuitous and, as it were, à propos of nothing.

Miss Hellman followed *The Children's Hour* with *Days To Come* (1936), which concerned itself with industrial conflict and, though completely unsuccessful on the stage, suggested that her central interest was in social forces. Then came *The Little Foxes* which was again a study of successful villainy though here some attempt is made to suggest that the wickedness of the central characters is somehow connected with the social system and we are asked to study it as a sort of malignant ulcer interesting for its diagnostic value rather than, as in *The Children's Hour*, to contemplate a flower of evil, a beautiful specimen of flourishing corruption. The two brothers and a sister who dominate the play exhibit various minor vices, including a sadism which leads one to maltreat his wife and to love a son who abuses horses, but it is acquisitiveness which dominates them and leads them to delight in attempts to swindle one another whenever it so happens that they are not for the moment united in the effort to swindle outsiders or to terrify the weak. Plainly the play is directed against contemporary society which is assumed to have acquisitiveness as its mainspring, and yet the action seems almost too extraordinary as well as too artificially contrived to serve as a very effective indictment, and one is again driven back upon whatever satisfaction can be obtained from the contemplation of unadulterated meanness and villainy wholly triumphant.

The fact that one tolerates *The Little Foxes* at all, that it, like *The Children's Hour*, is, indeed, as tense as it is disagreeable, implies no small tribute to the skill of the writer whose gift for characterization is superb and whose only defect as a craftsman is a certain tendency to over-contrive her situations. One does feel, however, that the plays are defective as works of art for the simple reason that the fables are not really suitable vehicles for the emotion which they are intended to carry. The rage which seems to dominate Miss Hellman is genuine; it seems to have its source in a sense of the world's injustice. But the stories she tells are too highly colored and too extraordinary to justify an attitude so inclusive as that which she has adopted. They seem invented to discharge an emotion generated by a vision of the world which they do not adequately represent. When their author has discovered a theme more truly central to her own concerns she may not unreasonably be expected to produce a genuinely important play.

CHAPTER IV

COMEDY

$SHORTLY$ before the War there flourished for a time in New York the vogue of the "bedroom farce." It prodigiously enriched the once famous Avery Hopwood, brought success to Philip Bartholomae and to Margaret Mayo, and it contributed to the stock of familiar allusions two titles, *Up in Mabel's Room* and *Getting Gertie's Garter*, still remembered for their quintessential vulgarity long after the name of Wilson Collison, only begetter of both, has been forgotten. But though "sophisticates" were for a time much intrigued by these plays which endeavored to achieve the maximum of naughty suggestion compatible with fables so constructed as to preserve the technical virtue of all the characters concerned, the most firmly established tradition of comedy was that "clean," homely, and fundamentally materialistic romance for which Winchell Smith and John Golden had perfected the formula.

Such typical examples of the genre as *The Fortune Hunter* and *Turn to the Right* fall outside the epoch covered in this volume, but as late as 1920

Frank Craven's *The First Year* achieved, with seven
hundred and sixty performances, one of the longest
runs of all time and its basic appeal is the same as
that exploited by Golden and Smith even if its picture of middle-class manners is shrewder and its
homely optimism rather less obviously synthetic. In
The First Year the troubles of a struggling young
couple reach a climax when their domestic arrange-
ments break down in the midst of a dinner given
for an important business acquaintance and the
wife, tired of struggling on too little a year goes
home to her mother. After she has left, the husband
gets drunk, finds new courage, realizes that the rail-
road company must have for its yards an otherwise
valueless piece of property which he happens to
own, and holds up its representative for a sum fantastic enough to serve as a symbol of permanent
comfort. Of course, the wife comes back and the
play ends on a note of tender sentiment.

All this, it must be remembered, took place in the
days when depressions were still assumed to be impossible and the general public, far from concerning
itself with the social meaning of any business enterprise, regarded "success" as the duty of all upstand-
ing young men and the "big deal" as the highest
form of human activity. Those—there were already some—who complained that *The First Year*
appeared less sweet if one described it as a play in
which a young wife leaves her husband because he

has too little money, and reconciles herself with
him after he has cheated a corporation out of a large
sum, were regarded as mere cynics. To make a lot of
money, to make it quick, and to make it by some
method which rendered the magnitude of the result
delightfully disproportionate to the effort involved
was regarded as the most inspiring possible example. Other young heroes had got rich by seizing the
right moment to open a garage in a sleepy village or
to modernize the paternal drug store with a soda
fountain. The hero of *The First Year* achieved the
same result in a few minutes by the even simpler
process of transferring money from another pocket
into his.

A new point of view was, however, about to make
its appearance. By 1920, ridicule of provincialism,
middle-class morality and the gospel of success was
beginning to play a large part in the work of
younger non-dramatic writers and *Dulcy* (1921)
served not only to draw conspicuous attention to the
collaborators, Marc Connelly and George Kaufman,
but also to introduce something novel on the stage
even though less so in other literary forms—satire
from a point of view rather "smart" than strictly
popular, and local rather than universal in its appeal. The central character was borrowed from
Franklin P. Adams's "column" where she had appeared from time to time as a self-satisfied retailer
of bromides, and the play, frankly farcical, merely

provided an opportunity for exhibiting at full length
the folly of a synthetic character who was little
more than a collection of all the empty common-
places which the authors most intensely disliked. It
was too much of the metropolis not to bewilder audiences unfamiliar with the smarter forms of journalism, but the authors returned to the attack with
To the Ladies (1922), a play about salesmen who
make speeches at Rotary Club dinners, and again
later in the same year with a dramatization of
Harry Leon Wilson's story, *Merton of the Movies*,
in which they once more exhibited their determination to satirize those typical American institutions
which the plain man was inclined to regard with
reverence.

Like George Kelly, whose *The Show-Off* was one
of the most talked-of plays of 1924, they also had
turned against what admirers of the young business
man called "pep" and a few days after *The Show-
Off* appeared, they produced *Beggar on Horseback*
(1924), based on a German book but completely
adapting to local conditions the fantastic story of a
sensitive young man who dreams that he has married the young woman with whom he is in love and
has been taken into big business by her wealthy father. The method is that of Strindberg's *The Dream
Play* which had been taken up by the expressionists in Germany but is here turned to the purposes
of extravagant farce. The young man witnesses con-

ferences at which exuberant directors toss twenty-dollar gold pieces about and decide that it is such fun they had better have another conference immediately. He also wanders endlessly from office to office trying to find someone with the power to authorize his requisition for the lead pencil without which he cannot do his work and in this as well as in various other ways discovers that nothing is less efficient than efficiency. When he wakes he naturally decides that business is not for him and the moral extends no further than that.

Beggar on Horseback is extremely effective, probably more so than any of the several other attempts which were made to adapt the method to satire, and it also marks the climax in the collaboration between the Messrs. Kaufman and Connelly. Indeed it exhibits a quality which could hardly have been achieved except through a combination of Mr. Kaufman's shrewd, sharp, cutting wit with Mr. Connelly's gentle, somewhat whimsical imagination. Some years later Mr. Connelly was to give his talents full play in the extraordinary poetic fantasy on Negro themes, *The Green Pastures* (1930), and Mr. Kaufman, with other collaborators, was to go on to become one of the most persistently and triumphantly successful of all recent American writers of comedy and farce. On the whole, however, the seriousness of his satire tended to diminish rather than increase so that he belongs now with the class of playwrights who tri-

umph in the commercial theater, whose pretensions
are non-literary, and yet who, despite frequent willingness to sacrifice artistic integrity to the crudest of
stage demands, often achieve an originality and an
incisiveness which less able if more scrupulous playwrights strive for in vain. As such he demands some
analysis.

Mr. Kaufman likes to work with collaborators,
seldom writes without one, and has produced plays
in conjunction with many different fellow-workers.
Occasionally the co-author is some little known
writer with a workable idea out of which Mr. Kaufman knows how to make the most; more often he is
a novelist or playwright who has already done successful work on his own and in such cases the pre-
dominant tone and mood of the play is likely to be
that of the collaborator. Thus when with Miss Edna
Ferber he wrote *The Royal Family*, which had a
very long run in 1928, the spirit of half-serious,
half-comic romance is precisely that of Miss Ferber's own popular novels and when, to take the example of a more recent effort, he staged John Steinbeck's *Of Mice and Men* nothing seems to be his
except the expertness of the adaptation to the needs
of the stage. In between came, among other things,
June Moon (1929), written in conjunction with
Ring Lardner, and the musical satire *Of Thee I
Sing* (1931) on which he collaborated with Morrie

Ryskind and in which the political tone is as certainly due to Mr. Ryskind as the dialogue of *June Moon* is certainly more like the dialogue of Lardner's stories than it is like that of Mr. Kaufman's other plays. Less witty in itself than Mr. Kaufman's dialogue often is, it exhibits Lardner's power to expose abysses of vulgarity in a single remark, and only he could have made the song writer say: "You needn't be afraid of me, girlie, I treat all women like they was my sister. Till I find out different." *Dinner at Eight* (1932) is merely sophisticated melodrama, the main outlines of which were certainly contributed by Miss Ferber, and the nostalgic sentimentality of *The Channel Road* (1929) is such pure Alexander Woollcott that Mr. Kaufman can have contributed nothing except his technical skill.

This does not mean, however, that Mr. Kaufman does not have qualities of his own or that he cannot exhibit them on frequent occasions. They are clearly defined in his first and, I believe, only independent play to be produced, *The Butter and Egg Man* (1925). They also show themselves so frequently in the results of collaboration that one has little hesitation in assigning to him responsibility for much that pieces written in conjunction with different co-workers have in common.

The first of these qualities is the result of an almost unrivaled instinct for dramatic construction of a sort which is seldom if ever really subtle or orig-

inal but is always precisely right at the moment.
No one can keep a play more continuously moving
or more unerringly place a laugh precisely at the
point where it is most needed, and this gift has made
him the nearly infallible expert whose deft "doctoring" of a script or equally deft staging can be
relied upon to save any potentially popular play
which seems just about to miss fire. His other outstanding quality is a kind of knowingness which
makes him admired and feared in any gathering of
those whose pride it is "to be on the inside."

Mr. Kaufman went from a newspaper office into
the theater; he is perfectly at ease when dealing
with the foibles of actors or men about town and his
best characters are those who belong in the lower
depths of "show business" or the related worlds of
night club and cabaret. Whatever knowledge he may
have of history or literature—and it is probably
considerable—he is careful to conceal. He would die
of shame if anyone were to call him "cultured" and
he would be as unlikely to quote Shakespeare as
Walter Pater would have been to talk cockney. But
if his characters know nothing outside their own
world, if they never read a book or have never so
much as heard of a play earlier than *Within the
Law* they know their world thoroughly. One may
rest assured that the argot they speak is the argot,
not of yesterday, but of today, and that if they refer familiarly to the bar of a certain hotel that is

the hotel which their kind really frequent at the moment. Mr. Kaufman would no more send the right people to talk over a deal at the wrong drinking place than a society editor would put a fashionable couple at the wrong hotel. He would be as ashamed not to understand the latest cant phrase as the president of a woman's club would be to be caught ignorant of the author of "Trees," and his wit is seldom beyond the comprehension of the kind of people about whom he writes. It is, indeed, what they would say if they could and what, having once heard, they probably repeat. His particular field is the "wisecrack" and if there is no better—if indeed, there is no other—name for the special sort of scornful observation or flippant repartee to which some unknown genius gave that name it still awaits exhaustive definition.

The wisecrack has, of course, certain things in common with more literary forms of wit. It is cynical, it is knowing, it is elliptical, and it is, very often, ironic—a sort of shorthand reference to facts or attitudes calculated to abash or annihilate the victim who stands convicted of a sentimental disregard for what every intelligent person knows. But the wisecrack is also all these things in a special way. In the first place its knowingness is of the kind previously described, a knowingness which is based wholly upon the moment and which, if it is actually part of the wisdom of the ages, is completely unaware of the fact. In the second place the wisecrack, instead of striving as the epigram does toward a perfection of elegance and polish in language, deliberately exploits the grotesque vocabulary and the syntactical vagaries of the sort of person into whose mouth it is commonly put. Many of Mr. Kaufman's wisecracks could be transferred without change from one of his characters to another quite as readily as the witticisms of Congreve or Oscar Wilde could be similarly taken from one character and given to another. But that is not because the wisecracks have no style. It is merely because his plays are as inevitably peopled with unlettered wits as those of Congreve and Wilde are inevitably peopled with mocking exquisites.

Sometimes, indeed, a new wisecrack is merely the rephrasing of a standard retort in such a way as to increase its indirectness. Thus in real life a smart Broadwayite who is treated to a "Possibly you don't know who I am?" would reply simply, "And what's more I don't care," but Kaufman has him remark with the innocent air of merely giving information, "That's only part of it." More often the speaker marshals all his contempt and defiance in one sweeping phrase which takes its point from a suggested analogy or a metaphor—as when the aging actress, still on her dignity, turns to the harassed manager who has paid her with a draft upon non-existent funds: "It's a check of yours, Mr. Lehman. It just came back to me for the third time. What does that

entitle me to—permanent possession?" To appreciate that, one needs a quickness of mind quite adequate to more literary witticisms but one needs no
knowledge except the fact readily learned from the
sporting pages that trophies often belong to those
who have won them thrice over.

Nothing is more typical or more revealing than
the reply attributed to Mr. Kaufman himself when
he was asked why, instead of such popular entertainments as he was accustomed to compose, he did
not try his hand at genuine and consistent satire.
"Satire," he said, "is what closes Saturday night."
Mr. Kaufman has said much funnier things but
none that more perfectly illustrates the nature of
the wisecrack and at the same time reveals his own
self-imposed limitations. In the first place the remark is shorter by almost two-thirds than "The
drama's laws the drama's patrons give, and we who
live to please must please to live." In the second
place, while it says just as much, it says it not only
in terms whose reference is to the moment alone,
but also in the idiom of those who close shows on
Saturday night. The "is what," the deliberate choice
of definition in the form which Teachers College
designates as midway between the moronic definition by iteration and the intellectual definition in
terms of essential qualities, is masterly. It puts the
remark on exactly the level where Mr. Kaufman
wants it. He is answering in character.

The remark also illustrates Mr. Kaufman's most conspicuous, most persistent, and apparently most cherished weakness, his willingness to subdue himself to the stuff he works in, to write plays of Broadway as well as about Broadway, to let the least worthy of the drama's patrons establish its laws. No one has ever satirized more keenly or more hilariously the absurdities of the synthetic play than he did in the scene in *The Butter and Egg Man* in which the producer recounts to the prospective "angel" the chief events in the plot of a new work marvelously combining all the worst features of the plays popular during the five years preceding. And yet Mr. Kaufman can go right on to work tricks just as shabby in that very play where the preternaturally innocent young man from Chillicothe gets the best of the city slickers for no reason at all except that he is turned into a sort of male Cinderella whose triumph will please those too naïve to appreciate the satire. Three of his other best known plays, *To the Ladies*, *June Moon*, and *Once in a Lifetime* utilize precisely the same plot scheme and each is simply a variant of the same perversion of the Cinderella story. In each, that is to say, the hero is a grossly incompetent boob of one sort or another, and in each case he blunders into a not very credible success. In the first—and to my mind most wholly unconvincing—he is a small clerk whose clever wife helps him to make an impression on the boss. In the

second he is an incredibly naïve youth from the
provinces who makes a miraculous hit as a theatrical "angel" despite all the wise guys preparing to
fleece him; in the third, he is a simple-minded vul-
garian who writes a song hit; in the fourth, he is a
second-rate vaudeville actor who sells himself so
successfully to the bewildered magnates of the new
talking films that they make him a director only to
discover that the film he has turned out is so bad
that the critics all hail it as the work of a new and
masterly technician. This gentleman's passion for
eating nuts has resulted in a constant tattoo accompanying the dialogue and his forgetfulness about
ordering the lights to be turned on has had the natural result of enveloping many important scenes in
an all but impenetrable obscurity. Nevertheless—
while in full flight from the scene—he discovers
from the reviews that all is well. The cracking of
the nuts is interpreted as a technical invention comparable to the drum in *The Emperor Jones*, and in
the words of one reviewer: "The lighting of the picture is superb. Dr. Lewis has wisely seen the value of
leaving the climaxes to the imagination of the audience. In the big scenes almost nothing is visible."

Yet despite the rather silly extravagance of such
an incident as this, and despite the plain sentimentality mixed in with *The Butter and Egg Man* and
To the Ladies, all these plays are rich with stretches
of dialogue and touches of characterization which

are amazingly shrewd and telling. Mr. Kaufman's comments are, in other words, on an entirely different level from that of the action itself, and he displays in them an intelligence which the main outline would certainly offend if he considered that outline as more than a necessary evil. Thus in *The Tangled Wildwood*, he can write a satire of the John Golden-Winchell Smith school of popular drama, but he can descend to the same level himself, and in either *June Moon* or *The Butter and Egg Man* produce something which is perilously close to a simple-minded success-story of the same sort.

Moreover, this willingness to descend to the lowest level of banality when the occasion seems to invite it is as ready in his latest work as it was in this relatively early one. *You Can't Take It With You* (1936), which he wrote with Moss Hart, won the Pulitzer Prize and had at least a considerable claim to that honor. Its central idea—that the good life consists in doing what you want to do rather than what is considered normal or reasonable—is a sound comic idea. It becomes thoroughly amusing when translated into terms of farce and embodied in a tale of the adventures of a mad family which keeps snakes on the mantelpiece and is furiously devoted to such hobbies as aesthetic dancing, playwriting, and the manufacture of fireworks in the cellar. But Mr. Kaufman, apparently afraid that a farce with

an idea is also "what closes on Saturday night," re-
members that a love interest is indispensable and
either invents or acquiesces in a story which delighted the movie-makers whom he had once so
hilariously satirized in *Once In a Lifetime* but at
which the judicious can do nothing except grieve.

Perhaps the most significant fact is that he has
remained essentially the "columnist" he was during
his early newspaper career—one, that is to say,
whose chief business it is to make brief random
comments upon a thousand things. Members of that
profession are not required to develop a philosophy
or to have anything independent to say. They are
supposed to sparkle a dozen times a day, not to throw
the steady light of sustained criticism upon either
society or life as a whole, and it is an exception
when one is found who has developed a consistent
point of view. Certainly Mr. Kaufman, for all his
brilliance, has not. He has said a hundred witty
things; yet it would be difficult after seeing all his
plays, more than a score in number, to say that they
tend in any one direction. One knows what Mr.
Lardner or Mr. Behrman stands for. The quality in
each case is almost as unmistakable as that of Eugene O'Neill. But in the case of Mr. Kaufman one
cannot be sure of anything—except that one will be
amused.

Shrewd flights of wit and shrewd touches of character are not enough to make a play. It has to be

held together by a plot and the plot must tend somewhere. But Mr. Kaufman, being primarily a wit,
does not know how to make a plot or even, probably, in just what direction he would want it to
tend even if he could concoct it. A wisecrack is usually what is known in the language of our generation as "a good comeback" and a good comeback is
something which not only arises out of the moment
but is intended only for the moment. It may imply,
perhaps, a philosophy in solution but it does not necessarily imply a consistently formulated attitude
and it is quite compatible with a complete inability
to expand any further the criticism which it suggests. Mr. Kaufman must therefore borrow his plots
and he borrows them from the sources nearest at
hand. He gives his play a conventionally sentimental ending because that is the way those plots have
usually ended before and also, perhaps, because he
has never explored his own mind thoroughly enough
to know what sort of ending would actually be consistent with the tone which the dialogue consistently
maintains.

At least once he apparently wanted to be taken
with complete seriousness and in *Merrily We Roll
Along* collaborated on a play treating a story peren-
nially tempting to very popular writers who are almost but not quite content with their popular ac-
claim—the story, that is to say, of the promising
talent which loses its way in the midst of worldly

success. It was told backwards, the first scene exhibiting the hero at a gathering of drunken wastrels,
the last showing him delivering a valedictory address full of high ideals at his own college com-
mencement; but the violent novelty of the device
was not sufficient to compensate for the banality of
the tale and the play was not the hit that its authors'
works usually are. Moreover, it suggests that if he is
ever to rise above his own level it will not be by
adopting themes radically different from those which
he has already treated with a large measure of success, but by inventing a fable really consistent with
the spirit of the wisecracks which enliven it; one,
that is to say, which is not only timely but caustic
and tough-minded as well.

All but one of Oscar Wilde's comedies exhibit in
exaggerated form what is essentially the defect of
Mr. Kaufman's plays. They are sprinkled with epi-
grams in every one of which the wit gives to the
fatuous moral of the play as a whole the lie direct.
But Wilde did not rise above his own habitual level
by returning to the style of *Vera*. He rose above it
by inventing, for once, the scheme of *The Importance of Being Earnest* in which action and moral
alike are as reckless and perverse as the dialogue can
manage to be. Mr. Kaufman happens to be as skillful as Wilde was clumsy in handling a conventional
plot. He is also a man whose wit is as racy as the wit
of Wilde was precious and literary. But he has

the same difficulty in imagining a story inspired throughout with the spirit of the talkers who act it. He puts his whole wit into a jest and then, as often as not, plants that jest in the midst of a play upon the fundamental naïveté of which only he could make the appropriate comment.

When judged as a whole Mr. Kaufman's work is seen to hesitate between pure farce on the one hand and, on the other, topical satire of the sort which made such early plays as *Dulcy*, *To the Ladies*, and *Beggar on Horseback* a part of the post-War revolt against current ideals and sentiments. Even at his most purposeful, however, his references are always exclusively to the local and temporary; he never pretends to go below the surface of manners, and on the whole his later tendency has been to turn either in the direction of sentimental melodrama or mere farce rather than in the direction of a more deep-cutting satire. Those of his plays in which he exploits the farcical possibilities of the metropolitan underworld suggest the work of several other playwrights whose success is exclusively a success in the popular theater and the transition from that aspect of his work to theirs is easy.

Notable among the writers whose work resembles that of Mr. Kaufman in its least serious aspect are James Gleason and George Abbott, two actors turned playwrights and similar to Mr. Kaufman in several respects. All three like to deal with minor figures in the worlds of sport and amusement; all cultivate a superficial air of tough sophistication; all actually exploit a vein of simple sentiment; and all are completely unliterary. Mr. Gleason was swallowed up by Hollywood some time ago and the great success of his sentimental farce comedies *Is Zat So?* (1925), *The Fall Guy* (1925) and *The Shannons of Broadway* (1927) is pretty well forgotten. Mr. Abbott, however, who collaborated on the second of these plays, went on to achieve the position he now holds on Broadway where he is generally regarded as second only to Mr. Kaufman himself in the art of writing, directing, or "doctoring" infallible successes.

Mr. Abbott was a moderately successful actor when he was asked to tinker with the script of John V. A. Weaver's experiment in colloquialism and sentimentality *Love 'Em and Leave 'Em* (1926). It was not, however, until he fell in with Philip Dunning, then a stage manager for a musical comedy, that he discovered the extent of his talents. Mr. Dunning had written a play about the night club as observed from behind the scenes and after Mr. Abbott had helped him to revise the script it became, under the title *Broadway* (1926), one of the outstanding hits of recent theatrical history. *Broadway* is a strange farrago of fast melodrama, good old-fashioned sentiment and knowing farce of a sort not wholly unlike that which Mr. Kaufman sometimes provides. It cannot possibly be taken seriously as drama but there are reasons why it demands some consideration in any discussion of the American theater during the last twenty years.

In the first place, few plays have been more successful in providing exactly what a large public wanted. For several years thereafter a whole school of playwrights was animated by no ambition except that of concocting a play as much like *Broadway* as possible and though no one, not even Mr. Dunning or Mr. Abbott himself, quite succeeded in repeating its success, "back-stage" drama became for a time a recognized genre. In the second place, Mr. Abbott discovered certain things in the course of his experience with that play which enabled him not only to become our most outstandingly successful producer of farce but to develop a recognizable style which is our chief contribution to the long history of farce itself.

What *Broadway* was when first conceived it is impossible now to guess. What it had become by the time it reached the first performance was an extraordinarily skillful exploitation, in terms which Broadway itself could understand, of the comedy, the romance, and melodrama of that underworld in which the gangster, the chorus girl, and restaurateur mingle. For the scene the authors chose the back room of a night club in which wholesale bootleggers pursuing their business and members of the homicide squad looking for evidence mingled with cabaret girls who come in quarreling to change their costumes and exit in the first step of their dance. Not only did they realize to the full the obvious picturesque possibilities of this scene but also turned the trick which is the secret of the most successful melodramas: they contrived a story centuries old in all its essentials but novel in all its external dress. Here is the sleek, sinister villain matched against the simple-minded hero for the love of the inexperienced girl; here is the unexpected murder done by the revengeful woman; and here, too, is the officer of the law who slips discreetly away when he realizes that justice, though irregular, has been done. But here as well is a locale new at least in the sense that it had never been so effectively used before, and here is dialogue whose liveliness, verisimilitude, and flavor constantly rise far above the intellectual level of the plot. The result is that even the sophisticated spectator found the old situations made surprisingly effective once more. To the general it was a perfect play; even to the judicious it was continuously entertaining.

Much of the popularity of *Broadway* was due to the fact that, for all the raffishness of its atmosphere, it took its sentiment seriously. Though fundamentally as naïve as it was superficially sophisticated, it gave the spectator the illusion that he was seeing life in the raw and that life in the raw was romantic enough to satisfy all reasonable demands. Technically, its great achievement was the discovery, or rather the rediscovery, of the theatrical value of mere speed in the simplest meaning of the word. Mr. Kaufman's plays give, to be sure, the impression of rapid movement. But in his case that means principally that the plot advances steadily to the continuous accompaniment of the rapid give and take of laconic conversation. It does not mean that the stage bustles with physical action. In *Broadway* however, characters rush in and out; the two or three plots become entangled with one another; everyone is being pulled in several directions; and no action is completed because it is always being interrupted by another. Mr. Abbott, in other words, here re-introduced the physical tumult characteristic of what used to be called "The Palais Royal farce" or, for that matter, of the "after piece" of our grandfathers, and he used it to heighten rapid melodrama as well as farce.

After *Broadway* Mr. Abbott tried with several different collaborators various experiments to discover new ways of exploiting the knack which is peculiarly his, succeeding with the sentimental drama *Coquette* (1927), and failing where he might have been expected to triumph with a straight melodrama *Spread Eagle*, written by George Brooks and Walter Lister. Probably, however, farce is the form to which his methods are most perfectly appropriate and more recently his name has been chiefly associated with a series of boisterous entertainments which have not only been repeatedly successful but all like enough to one another as well as different enough from most farces which preceded them to constitute a genre. Mr. Abbott commonly appears only as director or collaborator but there can be little doubt that he is largely responsible for the qualities which distinguish the various pieces and that the series from *Three Men on a Horse* (1935) to *Room Service* (1937) and *What a Life* (1938) owe at least as much to him as they do to the nominal authors. All involve the telling at top speed of a story in which probability is unhesitatingly sacrificed to grotesque action and all involve raffish characters of one sort or another.

Probably Mr. Abbott does not deserve credit for the original invention of the formula or even for that modification of it which consists of applying certain of the methods of *Broadway* to pure farce. That credit belongs more properly to Howard Lindsay who dramatized *She Loves Me Not* (1933) from a novel dealing wildly with a series of events beginning when a too chivalrous Princeton undergraduate undertakes to protect the innocence of a wandering night-club performer. But Mr. Abbott has since been associated with a whole series of highly successful entertainments which are all es-

sentially similar. *Three Men on a Horse* is concerned with the adventures of a mild-mannered little man forced to consort with race-track gamblers
because they would not permit him to waste his
magical gift for picking winners; *Brother Rat*
(1936) with the improbable scrapes into which a
group of students in a military school managed to
involve themselves; *Room Service* (1937) with the
misadventures of an harassed theatrical producer
trying to keep his quarters in a hotel where he cannot pay his bills; *What a Life* (1938), with the
troubles of a high-school student who cannot help
being a problem child despite all his desires to avoid
trouble. Mr. Abbott's students (like those in *She
Loves Me Not*) get into difficulties which might em-
barrass a gangster but, on the other hand, his deni-
zens of the lower depths of the amusement world
are often as innocently prankish as an undergraduate. Usually the situations involve something physically grotesque like the stuffed moose-head which
one of the characters in *Room Service* is trying to
save from both the rapacity of his creditors and the
enterprise of his companions who would like to
pawn it, or like the collection of stolen band instruments which the detective in *What a Life* returns
from a pawn shop. Essentially, the pieces are comedies of bad manners, farces determinedly impolite
rather than polite, but also as fundamentally inno-

cent as *Charlie's Aunt*—to which, despite all their superficial raffishness, they are more nearly allied than they are to the bedroom farce.

Sooner or later the possibilities of the style will be exhausted and the formula is already growing progressively more easy to recognize but no new vein has recently been struck and Mr. Abbott's nearest rivals are mere imitators of a method which no one else has managed to vary successfully. The farce hardly aspires to any high position in the history of dramatic literature, but Mr. Abbott is very nearly as original and as hilarious as a director of pure farce can be.

When set down in cold type there is probably nothing extraordinarily funny in the declaration made by the gentleman with the moose-head in *Room Service:* "I shot this moose myself and I ate him—up to the neck. But nobody is going to touch the rest of him." Coming as it does in the midst of rapid action and supported by the visual grotesqueness of the harried owner clutching the mounted trophy, it is the occasion of an amount of laughter reason would find it difficult to justify.

High speed farce of this particular kind has at least outlived the special variety of raucous but also sentimental melodrama which was born along with it when *Broadway* was produced. Back-stage dramas seem to have completely disappeared and along with them such even noisier farragos as *The Front Page* by Ben Hecht and Charles MacArthur and Louis Weitzenkorn's *Five Star Final*. It is hard to continue long in the faith that men who say "God damn" are necessarily deep-seeing realists and that the girls who fill the night clubs with music are necessarily longing for better things.

The two recent and very highly successful farce-comedies by Clare Boothe do, however, continue at least the extravagance and violence of this tradition. Miss Boothe was the author of two previous but already forgotten plays when *The Women* (1936) began its two-season run and she returned in the autumn of 1938 with the almost equally successful *Kiss the Boys Good-Bye*. The first, a sort of comedy of humors, exposes the vanity, vulgarity, and meanness of a group of smart but singularly depraved females; the second is an extravagantly irresponsible satire on the ways of the motion-picture industry and the foibles of the Southern belle. Critics and public alike have disagreed rather violently concerning the sincerity and the worth of Miss Boothe's satire. To some it seems hardy, bold, and devastating. To others—among whom I count myself—her plays seem deliberate and rather crude shockers, more blatant than witty. In *Kiss the Boys Good-Bye* one of the "sophisticated" characters explains to an outsider who is bewildered by the conversation on a Connecticut week-end that she will soon get the hang of it: all one needs to know is how

to be rude. This, I think, is a very dangerous conviction for a comic writer, and helps explain why
Miss Boothe's dialogue is so often crass rather than
funny. As one commentator put it, "The bludgeon-
ings of her wit left me bloody but unwowed."

Ten or twelve years ago it seemed that serious
comedy was most likely to develop in the direction
of the topical satire which the Messrs. Kaufman and
Connelly had begun to employ and which was, indeed, the basis of a number of now forgotten efforts.
But perhaps because the themes were treated in
terms so purely local, the vein was soon worked out
and satire tended either to decline into farce or to
grow bitter in the hands of politically minded playwrights. At one time or another various dramatists
did, it is true, attempt to treat social questions lightly
in the dubious form known as comedy-drama and
occasionally they achieved marked popular success
as Sidney Howard did with *Ned McCobb's Daughter* (1926) and Maxwell Anderson with *Saturday's
Children* (1927). Neither play—and they are the
two best of their kind—is, however, one by which
its author is likely to be longest remembered, and the
most substantial comedies written during the last
two decades are neither satires nor comedy-dramas
but works which at least tend in the direction of the
oldest and most honorable tradition of high comedy.

Such plays are frequently called "comedies of

manners" but in many, perhaps most, instances, the term is a misnomer for it suggests that they are concerned primarily with the superficialities of human behavior while the reverse is very commonly true. The ladies and gentlemen who people them do, to be sure, usually behave according to the laws decreed by the best society of the moment but they also tend to become abstractions and to act out stories which repeat eternal themes. Certainly Molière is not concerned primarily with the superficialities of behavior. His plays might be called "abstract comedies" rather more appropriately than they are called "comedies of manners" and the same may be said even of so much more limited a writer as Congreve. We are not interested in either chiefly because of the picture he gives of French or English society. We are interested because the characters, for all their local gestures, are abstract enough to represent persistent aspects of human nature, and the same may be said of the best recent American writers of high comedy. Mr. Kaufman—or even Mr. Abbott—is more deeply concerned with the mere manners of the moment than Mr. S. N. Behrman and less often criticizes them in the light of long human experience.

High comedy haunts the drawing-room because it is in the drawing-room that human nature in the abstract can best be studied. It commonly chooses as its protagonists cultivated men and women of the privileged classes because it is in those who have been most completely emancipated from material concerns that abstract human nature is most clearly revealed. And once this locale and these dramatis personae have been chosen, the formal characteristics which distinguish drawing-room comedy from all other kinds inevitably follow. It is a comedy in which, by premise, the characters are witty enough and sophisticated enough to understand themselves as well as the author himself does and to furnish their own comment upon their motives and behavior. It is also a comedy in which they have not only leisure enough to cultivate such comic understanding for its own sake but also material security sufficient to make the intellectual and emotional solution of their problems all-sufficient. Nor is it an accident that almost the only high comedies which do not take place in drawing-rooms take place in regions which, no matter what they may be called, really lie to the west of the moon, and that the Forest of Arden is merely a leafy salon. To whatever degree one so-called "comedy of manners" may differ from another in tone or spirit, it must be about intelligent people who can devote themselves to the cultivation of their intelligence, and it has remained the most persistently successful of comic forms for the simple reason that it provides both the circumstances under which comic intelligence can flourish most successfully and the problems to the solution of which comic intelligence is most obviously adequate. If it sometimes seems so detached from the immediate concerns of any particular epoch as to be dismissed as irrelevant that is not because it is so superficial but because it is so abstract.

The difference between high comedy of the sort under discussion and other related forms of merely "polite" comedy or drama is chiefly a difference in the degree to which it has been generalized and in the degree to which the spirit animating it has been purged of sentimentality and conventional, or merely fashionable, morality. Miss Rachel Crothers —the only contemporary American dramatic writer who has been turning out successful plays for more than thirty years and who still holds a secure place on Broadway—belongs in a continuous American tradition as old as Royal Tyler but her works are, for all their light touch, too definitely "problem plays" to be classed as pure comedy and her more recent works from *Nice People* (1921) to *Susan and God* (1937) are in most instances definitely topical.

Philip Barry and Mr. Behrman represent, on the other hand, an evolution in the direction of a more abstract high comedy and both are more cosmopolitan in their outlook. Though neither is lacking in fundamental originality both probably owe more than Miss Crothers, not only to English comic writers, but also to such continentals as Ferenc Molnar and Arthur Schnitzler. Plays by both these Central Europeans were performed during the early days of the Washington Square Players and the Guild, and they contributed largely to the "sophistication" of the American theater—which means, in so far as the term can be given a simple interpretation, that they encouraged dramatists to write and taught audiences to accept, situations rather more unambiguously racy than had been tolerated by a generation still proud to maintain that Anglo-Saxons had no reason to be curious about certain varieties of misconduct peculiar to continental races. Of the two, the achievement of the second is far more substantial as well as more unified, but Mr. Barry was a well-known playwright when Mr. Behrman first attracted attention and his very failures to fulfill early promises have their instructive aspects.

Mr. Barry was still a student with Professor Baker at Harvard when *You and I* won a five-hundred-dollar prize, was given a Broadway production, and in 1923 ran successfully for some months. Two other romantic comedies, *The Youngest* (1924) and *In a Garden* (1925), followed rapidly only to be succeeded with equal rapidity by two commercial failures—the much-praised but somewhat over-whimsical *White Wings* (1926) and the Biblical drama, *John* (1927). It was said that commercial failure stung him into the boast that he would prove to himself his ability to do pot-boiling when neces-

sary and that the long run of *Paris Bound* (1927)
was the result. However that may be, the last-
mentioned play not only exhibited substantial virtues
but was refreshingly free from a certain preciosity
which had previously beset the author and was to
beset him again.

The story of a loving wife who forgives her erring spouse just at the moment when she is sure that
he can never be forgiven skirts the edge of sentimentality but the morality which the play preaches
is fundamentally that morality of compromise which
is the essence of the comic spirit and the whole has
its being in a realm pleasantly illuminated by the
shrewd wit of civilized people. In certain respects it
suggests one of Miss Crothers' comedy-dramas because it is, for all the lightness of touch, intended as
a commentary upon a specific situation definitely
localized by the reference to strictly contemporary
manners and customs, including what was then the
vogue for Paris divorces. Hence it is, in one aspect,
topical or journalistic; but it is also high comedy all
but completely emerged.

Marriage, says the *raisonneur* of the piece, is too
serious a thing to be dissolved for trivial reasons.
Doubtless neither husband nor wife should ever
stray, but an adultery may be a very unimportant
thing, and only an essentially light mind would
consider it necessarily destructive of all the values
which a hitherto successful marriage has built up.

If a husband's extramural affair affects him so little that the wife does not even suspect its existence until someone tells her, then she can't have lost very much and it is she, not he, who is destroying the marriage if she clamors for a divorce. The lady in Mr. Barry's play first balks at this doctrine, but when she succumbs to an unexpected impulse to kiss an attractive young pianist with whom she happens to have spent an afternoon alone she learns how little such stray impulses may mean, and in a charmingly executed scene she forgives her husband because he, without knowing how much she knows about *him*, is so ready to forgive *her* for an infidelity of which he has reason to believe her guilty.

Now Mr. Barry's thesis is of course not new. The point of view from which it is developed is that which society has always held in those relatively rare periods when it has been neither so crude that it could not imagine any relationship between husband and wife except that of possessor and possessed, nor so romantically befuddled as to make a complete identification between the spiritual union of which it talked and the physiological process which it pretended to despise. Obviously the brutality of the peasant and the lyricism of the sentimental lover come to exactly the same thing if both agree in regarding exclusive physical possession as the *sine qua non* of successful marriage, and the best comic writers have always insisted upon this fact. Mr. Barry's point of view is, indeed, the only one from which true comedy (as distinguished from sentimental comedy as well as from tragedy) can be written because it is the only one which makes possible that triumph of the critical faculties over emotional impulses which is the essence of comedy. But true comedy is always rare enough to seem new, and so it is with the play under discussion. We have a dozen playwrights who can write acceptable drama or melodrama about the erring husband and we have a dozen playwrights who can write sentimental plays about the wronged wife who is big enough and tender enough to take back a thoroughly repentant sinner; but we have few who could sustain to the end the true comic spirit as Mr. Barry does when he makes the wife in his piece seal her lips, not because she is romantically forgiving (that, as the sentimental comedy says, "is woman's way"), but because she realizes that there is nothing important to forgive.

Mr. Barry's next play, *Holiday* (1928), carried him one step further along a road which looked, for a time, like the road to the best comedy yet written in America but which led instead to a very complicated frustration. The story of *Holiday* is concerned with a promising young man who loses his fiancée when she and her father discover that he has no intention of using his youth in making more money but is determined, rather vaguely, to "live" instead.

It need hardly be said that he finds in the course of the play another girl who understands him better and it is also probably hardly worth while to observe that this plot, by its very simplicity, reduces almost to fatuity the then current protest against the tendency to confuse the good life with material success. The plot is, however, extremely slight. The young man explains his own position with whimsical deprecation, and though the whole thing is tenuous to the last degree, it is also both delightfully witty and thoroughly humane as well.

Mr. Barry does not cultivate either the wisecrack or its more literary brother, the epigram. His dialogue is not of the sort which can be quoted in fragments, and it is almost too insubstantial to be subject to analysis. But it ripples in one continuous stream throughout the piece like the conversation which one hopes to hear (but never has actually heard) at some supernally well-selected dinner party. He tells no story that is really important and introduces us to no character very remarkable in itself, but he generates that atmosphere in which comedy lives, breathes, and has its being. The personages have less reality than those in *Paris Bound* and they are, as a matter of fact, too unsubstantial even for high comedy at its best, but they have something of the ease and gaiety and grace which that form requires. They make us believe, almost if not quite, in the real existence of that world of deli-

cate suavity, of free but decorous play of the intellect toward which sophisticated societies are always
striving. Though that world is never reached by any
beings of flesh and blood, it is the business of comedy to imagine it in order that we may have an
image of the ideal of civilized human intercourse
and, also, that we may find in this world of idealized manners some compensation for the crudities
of the real one in which we live.

After the success *Holiday* had enjoyed, both with
a large public and with the critics, one was hardly
prepared for *Hotel Universe* (1930) in which Mr.
Barry managed to display in all their fullness a defect of his understanding and a defect in his taste
neither of which had been more than hinted at in
previous work. The idea behind the play is simple
enough, once one has been permitted to glimpse its
outlines behind the mist which envelops it. It seems
that a collection of ever-so-rich and ever-so-sophis-
ticated people has gathered at a house party given
by a young girl devoting her life to the care of a
semi-insane father who used to be a physicist but
who appears to have lost his wits as the result of
some very loose thinking about space-time. It is a
subject which may be all very well for mathemati-
cians but which is disastrous for those who, innocent of mathematics, are prone to suppose that Professor Alexander is promising us all a kind of second
chance *(vide Dear Brutus)* in life. It seems, still fur-

ther, that each member of the company suffers from one kind of *Weltschmerz* or another because each has got himself "fixed" by an emotional experience in the past. Fortunately, however, there is something in the atmosphere generated by the physicist which liberates everybody. Each goes into a kind of trance, relives the crucial scene of his existence, and then awakes so completely purified and liberated that the whole party leaves, ready to begin a new life in the great world, while the physicist, his task completed, lies dead in a very comfortable chair.

The idea is passable and, I believe, sufficiently good Freudianism; but what the play needs desperately is more matter and less art. Every incident loses its outlines because every incident is swathed in layer after layer of fuzzy verbiage about Life, Death, the Great Beyond, and the fact (announced by a mysterious white cock given to apparently untimely crowings) that "somewhere it is always dawn." The dramatis personae are supposed to represent the intellectual as well as the social élite, but they indulge in the most appalling mystical chitchat and are responsible for a stream of discourse upon the surface of which float fragments of mangled Einstein together with all sorts of spongy, half-digested or completely indigestible bits which seem to be the remains of a meal formerly made upon some of the more repulsive varieties of New Thought. Such ideas pass current in Greenwich Vil-

lage salons when dusk and cocktails have combined
to elevate the spirits and depress the judgment, but
they are not taken seriously by captains of finance
and other authentic bigwigs, unless the upper classes
have degenerated further than even the more earnest satirists maintain.

Unfortunately, however, the pretentious pseudo-
philosophy of *Hotel Universe* was not the thing
most ominous for Mr. Barry's future career as a
dramatist. He might, as a comic writer, have pru-
dently resolved to keep the more misty of his no-
tions to himself and to devote himself to plays in
which thoughts about eternity did not have to enter.
But in the atmosphere of *Hotel Universe* there is
also a pervading air of unctuous snobbery which
suggests the mood of high comedy less than the
mood of those yellowbacks in which the author
seems to be perpetually engaged in inviting the
reader to share his surprised delight at finding himself received in such elegant society.

Mr. Barry went to Harvard; he is said to be
wealthy and to spend his life among people almost
as rich as those who inhabit his plays. These facts,
it would seem, ought to make it easier rather than
more difficult for him to understand the difference
between the useful convention which bestows upon
the personages of high comedy as much wealth,
leisure, and elegance as they can profit from, and
the assumption that wealth or fashionable manners

constitute in themselves the criteria by means of which an élite may be recognized. Modishness and elegance are the accidents, not the essentials of the comic hero, and it is absolutely indispensable that both he and his creator should recognize the fact. If that distinction is lost sight of then what ought to be comedy is bound to become, as Mr. Barry's loving analysis of *Weltschmerz* on the Riviera actually does become, mere vulgarity.

With *The Animal Kingdom* (1932) Mr. Barry made another attempt at high comedy. Fortunately, it is free from pseudo-metaphysical balderdash, but, unfortunately, it again reveals how completely the author had lost the power to distinguish between elegance and fashion and it introduces us to a set of precious puppets who might be the butts in a true comedy but could never be its protagonists. The play was, to be sure, hailed with delight. Critics and public seemed to agree that it was irresistibly charming. But it actually is, or at least ought to be, offensive in almost every feature from the coyly cynical title—which refers to the human species—on. Since the plot is of no moment only the tone counts and that tone, despite all the author's obvious efforts to be "authentic" or nothing, is distressingly hollow.

In *The Animal Kingdom* Mr. Barry wants to indicate that what he hates above all else is vulgarity. He wants to say that he despises the easy flippancy of Broadway no less than he despises the cheap sentiment of the uneducated, and that the blatant ostentation of the rich shocks him neither more nor less than does the middle-classness of the middle class or the proletarianism of the proletariat. He is always dreaming of some ideal milieu—of some purified Riviera or some intelligent Park Avenue—peopled with creatures really worthy of their gracious setting, and in pursuit of this dream he fills the play with characters who are fabulously "fine" as well as incredibly elegant, who combine the knowingness of the cosmopolitan fast set with the sensitivity of the artist as the artist is conceived in romantic fiction. But the result is merely that these characters are invariably a little bit "too" everything. They are too rich and too elegant to begin with, too preciously gay, and gallant, and sensitive as they develop. He is, besides, always telling us what they seem to be always telling themselves, namely, that never before were there any people so irreproachable from any reasonable standpoint. Park Avenue could not criticize their manners, Paris could not criticize their taste, and the Algonquin would hang its head in shame if it could realize how far it had been beaten at its own game. Even their morals are fundamentally as sound as their sophistication and their manners, for their essential "decency" is always flashing out from behind the flippant phrase; despite all the necessary complexity of their lives and sentiments they remain Boy Scouts at heart. Nor is there ever any danger that we shall fail to realize just how first-class everything is. With an accomplished casualness, characters and motives alike are always being unostentatiously turned up so that we shall not fail to see the mark. It is "Sterling," of course, but it is "Black, Starr, and Frost" besides.

If all this were purely extravagant and confessedly artificial, if Mr. Barry had his tongue firmly in his cheek and realized fully the ridiculousness of it all, then it might be amusing enough. But there is an undercurrent of seriousness which makes it evident that the author is determined "while laughing to teach." He reveals himself an essentially serious, somewhat sentimental man, and it is a pity that he should be seduced, as he obviously is, by the glamor of a kind of smartness really foreign to his nature. Because of it his people are unconventionally conventional and only escape one cliché to fall into another. They believe themselves free, spontaneous, and genuine; in reality they have only cultivated a more elaborate artificiality and stifled themselves with ultra-smartness while despising the smart. They like the right books and say the right things even though they have gone just one step ahead of the people who admit that they strive to do just that. They do not—to take a specific example—think the *New Yorker* really clever, but one is just as sure that they would think it cheap as one is sure that the group they despise would think it amusing; and they would be as ashamed to laugh at a drawing by Arno as their vulgar acquaintances would be ashamed not to. It is all too distressingly merely a matter of what "our set" is doing this year, and, to put it briefly, Mr. Barry falls into vulgarity as the direct result of his terrible fear that he might conceivably be vulgar.

Between *Hotel Universe* and *The Animal Kingdom* Mr. Barry had produced, without much success, a rather confused psychological study called *Tomorrow and Tomorrow* (1931). *The Animal Kingdom* was followed by two other unsuccessful plays, *The Joyous Season* (1934) and *Bright Star* (1935), which were followed in turn by an adaptation called *Spring Dance* (1936). More than two years of complete silence followed and when more than six years had passed since a successful play had appeared from his pen, one began to assume that a very promising talent had gone into permanent eclipse.

His was obviously a divided soul which took refuge, now in vague mysticism, now in an overvaluation of the "right" people and the "right" tastes because it could not wholly reconcile certain moralizing tendencies, evident from the beginning, with the comic spirit. He had been brought up in the Roman Catholic Church and by a happy acci-

dent the situation presented in *Paris Bound* was one
to which comedy and Roman Catholic teaching propose the same solution since both would agree that
a casual adultery is not necessarily adequate reason
for a divorce. But to say that is far from implying
that the two are identical in spirit or that they always or even usually concur so amicably in their
conclusions, and Mr. Barry's divided loyalties resulted in attitudes which neither could approve. A
man torn between religion and the ideal of gracious
living might not too surprisingly suppose that he
had found both in a society of elegant mystics looking at the stars from the Cap d'Antibes, but neither
theology nor the comic spirit is precisely comfortable there.

During the theatrical season of 1938–39 Mr.
Barry unexpectedly appeared with two plays very
different from one another but both rather more interesting and rather more successful than anything
since *The Animal Kingdom* had been. They were
called respectively *Here Come the Clowns* (1938)
and *The Philadelphia Story* (1939).

Here Come the Clowns (dramatized from his
own novel of the same name) is *Hotel Universe*
with a change of scene, and though the amateur
theology is even more persistently intruded, the atmosphere suggestive of that generated by a society
reporter is absent since this time the search for God
goes on, not at the Hotel Universe on the Cap

d'Antibes but in and about the Globe Theater (please note the symbolism) where minor vaude-villians gather.

As theatrical entertainment *Here Come the Clowns* was far better than anything Mr. Barry had written in some time and, some commentators not-withstanding, there is nothing obscure about the "message" of the play. Its much-troubled hero is a stage-hand who goes looking for God in order to find the answer to a few questions, but who falls instead into the hands of a charlatan and believes for a time that this faker's ruthless and destructive exposure of facts better left hidden is leading toward the truth our hero desires. In the end the charlatan is unmasked, and as the hero dies he proclaims his great discovery: God exists, but man's will is free, and man, not God, is responsible for evil and suffer-ing. The trouble with this idea, as an idea, is not that it is too complex but merely that it is too simple; and the trouble with the play, as a play, is merely that its author quite mistakenly supposes that the lives he is portraying seem more rather than less interesting and significant when they are "explained" in accordance with his intellectual scheme.

Both the dialogue and the situations are highly effective in a rather lurid and theatrical way. The play was well acted by an excellent company headed by Eddie Dowling, who played the hero with an innocent, rapt, and almost artless enthusiasm which clearly revealed his intense belief in his part. But it is unfortunate that a playwright, of all people, should not understand that human life and suffering as an artist can picture them are far more interesting mysteries than any likely to be revealed by the speculations of an amateur theologian. Theology is not a dramatic subject, though a myth may be; or rather, as one should perhaps say, myths are theology which has really been dramatized.

The Philadelphia Story, on the other hand, seems very pleasantly like the comedy which its author had been attempting, with something less than complete success, to write ten years ago in the days when he was very generally regarded as the ablest as well as the most promising of our creators of high comedy. Audiences on pleasure bent found it polite fun rather more than ordinarily delightful for reasons not immediately apparent but it has a flavor all its own which distinguishes it significantly from any of the other drawing-room comedies superficially very similar.

Mr. Barry has concocted a plot which involves the marital misadventures of the almost too charming daughter of one of the best of good families. He has added a female photograher who goes in the company of a writer for a magazine not too heavily disguised under the name of *Destiny*, and thus he has produced a scenario which might easily serve as

the basis for a raucous farce neither particularly
original nor particularly significant. But one gets
something very different from what this description would suggest—an almost exquisitely delicate
treatment of situations and themes which would
tempt almost any other writer into easy extravagance.

The piece has at least two themes. One is concerned with the daughter, superficially spoiled but
fundamentally decent, who comes to her senses
when three different men let her see how a kind
of spiritual pride has made her incapable of the
sort of human relationship she really desires. The
other theme, which runs just below the surface, involves the subtler aspects of that great truth which
W. S. Gilbert stated so bluntly when he announced
that the neighborhood of Seven Dials had no monopoly on hearts that are pure and fair. But neither
of these themes is, I think, the main concern of a
play which is struggling to illustrate in terms of
character and situation what is meant by such
words, at once cold and elusive, as refinement and
integrity and decency of soul. Any attempt to define any one of them is likely, as Mr. Barry had
demonstrated in previous plays, to end in the pre-
scription of a rigid code or, by implication at least,
in giving a false importance to mere fashion and
the *mores* of a fashionable class. Indeed, and as has
previously been suggested, it was just the failure

to draw clearly that fine line between decency and priggishness or between refinement of feeling and a mere familiarity with what is being thought, done, and said this season which constituted the chief defect of Mr. Barry's earlier comedies. But in *The Philadelphia Story* the confusion seems far less apparent. Certain of its characters are "nice people" and certain are not. But for once that vulgar phrase seems to have a real meaning.

Mr. Barry is said to resent the opinion that he is at his best in comedy rather than in those plays which are philosophical or moral in more conventional ways but *The Philadelphia Story* has made him once more a comedy writer of whom it seems not unreasonable to expect even better things than he has already produced. It suggests—and this is very important—that the fundamental defect of which he was previously accused may have been less a failure of feeling than an inability to express without shadow of ambiguity what was truly felt.

When the Theatre Guild produced *The Second Man* in the spring of 1927, S. N. Behrman, its author, was almost totally unknown. He had, to be sure, appeared as co-author of an unsuccessful comedy seen on Broadway shortly before, but his name meant nothing to the public and *The Second Man* was an astonishing revelation of a talent not only highly original but already sure of itself. Since

then Mr. Behrman has continued to write plays
which give him as sure a position in the contemporary American theater as any writer can claim.
No other has more clearly defined or more convincingly defended an individual and specific talent.

It is, as we shall see, difficult to discover in the
rather commonplace incidents of his career any
explanation of the fact that the whole cast of his
mind should be as different as it is from that of any
of his fellows, but from the very beginning it was
evident that he had accepted and assimilated the
Comic Spirit so successfully that he could write with
a consistent clarity of thought and feeling unrivaled
on our stage. Farce, burlesque, sentimental romance, and even satire are with us common enough.
They are, as a matter of fact, natural expressions
of that superficial tendency toward irreverence
which overlays the fundamental earnestness of the
American character. Embarrassed by deep feeling
or true comedy, we take refuge in the horse-play
of farce or the ambiguities of "sophisticated" romance, where the most skittish of characters generally end by rediscovering a sentimentalized version
of the eternal verities. But the remarkable thing
about Mr. Behrman is the unerring way in which
his mind cut through the inconsistency of these
compromises, the clarity with which he realized
that we must ultimately make our choice between
judging men by their heroism or judging them by

their intelligence, and the unfailing articulateness with which he defends his determination to choose the second alternative.

Several other American playwrights have hesitated upon the brink of the decision. One or two of them—Sidney Howard and Robert Sherwood, for instance—have written individual plays which all but defined their attitude and, indeed, Edwin Justus Mayer's almost unknown *Children of Darkness* is a masterpiece which may some day be rediscovered. But Mr. Behrman alone has been clear, persistent, and undeviating; he alone has emerged from the group by virtue of a surprising intellectual quality. One might have predicted him a generation hence. One might have foreseen that a definition as clear as his was bound to emerge and that someone in America would be bound to write comedy in the classical tradition—for the simple reason that such comedy is the inevitable product of a certain stage in the development of any nation's civilization. But the amazing thing was his sudden, unexpected emergence from obscurity with both attitude and technical skill fully formed.

The public was given no opportunity to discover Mr. Behrman until he had completely discovered himself, and *The Second Man* was not only a mature play—quite as good as anything he has written since—but actually a comedy about Comedy and therefore, by implication, the announcement of a program. All its accidental qualities were, of course, those common to nearly every work which even approaches the type of which it represents the fully developed form. The locale was luxurious, the people privileged enough to spend most of their time adjusting amorous or other complications, and the conversation sparkling with wit. But the theme was the Comic Spirit itself and the hero a man forced to make that decision between the heroic and the merely intelligent which must be made before comedy really begins.

Like Mr. Behrman himself, his hero belongs to a society which still pretends rather unsuccessfully to affirm its faith in idealism. Romantic love, for example, is still theoretically so tremendous a thing that no man or woman worthy of the name would hesitate to give up everything else in its favor. Life, below even the frivolous surface of fashionable existence, is supposed to be real and supposed to be earnest. But our hero—a second-rate story writer— has brains enough to know, not only that his stories are second-rate, but also that he does not really believe what he is supposed to believe. He can strike the heroic attitude, but the faith is not really there. A "second man" inside himself whispers the counsel of prudence, and common sense tells him that he does not really prefer love to comfort, or exaltation to pleasure. The only integrity he has is the only one which is necessary to a comic hero—the one which makes it impossible for him either to be a conscious hypocrite on the one hand, or, on the other, so to befuddle himself with sentiment as to conceal from even his own mind the fact that he is making one choice while pretending to make the other.

In terms of action the result is that he sends packing the determined flapper who wants to marry him, and returns to the wealthy mistress who can support him in the luxury to which he has been accustomed. "I suppose it's dreadful to take money from a woman. But why it's worse than taking it from a man I don't know. Do you?" Incidentally, and in the course of this action, the result is also to develop with bold clarity the whole philosophy of a hero who has surrendered the effort to be heroic and is ready to explain without equivocation why such as he must take themselves and the world as they find them without either trying to pretend that they are different or trying to make them so. The originality of the whole—so far as our particular stage is concerned—consists just in the fact that the play neither shirks the logic of its own conclusions nor presents itself as a simple "shocker" but remains essentially "serious" in the sense that it accepts and defends the premises of all pure comedy. "Life is a tragedy to those who feel and a comedy to those who think." Follow the emotions and you may reach ecstasy; but if you cannot do that, then

listen to the dictates of common sense and there is
a very good chance that you will be comfortable—
even, God willing, witty besides.

Mr. Behrman has concealed from the public the
inner history of his development and has not, so
far as I am aware, told us even what literary influences helped him upon the way to his exceptional
maturity, or enabled him to reach so quickly the
core of a problem toward which most of our dramatic writers are still only feeling their way. The
records say that he was born in Worcester, Massa-
chusetts, and that, as a stage-struck youth, he managed to get as far as Fourteenth Street, New York,
by appearing as an actor in a vaudeville skit which
he himself had written. Then he attended Clark
University and enrolled in Professor Baker's famous
course at Harvard. But since then the outward
events of his career have been much like those in the
careers of half the men connected with the New
York theater. For a period he worked on the *Times*
and for a period he acted as a theatrical press-agent
—being connected in that capacity with the resounding success of *Broadway*. Since his first play
he has spent a good deal of time in Hollywood and
he ought, it would seem, to share the weaknesses
as well as the strength of the typical Broadway
group into which he seems so obviously to fit. But
by now it is abundantly evident that *The Second
Man* was no accident. He shows no tendency to be-

come submerged in the common tradition, to write merely in the current manner. Instead, each of his succeeding plays has been quite obviously the product of the same talent and the same integral attitude.

It is true that once—in the comedy-drama *Meteor* (1929)—he fumbled the intended effect for the very reason that he had, apparently, not thought the situation through to the point where it could be stated in purely intellectual terms. This history of a rebellious and disorganized genius seen through the eyes of a bewildered but admiring acquaintance is not pure comedy because it is suffused with a sense of wonder, because its subject is a mystery, whereas comedy, almost by definition, admits no mysteries and adopts *nil admirari* as its motto. But since that time Mr. Behrman has not (except, perhaps, in his very latest play) faltered. He made a delightful play out of the delightful English *conte Serena Blandish* and then, in *Brief Moment* (1931) and *Biography* (1932), he extended his demonstration of the comic solution to the problem of civilized living.

Each of these plays—and especially the last—enjoyed a considerable run. At least *Biography*, moreover, was generally recognized by critics as one of the outstanding plays of the season. And yet neither, I think, was taken unreservedly to its bosom by the general public or given quite the whole-

hearted approval accorded to certain other plays
less relentlessly consistent in tone. The comic attitude—like any other consistent attitude—cannot be
undeviatingly maintained without involving a certain austerity. The time inevitably comes when
it would be easier to relax for a moment the critical
intelligence and to pluck some pleasant flower of
sentiment or—in other words—to pretend that
some compromise is possible between the romantic
hero and the comic one. But Mr. Behrman never
allows himself to be betrayed by any such weakness
and he pays the penalty of seeming a little dry and
hard to those pseudo-sophisticates who adore the
tear behind the smile because they insist upon eating their cake and having it too. Just as they giggle
when they find themselves unable to sustain the
level of O'Neill's exaltation—unable, that is to say,
to accept the logic of his demand that life be consistently interpreted in terms of the highest feeling
possible to it—so, too, they are almost equally
though less consciously baffled by Behrman's persistent anti-heroicism. Comedy and tragedy alike
are essentially aristocratic; only the forms in between are thoroughly popular.

Brief Moment is concerned with a very rich, intelligent, and disillusioned young man who marries
a cabaret singer because he fancies her somehow
"elemental," and then discovers that she is all too
capable of becoming a very convincing imitation

of the women of his own class—not only by adopting all their manners, but by developing a genuine enthusiasm for all the manifestations of fashionable pseudo-culture. One of its points, therefore, is that those "simple souls" which sometimes fascinate the too complicated are really less "beyond" than simply not yet "up to" the follies from which they seem so refreshingly free; but the real theme of the play is larger. Its hero is an inhabitant of that Wasteland described in so many contemporary poems and novels. He is the heir of all our culture, the end product of education and privilege, eclectically familiar with so many enthusiasms and faiths that there is none to which he can give a real allegiance. But instead of gesturing magniloqently in the void, instead of trying, like most of his prototypes in contemporary literature, to turn his predicament into tragedy despite the obvious absence of the necessary tragic exaltation, he is content, first to analyze the situation intellectually, and then to compensate for the absence of ecstasy by the cultivation of that grace and wit which no one can be too sophisticated to achieve.

Biography is again the vehicle for a comment made by the Comic Spirit upon one of the predicaments of contemporary life. Its heroine is a mediocre portrait painter with a genius for comely living. Her dilemma arises out of the apparent necessity of choosing between two men—the one a

likable but abandoned opportunist in public life,
the other a fanatical revolutionary idealist. Her
solution is ultimately to choose neither, and the
play is essentially her defense of her right to be a
spectator and to cultivate the spectator's virtue—
a detached tolerance. The revolutionist says everything which can be said against her attitude. He
denounces it as, at bottom, only a compound of
indolence and cowardice which parades as a superi-
ority when it is really responsible for the continu-
ance of all those injustices of the world which the
intelligent profess themselves too wise to correct.
But the heroine sticks to her contention that a con-
templative, understanding neutrality is "right" for
her. She may be wholly ineffectual. The world's
work may be done by persons less reasonable and
less amiable than she. But wit and tolerance are
forms of beauty and, as such, their own excuse for
being.

Mr. Behrman's plays are obviously "artificial"
—both in the sense that they deal with an artificial
and privileged section of society and in the sense
that the characters themselves are less real persons
than idealized embodiments of intelligence and wit.
No person was ever so triple plated with the armor
of comic intelligence as his heroes; no society ever
existed in which all problems were solved—as in
some of his plays they are—when good sense has
analyzed them. Just as the tragic writer endows all

his characters with his own gift of poetry, so Mr.
Behrman endows all his with his own gift for the
phrase which lays bare to the mind a meaning
which emotion has been unable to disentangle. No
drawing-room ever existed in which people talked
so well or acted so sensibly at last, but this idealiza-
tion is the final business of comedy. It first deflates
man's aspirations and pretensions, accepting the inevitable failure of his attempt to live by his passions
or up to his enthusiasms. But when it has done this,
it demonstrates what is still left to him—his intelligence, his wit, his tolerance, and his grace—and
then, finally, it imagines with what charm he could
live if he were freed, not merely from the stern
necessities of the struggle for physical existence, but
also from the perverse and unexpected quixoticisms
of his heart.

The theme of *The Second Man* was abstract and
timeless, concerned with nothing except the effort
of an individual to preserve the integrity of his own
unheroic soul through honesty and self-knowledge.
It assumed the stability as well as the homogeneity
of the comfortable world which its personages inhabited and, after the usual fashion of high comedy, presented no problems whose origin and solution were not both included within the framework
of the play itself. On the other hand, Mr. Behrman's four most recent plays—*Rain from Heaven*
(1934), *End of Summer* (1936), *Wine of Choice*

(1938) and *No Time for Comedy* (1939)—develop much further a tendency of which the beginnings are clearly observable in *Biography*. He had become aware—as who had not—of disturbing forces at work in a world where comedy seemed less and less at home and his problem became the problem of recognizing those forces without completely disrupting the pattern of plays. He had to discover what, if anything, the comic spirit could add to the discussion into which everyone was being compelled, willy nilly, to take some part.

In *Rain from Heaven* (1934), the first of this new series, the internal strain (if one may call it that) is most clearly apparent. Indeed, the piece is not comedy at all, if by that term one means either a play whose sole purpose is to amuse or even one in which all the conflicts are resolved through the benign offices of rationality. Here the dramatis personae include one figure whose predicament is almost inescapably tragic and here there is no solution wholly happy for the general problem whose existence the specific problems of the play suggest. In retrospect one realizes that the theme of the play— even, indeed, the situation—is surprisingly similar to that of *Biography*. Again we have a wise and clever woman brought into conflict with two men each of whom is capable of a certain fanaticism incomprehensible to her, and again it is her perception of a basic incompatibility which separates her from

both. Yet *Rain from Heaven* is by no means the
same play as *Biography;* and it is different not
merely because the concrete embodiments of the
situation are entirely different but, more importantly, because the problem has become more acute
and the issue more pressing. In the earlier play
neither the Communist nor the "practical" politician can be taken too seriously for the simple reason
that both are operating in what is nearly a vacuum,
and the discords between them are discords of temperament and ideology alone. But in *Rain from
Heaven* another sort of crisis is nearer. The scene
has been moved to England and to an atmosphere
charged with the possibility of proximate conflict.
One of the chief male characters is a popular American hero being exploited by his brother in the interests of a vague fascist scheme; the other is a German
refugee. Thus one comes face to face with tangible
results brought about by the two opposing temperaments; and if the heroine elects again to remain to
some degree "above the battle," there is here, as
there was not in *Biography*, a very real battle to
remain above. For this reason the action which begins on the level of pure comedy grows steadily
more tense, and the last act, while still managing
not to violate comedy's necessary allegiance to common sense, achieves real power in the drunken confession of the financier and the determination of

the refugee to return to participate in the conflict he had once thought no business of his.

As in *Biography* there can be no doubt where Mr. Behrman's own sympathies lie. It is safe, I think, to assume that here also the lady speaks for him. But the situation is no longer quite so clear, and the refugee makes out a much better case for himself than either of the men in the earlier play was able to do. While you are trying to understand your enemy, he says, that enemy will kill you— unless you kill him first. And to this the lady can only reply sadly that though it may be so her kind will, nevertheless, not perish utterly; they will somehow survive the storm, and when the storm has passed they will be there ready to play the only part they are fit to play—that of helping to re-establish the only kind of world really worth having.

In one respect the increased interest in world events which *Rain from Heaven* exhibits is a healthy sign even from the standpoint of those whose concern is ultimately with formal literary virtues. It means that the wit must be exercised in connection with fresh situations and that the curse of pure comedy, the tendency of its "sophistication" to become mere convention and its "wisdom" something merely borrowed instead of achieved, is escaped. But there is, on the other hand, no doubt that the intrusion of a situation so nearly tragic as that of the refugee does threaten to render comic treatment almost impossible. One step further in that direction and Mr. Behrman would have been compelled to abandon the very form of comedy for that of sociological discussion or genuine tragedy. That he had, however, no intention of doing anything of the sort was made clear by his next play, *End of Summer* (1936), where the subject is again related to current problems but where two devices are employed to keep the action upon a comic—at times almost a farcical—level. In the first place both the radical and the reactionary enthusiasts are again chosen, as they were in *Biography*, from among those whose connection with either radical or reactionary movements is largely intellectual and emotional and who are, by consequence, grotesque rather than dangerous. In the second place the central figure, again a triumphant woman, is this time presented in a manner wholly satirical.

The part was probably written for Miss Ina Claire who had acted the chief role in *Biography* and once more she is surrounded by a group of passionate men whose verbal bombs—often hurled at one another with the most vicious intent—somehow burst harmlessly over her head like so much fireworks. Anxious only to be loved, she is equally willing to endow a hospital for the sinister psychoanalyst—played with diabolical suavity by the late

Osgood Perkins—or to finance a radical magazine
for the two nice college boys determined to put an
end to her and her kind. And while the world rocks
around her—or at least while the other characters
assure her that it does—her only contribution to
the solution of its problems is the brilliant suggestion that calamities are on twice the scale they used
to be simply because the women (who make up one-
half of the population, remember) insist on taking
part in them now instead of staying quietly at home
as they used to do.

If among all Mr. Behrman's recent plays *Rain
from Heaven* is the most nearly tragic, *End of
Summer* is the most nearly farcical. It might be
argued indeed that when he degraded the character
of the *raisonneuse* of *Biography* to make the addle-
pated heroine of *End of Summer*, he was not only
abandoning comedy for farce but, by implication,
confessing to a loss of faith in the ability of the
comic spirit to play any really significant role in a
world got somehow beyond its ministrations. But
the play as a whole does not make any such confession for the simple reason that the farcical plot
is used merely to provide occasions for talk, all of
which is brilliant and much of which is profound.

What the personages talk about is precisely what
everybody talks about today: the blessing or the
curse of wealth, the problem of unemployment, the
brave new world which either is or is not about

to emerge; and they manage to say nearly everything upon those subjects which is either thoroughly foolish in a recognizably current fashion or genuinely wise in the fashion of all times. There are of course those who always rise to remark that even the best and most pointed discourses do not make a play, but the excellence of Mr. Behrman's talk has the effect which any particular excellence always has—provided of course that it is really excellent enough. It makes one forget for the moment whatever other kinds the universe may afford and becomes, for the time, all that one could ask.

It is true that all this talk leads the characters to no real solution and to that extent comic wisdom is admitted to have failed in these particular cases. The conclusions reached are no more conclusive than those which were being achieved in a thousand drawing-rooms at precisely the same moment. Indeed, the conclusion of the play finds everybody very much as he was found at the beginning. There was never much doubt that the daughter of wealth would end by taking the young radical suitor and hoping for the best. If the Machiavellian psychoanalyst does make one serious mistake, he is merely convinced that he will not make it again; and Miss Claire, of course, is beyond the reach of argument or fact. Whatever fate—and it is all still dark—the others may meet, one is certain that her invincible triviality will carry her through. Hers is the last word; for at the end of the play she is developing a lively personal interest in the second of the young radicals. It is true that, for the moment, she doubts the propriety of financing an enterprise whose chief aim is the destruction of her and her world. But the eager editor explains that to do so would only be, after all, to "anticipate the inevitable" and upon her bright exclamation, "Now wouldn't that be clever of me," the curtain goes down.

Yet even if this addle-pated lady represents in its last degradation the character of the liberal spectator and even if the wiser talkers of the play achieve no solution of their own problems, it remains clear enough that nothing else is likely to succeed where even reason is failing and to that extent Mr. Behrman's allegiance to the spirit of comedy remains. It is failing in a world where everything else is failing also, but it is still the only thing to which it will be worth-while to return if the world should ever recover from the sicknesses which afflict it.

Though frequently brilliant in dialogue *Wine of Choice* (1938), which is Mr. Behrman's most recent comedy but one, exhibits no new facets of his talent. The scene is again a sumptuous drawing-room through which the characters move with their accustomed ease and the subject under discussion is not unrelated to subjects which similar characters have taken in hand on similar occasions. That is no doubt the reason why the play was, on the whole, somewhat less favorably received by reviewers than some of its predecessors, but it seems unjust to with- hold admiration so long as Mr. Behrman can dis- course with the wit and incisiveness displayed in *Wine of Choice.*

His method, like every other method, has of course its limitations. Certain dramatic aspects of the conflict between the philosophy of those who have and the philosophy of those who have not obviously cannot be observed in a drawing-room. If, as the proponents of the left-wing drama main- tain, the real significance of that conflict does not emerge except on the battlefield where concrete things are being fought for, then it is plain enough that only plays which move through the factory and the field can communicate that significance. But a fundamental assumption of intellectual comedy is that one kind of understanding of any conflict is possible only on the sidelines, or at some other place where, for the moment at least, the battle is not raging. And Mr. Behrman's drawing-rooms are merely realistic substitutes for a spot of enchanted ground upon which deadly enemies can meet, frag- ments of neutral territory over which flies the flag of social convention guaranteeing against any breaches of the peace other than those which come within the definition of the "scene" as opposed to

the brawl. Here the contented sybarite can ex-
change thrusts with the reformer, but here also the
revolutionist can, not too improbably, come to express his inclusive contempt for all the rules of a
game which is not, to him, worth playing.

Mr. Behrman's clarity and wit being what they
are, the result is an exhilarating exploration of
minds and temperaments which can be as clear and
stimulating as it is only because he has adopted still
another convention—that by virtue of which each
character is permitted to speak as wittily as the
author can make him. For this same reason the battle is, moreover, almost necessarily a draw. That
does not mean that Mr. Behrman conceals the direction in which his own sympathies lie. He is, as
clearly here as in the other plays, among those who
hold that the sensibilities and loyalties of his lib-
erals—"inhibited by scruple and emasculated by
charm," as one character puts it—are indispensable
to any possible good life, however insufficient they
alone may be to guarantee it. But this revelation
of his own conviction does not involve any failure
to give the revolutionist an opportunity to make the
best possible statement of his case, and there is no
reason whatever why many spectators should not
conclude that he actually has the best of the argument.

Had Mr. Behrman happened to live in a more
stable society he would doubtless have written com-

edies even more strictly in the line of the great
comic tradition than these later works are. Faced
with the problem of writing comedy in an atmosphere which so many are ready to say makes pure
comedy either impossible or at least impertinent, he
has evolved something which it might not be improper to call the Comedy of Illumination—a kind
of comedy in which grave issues of the moment are
touched upon but which differs from sociological
comedy on the Shavian model in two respects. In
the first place there is a less consistent tendency to
beg the question in order to favor one side in the
debate; in the second place—and this is more important—the moral is not the moral of an enthusi-
ast, but a moral appropriate to a comic intelligence
which cannot but feel that the solution of all problems is ultimately to be discovered by tolerance and
common sense no matter how completely impossible
it may be to employ either effectively during certain moments of crisis.

After his first play *The Second Man* it apparently
became increasingly clear to Mr. Behrman that he
did not wish to continue to deal merely with the
timeless themes which have served for the whole
tradition of artificial comedy; and there was the
period to which *Meteor* belongs, during which it
seemed possible that he might sacrifice his particular gift to the conviction that he must be "important" in a way that comedy of his sort cannot

possibly be. A less sure instinct than his would either
have followed this false lead or in some other way
perverted his genius for a kind of wit which is essentially a pure and disinterested illumination. He
might, for example, have turned to tendentious
satire, for which he is temperamentally too skeptical and too balanced; or he might, on the other
hand, have fallen into a merely cynical nihilism
equally foreign to his urbane and generous spirit.
Instead, however, he happily invented this novel
kind of comedy which deals in no merely trivial
fashion with controversial issues and yet affords full
play to his essentially critical and skeptical mind.
It is a kind of comedy in which the protagonists
of various points of view, each equally endowed
with eloquence and intelligence and wit, state their
cases and expose the weakness of their adversaries
while the spectator stands by, not so much cynically
enjoying the discomfiture of each as delighting in
the insights which are afforded into both the problems themselves and the characters of those who are
trying to solve them. Such comedies are neither
tendentious on the one hand nor trivial on the
other. They are comedies of illumination. They
turn to the uses of the moment the most valuable
of comedy's gifts—the gift of disinterested insight.

From what has been said it must be evident that
the path which Mr. Behrman has been following is
one surrounded by pitfalls and that his success in

avoiding all of them is, in the case of each of the recent plays, almost miraculous. In his latest work *No Time for Comedy* (1939) the miracle was not, unfortunately, vouchsafed him.

As the title suggests, the problem is specifically that with which Mr. Behrman himself has been repeatedly faced—the problem of a comic writer living in an age forcing upon his attention conflicts which the comic spirit seems incapable of resolving. Such a writer seems, therefore, to be faced with an unhappy choice: either he must abandon the form and spirit of pure comedy, or he must confine himself to subjects which are bound to seem remote for the simple reason that they are bound to avoid reference to the topics most persistently under discussion. In the past Mr. Behrman has got around the difficulty in more than one way. In *Biography* he eluded it by making the two proponents of conflicting political philosophies so plainly mere talkers that they could be satisfactorily disposed of by the talk of the brilliant woman who embodied the comic philosophy. In *Rain from Heaven* he sent the German exile back to his native land to fight the battle which he could no longer honorably avoid, while he left his heroine to continue life in her own land, where, for the time being at least, the comic virtues of tolerance and common sense still have their place. Both of these plays were successful, but *No Time for Comedy* ceases almost to be comedy at all while failing to become very much more than a rather tepid problem play.

The central situation is decidedly promising. It concerns the dilemma of a brilliant young writer who, just as he is beginning to be tired of writing smart comedies for his actress wife, falls into the hands of a sort of up-to-date Dulcy, a rich woman who goes in for serious problems and is accustomed to use as a technique of seduction the discovery that successive men are wasting their talents by not realizing the depths of their souls. Inevitably our hero writes a play about death, asks his Dulcy to marry him, and plans to go off to Spain to fight for democracy. But when he realizes that the play is wretched stuff, it is almost equally inevitable that he should return to his wife and, presumably, forget about Spain.

Perhaps the fundamental trouble with the play is that it has really two themes, here related but not identical, which are never clearly distinguished and which get in one another's way. One theme, specifically stated, is concerned with a conflict over a man between two women representing two types—the shrewd, intelligent critic and the yearning flatterer or, as the former puts it, the tearer-downer and the builder-upper. The other theme, and the one to which the title of the play refers, is concerned with the question whether or not the comic virtues have any place in a world where, as the character in

Rain from Heaven had remarked, "while you are trying to understand your enemy he will kill you." This second theme Mr. Behrman takes seriously and seems by no means willing to dispose of out of hand. Yet he has begged the question and made the conclusion inevitable by making the protagonist of the graver view a pretentious imbecile while still permitting the hero's choice of an attitude to depend largely upon his choice between the two women. Perhaps because the two themes are confused, neither of the issues is ever directly faced, and at no time does either conflict really come to a head. The play is brought to a close by an ingenious theatrical trick, but brought to a close while one is still waiting for the decisive confrontation of the problem with which it ostensibly proposes to deal. The big scene has simply not been written, and even the hero's conclusions concerning the place of comedy in his world are left almost sentimentally vague.

Only occasionally does the dialogue exhibit the crisp and witty precision one has come to expect from Mr. Behrman, and it may be that the central confusion is also responsible both for that and for the fact that the characters seem to lack the charm which even his rattle-brains have managed so often in the past to suggest. Under the transforming touch of pure comedy even bores become entertaining, though we still recognize the fact that they would be intolerable in any drawing-room except the enchanted one which the comic writer has conjured up, and in the same magic realm even fools make themselves welcome. But in *No Time for Comedy* Mr. Behrman's characters are seen without enchantment. Katharine Cornell could not make the heroine as charming as she ought to be and Margalo Gillmore, though she played extremely well, could not make the solemn seductress amiable. Much the same might have been said of Lawrence Olivier as the playwright. We were asked to believe that, though we saw him in a bad mood, he was really a young man of graciousness and charm as well as intelligence. Yet it was difficult to see him as other than a pouting and ill-humored puppy. Probably Mr. Behrman was not very happy in writing this play, and he did not make either the spectator or the reader very happy either.

Except in the works of Mr. Behrman and, to a lesser extent, in one or two of the best comedies of Mr. Barry, American playwrights have seldom succeeded in combining the qualities which make for successful plays in the genre which these two have cultivated. "Polite" comedy on the one hand and, on the other, comedy which exploits the most characteristic aspects of the contemporary scene have tended to remain separate from one another and both have suffered as a result. From the days of Charles Hoyt, through those of Kaufman, Dun-

ning, Abbott, et al., the writers who have best
caught the superficial gestures of our civilization
have been unable to rise above the level of their
subjects. Their forms have been crude, their spirit
essentially naïve, and their wit of the sort which
expresses itself in the wisecrack. Those who, on
the other hand, aspired toward literature have generally suffered from a derivativeness which made
their work seem artificial and thin. Even Mr. Barry
and Mr. Behrman write plays one of whose characteristic virtues consists in an abstractness which
permits only the most highly generalized representation of contemporary manners. For that reason
deserved attention has been attracted by four rather
slight, isolated comedies remarkable for the success with which they managed to preserve a strong
local flavor while maintaining an attitude more
consistently and maturely comic than Mr. Kaufman
or Mr. Abbott has ever been capable of.

In 1929 *Strictly Dishonorable*, by an almost unknown young author named Preston Sturges, won
instantaneous and continued popularity because the
public appreciated if it did not analyze the originality of a little comedy which not only set its scene
in a "speakeasy"—then one of the most characteristic metropolitan institutions—but exploited the
picturesque possibilities of the locale without falling into the sensational romanticism of *Broadway*.
Instead, it caught the atmosphere in a fashion which

seemed veracious to a public less naïve than the
public which delighted in *Broadway*, and told a
story which the same audience found more credible.
The chief characters are a bibulous judge, an Italian
tenor, and a young lady from Mississippi stranded
in this unfamiliar environment; but none of these
facts is sufficient to explain the charm of the play
which depends upon bubbling dialogue and upon
the serene humor of the author's implied comment
upon the meetings which the strange social customs
of the speakeasy era made possible.

Mr. Sturges did not immediately achieve a second success in the theater comparable to that of
Strictly Dishonorable and he was taken away to
Hollywood where he has apparently become so completely naturalized that he will probably write no
more plays for the stage. Mr. Samson Raphaelson,
author among other works of *Accent on Youth*
which was produced in 1936 and which, despite a
somewhat greater artificiality, deserves mention for
its genuinely comic treatment of contemporary life,
is also chiefly occupied with moving pictures.

Mr. Mark Reed, on the other hand, has been continuously associated with the theater and for that
reason possibly promises more for the future than
either of the other two. In one respect at least, his
Yes, My Darling Daughter (1937) suggests comparison with *Strictly Dishonorable*. Both are rich
with local color and both solve their problems in

purely comic terms. Mr. Reed's heroine is a now
sedate woman who has almost forgotten the role she
had once played in the Greenwich Village renaissance, but who finds it difficult to explain away her
legend when "darling daughter" offers it in justification of her own proposal to dispense with the
formalities of marriage. Here we have the eternal
comic predicament of those about to be hoist on
their own petard greatly enriched in this instance
by the author's fine sense of the subtle differences
between the "emancipation" of the nineteen hun-
dreds and that of the young rebels of today. Some
playwrights would have made the tale merely
naughty, others—Miss Crothers for instance—
would have preached a gentle sermon, but Mr.
Reed arrives at a satisfactory solution without ever
violating the tone of comedy and allows the young
lady to surrender without sacrifice of principle.
The young man has been, all along, as uncomfortable as young men so often are, and to his
middle-class prejudices she finally agrees to yield.

Arthur Kober's *Having Wonderful Time*
(1937) exploited in dramatic form the milieu
which the author had previously described in a
series of sketches published in the *New Yorker*,
and it enjoyed a run of more than a full year. The
scene is a summer camp frequented by Jewish office
workers who save throughout the winter for their
two weeks of romantic leisure, and the play was

remarkable for its keen yet always kindly satire. For it Marc Connelly turned producer and the reason for his enthusiasm is easy to find. Mr. Kober's gentle shrewdness is of a sort which has hardly existed elsewhere in the recent American drama except in the plays of Mr. Connelly himself. Another very successful comedy in an unfamiliar manner was Lawrence and Armina Langner's *The Pursuit of Happiness* (1933), a sort of historical farce in the course of which a foreign idealist come to join the American revolutionary forces is introduced to the pleasant custom of bundling. The situation was handled with broad humor which did not, however, obscure the quaintness of the folk material, and the play deserved its long run.

Only two other American writers so far not alluded to have achieved both distinction and repeated success in comedy during the two decades just past and each has cultivated a manner so completely individual as to place each in a classification of his own. The first, Edwin Justus Mayer, invented a kind of half historical, half mythical, costume comedy of which he has produced only two examples, but in one of which he achieved a kind of ironic masterpiece which may yet be rediscovered and properly recognized. Before it was written, he had enjoyed considerable popular success with *The Firebrand* (1924), in which an invented escapade involving Benvenuto Cellini was used as an excuse for a fantasy on the theme of Renaissance manners and the total depravity of the Duke Cosimo made the occasion of somewhat grisly humor. Apparently this play enabled its author to discover his manner but it was not until the beginning of 1930 that *Children of Darkness* appeared briefly and demonstrated that though its fantastic irony delighted those capable of appreciating the literary and highly artificial product of an original imagination, it was unmistakable caviar to the general.

The original title of the play, *The Jailer's Wench*, suggests rather better than does *Children of Darkness* something of its mood but neither would prepare one adequately for what is in store for the spectator or reader. The scene is the private apartment where an eighteenth-century jailer keeps those of his unwilling guests who are able to pay for the privilege. Here a choice collection of villains practice upon one another the arts they had formerly cultivated in a wider sphere and, here, with the aid of the jailer's wanton daughter, they manage to find full scope for their genius. But wit flies back and forth—for these are accomplished scoundrels. Cynicism, refined and perfected, is carried to ineffable heights. Vice achieves a consistent code so perfect that it becomes an independent art, and man, deprived of everything except malice and wit, becomes an amazing creature whom one may admire with-

out scruple for the simple reason that his victims
are no better than he himself.

Success in a work of this kind depends, of course,
upon the ability of the author to maintain a mood
of ironic detachment, and this Mr. Mayer has found
himself quite capable of doing. One of the characters remarks that "the most eminent poisoners have
generally been of good family" and this observation will serve to suggest the tone consistently maintained and supported by a steady flow of brilliant
phrases, sometimes as brittle and almost as cun-
ningly wrought as those of Congreve. When a thief
has reminded the wanton daughter of certain amorous favors which she has granted him, she reminds
him that it is "a lady's privilege to remember, but
a gentleman's duty to forget," and nothing could
be better than that unless, perhaps, it is the reply
of the same daughter to another declaration of love,
made this time by a poet: "There are three things
which a man says with equal ease: 'I love you.'
'Madam, I regret that it will be impossible for us
to meet again.' And, 'By God, she was as pretty a
wench as ever I bedded with!' "

Yet polished phrases are only the ornaments of
Mr. Mayer's writing. His greatest gift is a gift for
comedy of the purest and most artificial kind, in
which he leaves any real scene in order to create
an imaginary world in which his fantastic yet clear-
cut characters can function perfectly, and where,

besides, they need be judged by no standards extraneous to themselves. He may call this world Renaissance Italy as he did in *The Firebrand*, or eighteenth-century England as he does in the play at present under discussion, but for him history is only a device for escaping from actuality, and the scene is really laid in one of the many provinces of the Realm of Comedy—in, to be precise, that particular province where nothing except wit and villainy count, and where, therefore, wit and villainy can achieve a perfection wholly delightful because they are, in that world, the measure of all things.

No one incapable of appreciating the comic possibilities of total depravity could enjoy this play, and obviously the Broadway audience was unable to do so. It did not perceive the charm of even Lord Wainwright (committed to prison because an inability to endure cant compelled him to poison "my wife and a few of her intimate friends") and it failed to understand how a comedy which contains nothing except wickedness can be wholly exhilarating. It failed to understand because it was unable to do what Congreve and Wycherley as well as Mr. Mayer invite their audiences to attempt—namely a moral holiday for the mind more complete than any it can ever enjoy outside the realm of art where all things may, for the occasion, be judged by the intellect alone and as though the intellect's burdensome spouse, the heart, had never existed.

The trouble with the real world is that it is too badly mixed. In it neither goodness on the one hand, nor wit on the other, is quite enough by itself. Mr. Mayer gives us here a microcosm ideally corrupt and somehow delightful because, perhaps, when we are in it we at least know where we are. His only mistake is that he thought it necessary at the end to introduce a touch of sentiment as out of place as it would be in *The Country Wife*. To suggest in such plays the possibility of virtue does not so much temper corruption as merely destroy the harmonious effect produced by consistent depravity.

To Burns Mantle, the drama critic, Robert Emmet Sherwood once wrote: "I have come to the conclusion that to be a successful playwright you have to cheat a little." Perhaps that conviction helps to explain why the form which Mr. Sherwood invented for his two most recent comedies distressed some critics almost as much as it delighted a very large and profitable public, but for ten years he has enjoyed an enviable reputation on Broadway and his very considerable talents are not likely to be denied even by those who sometimes wish he were a bit less ready to "cheat a little."

His first comedy, *The Road to Rome* (1927), achieved a resounding success. Hannibal was the hero and the story was treated somewhat in the manner of Shaw's *Caesar and Cleopatra*, but rather more in that of John Erskine's *The Private Life of Helen of Troy*. It was followed by *The Love Nest* (1927), an unsuccessful dramatization of a story by Ring Lardner, *The Queen's Husband* (1928) and *Waterloo Bridge* (1930), an unsuccessful attempt at sentimental drama. Then, in 1931, Mr. Sherwood re-established and confirmed his Broadway reputation with *Reunion in Vienna*, a comedy remarkable not only because it provided a very highly entertaining vehicle for the Lunts but also because it is so successful an imitation of the tone and manner of Molnar that it might almost have passed as a translation of a new work by the author of *The Guardsman*—from the situation as well as from the tone of which play it did, to tell the truth, take a broad hint.

Mr. Lunt played the role of an exiled Hapsburg who returns to renew acquaintance with Miss Fontanne, formerly his mistress but now the happily domesticated wife of a famous psychoanalyst. The Hapsburg maintains that in order to lay the ghost of memory it is necessary that he should spend the night with his former sweetheart. The psychoanalyst is obliged to confess that it would be fatal for him to forbid this therapeutic measure and so, leaving the two together, he informs his wife that she must decide for herself. Next morning no questions are asked and the audience is left, like the husband, to guess what really happened. Did Miss Fontanne consent or did she not? The only clue is given by a certain blank expression which Miss Fontanne permitted to occupy her countenance at the instant when she had just said "No" so effectively that the departing Hapsburg shut the bedroom door behind him with a fine air of finality. At that moment the curtain descends upon the second act and when it arises on the third the next day has arrived. But that blank expression above referred to should make it clear what was about to happen. Temptation is never so seductive as at the precise instant when we are struck by the fear that we have just succeeded in conquering it once for all. It leaves an emptiness behind which only the forbidden can fill, and it is at that moment that we begin to hunt through the tall grass for the apple we have just thrown away.

Undoubtedly the play owed a very great deal to the performances. Mr. Lunt was reckless, dashing, and impudent; Miss Fontanne, sly, capricious, and deliberately provocative. But to these qualities each added a certain knowingness which belongs with the racy sort of comedy they were called upon to play. Though the pattern of their conduct is romantic enough, it is always plain that each knows very well what it is all about, and plays the game for the game's own sake. The one is no simple maiden startled out of dreams of innocence; the other no passionate pilgrim deluded by his own eloquence. The battle is sham because neither has any real intention of holding out and the joke is inherent in the fact that the struggle is over nothing except those inessentials invented for the purpose of keeping the game from being either too simple or too soon over. Thus Mr. Lunt, Miss Fontanne, and Mr. Sherwood give lessons in the art of preventing sophistication from taking the fun out of life. They show how the uniforms may be very splendid and the military bands very stirring even though no real battle is to be fought.

Reunion in Vienna may not be intrinsically very important or even, in view of its close approach to the spirit of mid-European comedy, very original. With some show of reason one might, however, hail it as marking an epoch in the history of one of those minor folk ambitions which are seldom recorded even in histories of culture. From their earliest days the Washington Square Players were wistfully anxious to be, among other things, "continental," and the American intellectual often exiled himself in Europe for no better reason than that American authors were incapable of treating a chronicle of light love lightly. Here at last Mr. Sherwood had succeeded completely where others had failed; he was as "continental" as though he had been born in Budapest. One more of the reproaches tradition- ally leveled against American culture had been tri- umphantly answered. The works of Mr. Molnar need make us feel inferior no longer.

Possibly Mr. Sherwood himself decided that, hav- ing demonstrated his talents in this direction once, it was not necessary to demonstrate them again. In any event he soon proved that he could invent for himself a form as thoroughly American as it was novel, and he produced with great success two plays of which the second at least may perhaps best be described as a didactic vaudeville—a melodramatic farce-with-a-moral in which the author manages to discuss a current problem while maintaining all the superficial excitement, all the bustle and all the raf- fish humor, of *Broadway*. Mr. Sherwood is an intel- lectual by education as well as by temperament, but he has demonstrated that by taking thought he can beat more naïve dramatists at their own game.

Of the two plays, the one which it is most easy to take with complete seriousness is *The Petrified For- est* (1935), which came first. Its brilliant and in- stantaneous success need surprise no one. Writing so suave and acting so ingratiating would have been enough to insure the popularity of a play far less in- teresting in itself, and even now, indeed, they make it difficult to be sure just how substantially good it really is. Mr. Sherwood had something to say and he was obviously in earnest. He was also, however, too accomplished a craftsman to ask indulgence from any Broadway audience, since he knows the tricks of his trade and has a witty fluency quite sufficient to make something out of nothing. He could fool us to the top of our bent if that was what he wanted to do, and we may take it for granted that at least half of his delighted audience would have liked the play for reasons which have little to do with its theme. *The Petrified Forest* could succeed upon its superficial merits alone, and one has some difficulty in deciding whether or not one has been charmed into granting it virtues deeper than any it really has.

To begin with, the play is quite capable of standing on its feet as a simple comedy melodrama of a familiar type. The lonely filling station on the edge of the desert has been used before, and so has the band of fleeing desperadoes which descends upon it to take charge temporarily of the assorted persons who happen to find themselves there. In itself all this is merely sure-fire theatrical material, and so is the fresh and innocent rebelliousness of the budding young girl, who happens in this case to be the proprietor's daughter. Add, for love interest, a penniless young man who has made a failure at writing, and there is still little to distinguish the play from very ordinary stage fare. Imagine further that the dialogue is bright and the characterization crisply

realistic. You have now a play admirably calculated
to please anyone intelligent enough to prefer that
even the routine should be well performed. What is
more, this routine play can easily be detached from
all the meanings which Mr. Sherwood has given it.
It is complete in itself and it is, as I remarked before, quite capable of standing alone.

Yet for all this, it is plain enough that the play is
double and that the familiar situations may be taken,
not at their face value, but as symbols. Solidly realistic as the filling station is, it is obviously intended
also as a place out of space and time where certain
men can meet and realize that they are not only individuals but phenomena as well. Though there is
no obvious patterning, no hint of plain allegory
even for an instant, the characters represent the protagonists in what the author conceives to be the
Armageddon of society. The young man is that civilized and sophisticated intelligence which has come
to the end of its tether; the young girl is aspiration
toward that very sensitivity and that very kind of
experience which he has not ceased to admire but
which have left him bankrupt at last. About them
are the forces with which they realize they cannot
grapple: raucous bluster in the commander of the
American Legion, dead wealth in the touring banker,
primitive anarchy resurgent in the killer and his
gang. By whatever grotesque name the filling station may call itself, and no matter how realistic the

hamburger being served across its lunch counter as "today's special" may be, the desert tavern is also Heartbreak House, a disintegrating microcosm from which the macrocosm may be deduced. And the moral—or at least the only one which the only fully articulate person in the play can deduce—is a gloomy one. What Mr. Sherwood calls Nature, and what a poet once called Old Chaos, is coming again. We thought that she was beaten. We had learned her laws and we seemed to manipulate her according to our will. But she is bound to have her way again. She cannot get at us with floods and pestilence because we are too clever for that. But she has got us through the mind and the spirit. Intelligence can no longer believe in anything, not even in itself. It can only stand idly by with refinement and gallantry and perception while the world is taken over by the apes once more. And so when the bullets of the posse begin to shatter the windows, the young man and the young woman drop to the floor in each other's arms. It is a symbol of all they know or can still believe in, but they have no illusion that it is enough.

When Cervantes had finished the first part of *Don Quixote*, he was visited, so he says, by a friend to whom he confessed his inability to describe in any Introduction what his aim in the book might be; and upon this the friend replied that he should not worry about either explanations or meanings.

"Strive," said he, "that the simple shall not be wearied and the great shall not disprove it." One can hardly deny that the method worked in that particular instance, and it works again in the case of Mr. Sherwood's play. I have, to be sure, a lingering feeling that there are dangers inherent in the effort to write on two levels at once, and some scruples about accepting as symbols things as familiar in their literal use as some which *The Petrified Forest* employs. There is an unresolvable ambiguity at times, not only concerning the meaning but also concerning the emotional tone, and the melodrama as such sometimes gets in the way of the intellectual significance. But such objections are purely intellectual. Mr. Sherwood achieved the almost impossible feat of writing a play which is first-rate theatrical entertainment and as much more than that as one cares to make it.

Idiot's Delight (1936) takes the simple theme of the horrors of war and treats it in a play remarkable for the extent to which certain tendencies observable in *The Petrified Forest* are exaggerated until the manner becomes, at least in the light of all the conventions to which we are accustomed, monstrously incongruous with the subject matter. Here again Mr. Sherwood is discoursing upon one of the grimmest of topics—namely, the social and spiritual bankruptcy of modern life and one expects that a man who goes about crying "Woe to Israel" shall behave, not only with a prophet's earnestness, but also with something of a prophet's disregard of the arts of pleasing. But even in *The Petrified Forest* it was somewhat disconcerting to find the author delivering his message with all the disarming facility of the parlor entertainer. He was not merely skillful; he was positively slick; and in *Idiot's Delight* he is the same, only more so.

In that play audiences found even greater amusement than they had found before, the actors—this time Mr. Lunt and Miss Fontanne headed the cast —were even more perfectly suited, the producers even more substantially enriched. At the same time the theme is, if anything, even more grim, while the manner and methods are even more conspicuously those of the slickest contemporary stagecraft. Whatever else *Idiot's Delight* may or may not be, it is the result of the most accomplished showmanship exhibited in New York since *Broadway* and, indeed, there is much in both the pace and the methods by which the pace is maintained to suggest those of that phenomenal melodrama. Leaving aside for a moment the question of Mr. Sherwood's ultimate seriousness, the chief difference is that whereas *Broadway* used its theatrical virtuosity to make a shabby and conventionally sentimental tale acceptable to an audience which would have laughed it off the stage had the presentation been anything like as ingenuous as the story, *Idiot's Delight* uses a very similar virtuosity to enliven a theme which, for all its pertinence, is not very well suited to the purpose of enticing into the theater those who demand entertainment along with whatever else they may get.

The scene is a resort hotel high in the Italian Alps. The chief characters are the leader of a group of night-club entertainers (Mr. Lunt), an international munitions magnate, and his mistress (Miss Fontanne)—later revealed as an erstwhile vaudeville performer who had been the great love of Mr. Lunt's varied life. Imminent war hangs over the proceedings, and the final curtain descends upon the reunited lovers clinging together while bombs rain down upon the airplane base just outside the window.

None of the gaudy situations obviously possible from this set-up is missed, and much of the time the action is kept going by means of a series of "gags," both verbal and practical, some of which are clever and original, some of which—for example, the verbal one consisting of Mr. Lunt's remark, "I'm afraid you've been betrayed," to the girl who asks the value of a coin given her by an Italian admirer, and the practical one executed when he demonstrates excitement by putting his fist through a straw hat—are adaptations of material very decidedly in the public realm. The fact remains nevertheless that the effect is irresistibly lively and—what is more important as well as more puzzling—that despite all the gags Mr. Sherwood manages frequently to treat his serious theme with no little effectiveness. The speech in which Miss Fontanne describes an air raid to her munitions-selling lover is, to take a single example, hair-raising, and if the author's main contention—namely, that men are too emotional and too childish to carry to a successful issue any plan for abolishing war—is not especially encouraging, it is at least tenable enough as well as grim enough. When all has been said and done, there is no doubt about the fact that despite all the comic interludes the sense of the folly and the horror of war has been conveyed almost as effectively as it has ever been conveyed upon the stage.

Perhaps to those who object that the two aspects of his play are radically incongruous, Mr. Sherwood would reply what the Salvation Army is said to have replied when criticized for its habit of singing hymns to the latest and sometimes the least respectable of contemporary airs : "We see no reason why the devil should have all the best tunes." Leaving aside the question of artistic integrity, I do not know just how much practical justification there is for this attitude. I do not know whether or not "The Saloon Must Go, Boom, Boom" has actually saved more souls than the Gregorian Chant. It is a nice problem, implying a great deal with which those who are concerned primarily with social effectiveness will have to deal; and I can only say that I am at least pretty sure that—whatever the result—a great many more people will expose themselves to *Idiot's Delight* than usually expose themselves to treatments of similar subjects by our more uncompromising dramatists.

A great part of *Idiot's Delight* is not comedy but farce. Perhaps the rest would have been more appropriately discussed in the chapter which follows.*

* See p. 316 for mention of Mr. Sherwood's historical drama *Abe Lincoln in Illinois* (1938).

CHAPTER V

THE DRAMA OF
SOCIAL CRITICISM

MANY of the plays already discussed imply a criticism more or less fundamental of the social and moral order. In some cases—notably those of Eugene O'Neill and Sidney Howard—the authors had had intimate contact with definitely radical groups; in others they had merely breathed the atmosphere of protest in which the post-war intellectual was immersed and had written plays whose iconoclasm was all but taken for granted by audiences for whom certain unorthodox opinions were rapidly becoming orthodox. In few instances was the explicitly didactic and hortatory element conspicuous or the implied comment upon contemporary society much more than is inevitable in any work of art purporting to deal with contemporary lives and firmly rooted in its own age.

It was not, indeed, until the late twenties that much effort was made to use the stage as a soap box from which specific political doctrines could be preached, and the propaganda theater, frankly so called, developed chiefly as a result of that hardening of political convictions which the depression produced. Long before that, however, a few playwrights were discernibly more concerned than most of their fellows with deliberate social criticism, and more inclined to regard such criticism as the primary function of the theater. Notable among them were Elmer Rice, author of many successful plays, and John Howard Lawson, remembered chiefly for one; but the remarkable fact is that between 1916 and 1929 the American playwright was not more often consciously carrying on according to the gospel which Shaw had proclaimed and of which he had made Ibsen, willy nilly, a prophet.

The explanation seems to be that by 1916 the revolution, in so far as it was merely a matter of transvaluating certain intellectual values, of winning acceptance for certain moral attitudes, had been accomplished. In so far, on the other hand, as the teaching of Shaw and his interpretation of the teaching of Ibsen and others implied a revolution in social or political organization, the revolution he had proclaimed was unmistakably stagnating. The post-war world was apparently returning as rapidly as possible to "normal." Direct attack upon its fundamental institutions seemed hopeless even to most of those who theoretically opposed them, and the radical who got a hearing was the radical whose criticism was directed rather at the culture than at

the political organization of America. If he described
the lives of the poor, it was more likely to be for the
purpose of inviting compassionate or ironic contemplation of the contrast between such lives and the
lives of the more fortunate than it was to be for the
purpose of summoning the audience to the barricades. If he looked with a jaundiced eye upon the
rich it was more often to expose their vulgarity or to
satirize their intellectual and aesthetic limitations
than to attribute such defects to the capitalistic system.

One result of this was that, though the groups
out of which both the Washington Square Players
and the playwrights and actors of the Provincetown
Theater emerged were known then as "radical,"
they would be described by radicals of today as more
conspicuously bohemian than revolutionary. They
were homogeneous only to the extent that all dis-
senters were good-humoredly accepted by all others
for no reason except the fact that their opinions
were, in any event, not conventional, and even the
Provincetown group, from the beginning somewhat
grimmer than the Washington Square Players,
could include Mike Gold on the one hand and Edna
St. Vincent Millay on the other. The rise of Communism changed all that, not merely because it
made specific doctrines so important that the Communist radical soon came to hate all other radicals
even more vehemently than he hated members of

the bourgeoisie, but also because he had come to regard that aestheticism to which many of his former fellows had been attracted as a peculiarly vicious form of decadence and now proclaimed, not the freedom of art, but the doctrine that art was above all "a weapon." These facts explain why the political theater which emerged after 1929 was regarded as a phenomenon distinctly new. They also explain why such writers as Rice and Lawson, though more directly concerned than most of their contemporaries with social criticism, seemed at the time when they began to write rather part of the general movement than prophets of a different one.

Though both are, in a sense, links between the earlier and later groups of dissident playwrights, the career of neither has continued to prosper under changed conditions. Mr. Lawson went over wholeheartedly to the Communist group, but has achieved no great success with any of the plays written to preach its doctrine. Mr. Rice responded to the increased concern with political and social questions by intensifying the didactic element in his recent plays but did not proclaim himself a Communist and, after the failure of several plays, sulked for a time in his tent. Nevertheless both Mr. Lawson, because of one play, and Mr. Rice, because of several, occupy secure places in the history of the theater since the War. We shall first consider that part of the work of both which antedates 1929.

Mr. Rice's first produced play was *On Trial* (1914), a courtroom melodrama, novel chiefly because it called for a revolving stage which made possible the "flash back" technique borrowed from the moving picture. It earned him a modest fortune and the next few years were devoted to another melodrama, to the dramatization of a short story, and to a collaboration with Hatcher Hughes on the comedy *Wake Up, Jonathan* (1921). None of these efforts was conspicuously successful and none except the last of any particular interest. Then, in 1923, the Theatre Guild produced *The Adding Machine* and Mr. Rice became the Guild's first American "discovery."

Mr. Zero, the hero of this play, is an aging nonentity employed as an office worker, and also, as his name suggests, a symbol of all the depersonalized helots who perform the routine tasks of a commercial civilization. When he is discharged from his job because an adding machine has made him unnecessary, he rebels for once in his life, stabs his boss to death, is executed for murder and ascends to a heaven in which he is put to work at a machine of the very sort responsible for his downfall. But even heaven cannot use him as he is, and when the curtain falls he is on his way back to earth to try again.

Mr. Rice may or may not have remembered the button maker in *Peer Gynt* but *The Adding Machine* is not so much an imitation of anything—not even of the German expressionistic drama from which the technique was doubtless borrowed—as it is an original synthesis of half a dozen elements all of which were characteristic of current rebellion in the arts. In the first place there is, of course, the concern with human nature at its nadir, with the cipher not the great man as hero. What one gets is accordingly not tragedy but anti-tragedy and the story of a man without even the brute strength which had given *The Hairy Ape* at least one distinction. But, as in the case of *The Hairy Ape*, the dream world is called upon to contribute irrational elements capable of intensifying the atmosphere of a play which would otherwise fall as flat as a day in the life of Mr. Zero himself, and the whole becomes, not a series of rational events, but a nightmare.

It begins with a long soliloquy in which the wife of the hero reveals her soul in the course of some meditations on marital fidelity and the movies. Like the meditations in James Joyce's *Ulysses* it is ostensibly the stenographic report of a "stream of consciousness" but actually so intensified and formalized that it becomes a fitting introduction to the Walpurgis night which follows. The very monotonous insistence of its vulgarity hypnotizes the imagination and one passes easily into the world of half-insane fantasy where the main action takes place. Moreover, the formal unity and hence the artistic

success of the piece depends upon the fact that the
spell of the nightmare is never broken and no attempt is made to interpret it in fully rational terms.
Ten years later Mr. Rice, like many of his fellows,
would have been unable to write the play because he
would by then have been too sure that he knew precisely what it meant, and the nightmare which has
here all of a nightmare's not quite definable logic
would have become a mere allegory with all of an
allegory's childishly mechanical symbolism. In *The
Adding Machine* the author was describing a vision
in which he saw a typical human cipher rendered
contemptible by his own spiritual nullity and then
destroyed by a machine capable of performing his
absurd little function better than he could perform
it himself. Ten years later Mr. Rice would have
been capable only of explaining a theory which
made spiritual nullity the product of a society which
misused its mechanical tools. And the fact remains
—however lamentable it may be—that visions still
make better plays than theories ever have.

Mr. Rice devoted the next few years to adaptations and collaborations which added little to his
reputation. Then in *Street Scene* (1929) he returned again to the life of the urban proletariat for
a theme to be treated in a very different manner and
in a very different mood. In *The Adding Machine*
he had made his central character not an individual
but a symbol because the story of a cipher can be

made to seem even dubiously important only if one is made to feel that the story of one is the story of thousands. But Mr. Rice is not by temperament a man given to either abstraction or despair and he turned in *Street Scene* (instinctively, no doubt) to the opposite but more familiar method of dignifying the story of humble folk. He sought, that is to say, to discover even in the squalor of the slums men and women with character enough and passion enough to make them respected as individuals, and he wrote in consequence a melodrama with genuinely tragic implications. In one sense it is, therefore, the antithesis of *The Adding Machine*.

The method is the method of that realism which strives for the typical and yet stops just short of the point where all sense of particularity is lost. The entire action takes place in front of a typical New York tenement. The intent is to present a cross-section of the life in such a metropolitan microcosm, and the curtain rises upon a neighborly group on the front steps exchanging platitudes about the heat. Presently the janitor deposits the ashcan upon the sidewalk, a boy on roller-skates shouts to his mother on the third floor for a nickel to buy an ice-cream cone, and by a dozen such trivial incidents the rhythm of tenement existence is established. For a time we admire the accuracy with which these routine events are mimicked, but as the play proceeds the stress is laid more and more upon the lives and

characters of certain individuals. Before mere recognition has palled as a source of pleasure, various
little domestic dramas begin to emerge; then the attention is gradually focused more and more upon
one of them; and the play reaches its climax in a
melodramatic scene of unusual intensity—a scene
of violence which made even the hardened playgoer
grip his seat and stifle the involuntary and agonized
"Don't, don't!" which he was about to shriek across
the footlights. The events which lead up to it are
artfully managed, the tension grows tighter and
tighter as the moment approaches, and the scene itself is as vivid as such a scene can possibly be.

Obviously, a part of the interest which the play
holds is the result of this mere melodramatic tension which the author has managed to generate by
the use of devices as old as melodrama itself. Equally
obviously he intended that it should take on an addi-
tional importance by virtue of the fact that the scene
presented and the manners delineated are typical
enough to constitute a commentary upon a portion
of our civilization—even indeed to suggest a criticism of a society which generates slums and compels
human beings to live in them. But this is not all, for
the central story of the oppressed wife and of the
pathetic little love affair which precipitates the catastrophe also suggest the irrepressible aspiration of
human nature toward some sort of self-fulfillment.
She is not a mere Zero. She is capable of resolution,

of courage, and of choice. She is therefore capable also of dignity and the story of her fate is the possible subject of a genuine tragedy.

Mr. Rice never wrote again so good a play because he never again showed himself capable of being equally serious without sacrificing his interest in character to his interest in a theory and a lesson. *Street Scene* is a "proletarian" play in the simple sense that it is a play whose dramatis personae are all members of the proletariat. It is also a "proletarian play" in the sense that the form taken by the conflict and by the catastrophe is determined in part by the physical environment amidst which the characters live and the economic conditions against which they struggle. But the attention is centered upon the interplay of passions, and the personages are interesting chiefly, not because they are oppressed, but because, despite oppression, they have remained human beings.

After *Street Scene* Mr. Rice produced in rapid succession three plays lighter in tone and rather obviously intended primarily as contributions to the popular theater. Of these, *See Naples and Die* (1929) was a failure; *The Left Bank* and *Counsellor-at-Law* (both produced in 1931) conspicuously successful. Both the latter are narrowly topical in a way that neither *The Adding Machine* nor *Street Scene* had been since both deal with what used to be called "the humors" of a specific milieu—in one case that of the tourist's Paris; in the other a New York lawyer's office. But both are also characteristic of Mr. Rice because they exhibit his great skill as a practical playwright and, what is more important for the present discussion, because they spring out of that eager concern with the phenomena of contemporary life which, in the case of these two plays, renders even its trivia interesting to him.

No contemporary dramatist has (or rather had) a keener ear or a shrewder eye. No matter what milieu he chose to present in a play, one might be sure that its salient features would be recorded with an exactitude which both the camera and the phonograph might envy. What most of us have only seen or heard he has noticed; and the result is a spectacle at once novel and familiar—familiar because we have met every one of its elements before, amusingly novel because we have never previously realized just how characteristic these familiar things were. The titter of recognition is the response which he is surest to win, and realism of a kind could hardly be carried further. In *The Left Bank* his room in a cheap Parisian hotel is perfect in its verisimilitude and so too are all the things that go on in it. The bathroom two flights up and the telephone three flights down are nature herself; so too are the obsequious but incompetent male chambermaid, the light which goes on over the bed when it is turned off in the room, and the hideous wallpaper which is convincingly declared to be worse in the next room than in this. Whoever has taken his course at the Dôme—and what American under fifty has not?—will smile with malicious pleasure and feel, besides, a certain pride in the realization that he too is in a position to appreciate the jest. For a time the Left Bank was, hardly less than Kansas, a part of the American scene. "Et in Arcadia ego," murmured the spectator. He too knew whereof Mr. Rice was speaking. He too had tried to forget a damnably inadequate bath by reflecting on the superiorities of European civilization, and he too had babbled of the graciousness of Parisian life while munching stale *croissants* beside a bed of incomparable hideousness. But none of these reflections quite last the evening out, and as the minutes rolled by, one became more and more acutely aware that Mr. Rice had nothing new to say concerning the problem of the expatri-ates.

Obviously these latter are running away from themselves and obviously that is something which no one can do successfully. Their roots are in Amer-ican soil and can draw their sustenance from no-where else—even though, perhaps, it is just as well that every rebel should find out that fact for him-self. If they want a different civilization they will have to build it for themselves since, as the *raison-neur* of the play remarks, "It seems to me that we have got to go where the world is going, not where

it came from." All this and more along the same
sensible line is said well in *The Left Bank*; but
something less familiar would be necessary to make
the play more than the rather amusing comedy it is.
If the scene is to be familiar and the characters are
to be typical, then there is a crying need for novelty
somewhere, for the pleasure of recognition, genuine
though it be, is not by itself enough for a great or
really stirring play.

All that has just been said of *The Left Bank*
might be applied with very little change to *Counsellor-at-Law*. The latter play, to be sure, professes
to be serious in its undertone since it is concerned
with the personal tragedy of a self-made lawyer
who is compelled by force of circumstances to wan-
der through certain not too attractive back-alleys of
practice; but the effect is primarily the effect of
comedy, and there is an entire gallery of characters
so justly drawn that one recognizes them immediately as exquisitely lifelike. Certain sections of the
play——notably the first scene of the first act which
establishes the atmosphere——succeed so admirably
that they might stand by themselves as complete
sketches. Time and time again the spectator is moved
irresistibly to laughter by the perfect rightness of
some remark made by an office boy, a telephone
operator, or a dowager from the East Side. Few will
remember the plot; many probably remember the
youth in whose possession was always to be found

the volume from the law library which dealt with rape.

We shall return to Mr. Rice's latest—and very different—work in connection with the frankly didactic drama, but before discussing that drama it will be more convenient to consider Mr. John Howard Lawson whose one conspicuously successful play belongs, like *The Adding Machine*, to the period before the radical dramatist had a specific doctrine which he felt it his first duty to preach. Mr. Lawson first attracted attention with an expressionistic drama called *Roger Bloomer* produced in 1923. Like many works of literature roughly contemporary, it was concerned with the problems of the "sensitive" adolescent growing up in the American environment, and though it attracted a good deal of praise from critics it was not a commercial success. Then in 1925 came *Processional* which the Theatre Guild produced and which remained for some time one of the most discussed plays of the contemporary American theater.

The method was again the method of that expressionism which abandons all pretense of literal representation in favor of a symbolism sometimes borrowed from the dream world, sometimes, it would appear, merely at random from the whole mixed tradition of allegorical representation including the political cartoon and the comic strip. The method had been made familiar to at least a certain number of Americans through the Theatre Guild's production in 1922 of *From Morn to Midnight* by the German, Georg Kaiser, as well as through *The Adding Machine*, and it was widely hailed for a time as the most important contemporary contribution to the theater. That the possibilities of the method were very rapidly exhausted is a fact of history, but for the moment it seemed capable of expressing as no other method could the confused emotions of that section of the intellectual public which agreed with Mr. Aldous Huxley when he said : "The mind has lost its Aristotelian elegance of shape." It seemed the only way in which Mr. Lawson could say what he had—or seemed to have—to say.

What Mr. Huxley meant by his tantalizing phrase it may be difficult to state precisely, but he may have meant that the enormous increase in both our knowledge of the natural world and the extent of our familiarity with mere details of "the news" has made it difficult any longer to arrange that knowledge into a comprehensive or meaningful pattern. *Processional* is not a completely successful attempt to mirror this state of mind. The author does not, in his own way, do it so well as Aldous Huxley and James Joyce had done it in theirs; but it was something of the sort which he wished to do, and he came close enough to success to awaken the highest interest and the most generous admiration. Taking a story based upon an incident in the West Virginia coal region, he delib-

erately threw realism to the winds. Basing his technique now upon the expressionistic drama, now
upon the rough caricature of vaudeville, he mingled tragedy and satire, pathos and burlesque into a
phantasmagoria of diverse elements which does
somehow suggest both the wild disorder of contemporary life and the emotional exasperation which it
produces.

The figure of the tragic hero is almost realistic,
but all the subsidiary ones belong to some region
which lies between genuine symbolism and the
rough-and-ready caricature of the comic strip. The
silk-hatted master of the mine; the Polish laborer
eager to explain in a continuous discourse of two
weeks' duration the place of the workingman in history; the broad-mouthed Negro with his banjo; the
heroine, a flapper of the slums ready at every moment to go into the nervous convulsions of the jazz
dance——these and many more are figures grotesque
to the last extreme, yet undoubtedly veracious in
their exaggerated outline, and they perform all
sorts of fantastic acts which are nevertheless no
more than caricatures of their normal behavior. The
white-robed members of the Klan respond in uni-
son, "God's will be done" when their master announces that "the tar and feathers are ready"; but
they break up their meeting in a fox-trot. The soldiers, under the orders of the master of the mines,
knock down the Pole and search him; but when they

come across the photograph in his pocket they leap to attention and, taking off their hats, declaim with exaggerated sentiment: "His mother!" These acts are no madder than those daily performed, but they are simplified until their grotesqueness stands nakedly forth.

Such an extravagant method can be justified only if it obtains effects which a more conventional one could not produce. Mr. Lawson's play does, it seems to me, thus justify itself. The things which he definitely says could be and have been said in straightforward plays dealing with social themes, but the emotional effects could not be duplicated by any drama of conventional structure. His various types with their recurrent and characteristic utterances are less protagonists in any definite story than different instruments, each with a characteristic range and timbre, composing the orchestra upon which is played the jazz symphony of contemporary life. Each seems almost unaware of the other and yet each is obedient to an underlying rhythm, set by the lust of life, which makes them, without knowing it, play in a sort of wild harmony. What one gets from the performance is not the particular story which the play has to tell but the sensation which it gives of the cries of disorganized humanity orchestrated into the form of a nearly formless jazz symphony.

Mr. Lawson's next work, *Nirvana* (1926), was a

cloudily mystical play about a scientist who finds it
difficult to adjust his spiritual life to the world
which the laboratory reveals. It was not a success
with either the critics or the public and is interesting chiefly in revealing how far Mr. Lawson then
was from supposing that there was a political solution for all the problems which concerned him. After
the failure of *Nirvana* he associated himself with a
group of young playwrights and performers who
had committed themselves to experimentation, and
in 1927 produced at a little theater on Fifty-second
Street *Loud Speaker*, a wild harlequinade in which
clowns caricaturing such familiar modern types as
the politician, the flapper, and the tabloid reporter,
tumble about a series of elevated platforms or make
their entrances down a chute reminiscent of Coney
Island. Apparently *Loud Speaker* was not intended
to be very specifically "important," but in a later
play, *The International* (1928), Mr. Lawson attempted to report in a sort of futuristic shorthand the
course of a world revolution of Communists.

The International is not calculated to give the
spectator much pleasure or even to provide more
than occasional moments when he is sure that he
knows precisely what is supposed to be going forward, but it reveals the definitely political direction
taken by Mr. Lawson's interests and it may stand as
typical of a whole series of dramas written by various
authors and produced during a brief period when the

group with which Mr. Lawson was associated occupied a little theater on Commerce Street in Greenwich Village. By comparison with some of them— for example Mr. Emjo Basshe's *Earth* (1927) — *International* was almost classic in its clarity and decorum and it was also at least as pointed as *The Moon Is a Gong* (1926) or *Airways, Inc* (1929), both contributed by John Dos Passos. The unconventionality of these new playwrights soon hardened into a very monotonous convention and it was revealed that chaos as a dramatic subject has a very serious limitation : one cross section is bound to look very much like another. Performances at the theater on Commerce Street were sometimes witnessed by as few as a dozen spectators but the enterprise was enabled to continue for a time chiefly, it was said, because of the patronage of Mr. Otto Kahn whose desperate determination to patronize the adventurous artist survived even one production in the course of which young ladies dressed to represent monkeys ran down the aisles and distributed lollypops among members of the audience.

Even *a priori* it would appear that the method of expressionism was more suited to communicate moods of confusion, disillusion, and despair than it was to afford a means whereby the political reformer can propagate his faith. It had, however, been taken up in post-revolutionary Russia where it was regarded as the most typical contribution of the revolutionary spirit to dramatic art and consequently it was adopted in America by that group of American writers which was finding in its sympathy for Russia the beginnings of a new and dogmatic faith. The audience for many of the half-futuristic, half-communistic plays written by members of this group was, however, very nearly non-existent and the absurdity of attempting to appeal to the proletariat via plays so eccentric that only the most self-consciously "advanced" of intellectuals could even pretend to understand presently became apparent. Certain of the devices of allegory which expressionism employed have continued to be used cautiously in some of the most recent propaganda plays—notably in the "Living Newspaper" productions of the Federal Theater and in Mr. Marc Blitzstein's *The Cradle Will Rock*—but the final abandonment of the theater in Commerce Street marked the end of the brief period during which expressionism was regarded as the almost inevitable method of the playwright with a radical social message. As the aims of the didactic playwright were clarified and as he came to separate himself more and more clearly from the merely skeptical protestant of the type familiar during the twenties, he turned, sensibly enough, to more direct and less ambiguous forms of expression. And to such plays we also shall turn.

The drama which exists for the sake of a simple, specific, and clearly defined moral is, of course, at least as old as *The London Merchant* but until after the World War the moral was, in America at least, likely to be neither political nor unorthodox. On the other hand, much of the drama of the post-Ibsen period in Europe had been—like the plays of Brieux as well as some of the earlier "unpleasant" plays of Shaw—primarily didactic though concerned with "advanced" doctrines of one sort or another. It is therefore surprising that there were not in America more plays—Miss Susan Glaspell's *The Inheritors* (1927) in which she dealt didactically with the problems of patriotism was one—following the method of *Damaged Goods* or *Widowers' Houses*.

After 1929 there began, however, to appear sporadically on Broadway various plays which either dealt specifically with some social problem or dramatized under intentionally thin disguises some current *cause célèbre*. The way had been led by *Gods of the Lightning* (1928) in which Maxwell Anderson and Harold Hickerson had made a sort of chronical-melodrama out of the Sacco-Vanzetti case. It was followed by John Wexley's *The Last Mile* (1930), *Steel* (1931) and *They Shall Not Die* (1934), the last dealing with the Scottsboro trial; also by Elmer Rice's *We the People* (1933), a sort of pageant of the depression. Meanwhile two new producing organizations known respectively as The

Group Theatre and the Theatre Union had emerged to devote themselves primarily to plays of social criticism from the point of view of the left and, as a result, "propaganda plays" "revolutionary dramas" and "plays of social significance" came to constitute a recognized department of contemporary playwriting.

Those whose interests are primarily political and only secondarily in the theater are inclined to lump all such plays together and either to praise them indiscriminately as examples of a healthy protest against what is assumed to be the decadence of any literature not primarily concerned with remolding society or, if distinctions are drawn, to base favorable or unfavorable judgment upon them in accordance with the degree to which the political opinions of the author do or do not coincide with those of the political group to which the critic belongs. But though the plays are alike in that they professedly aim at producing political change they vary greatly in effectiveness and to the critic of the drama they seem, moreover, to represent several different solutions or attempted solutions of the formal problem facing a dramatist whose aim is primarily didactic.

A certain number are "problem plays" not differing greatly in method from *Widowers' Houses* or even *Ghosts*. Like the earlier sociological plays they propose to enlarge the spectators' understanding of the effect of basic social or economic conditions upon individual lives; they strive for some psychological subtlety; and they depend for their effect, in part at least, upon such richness of characterization as the playwright has been able to achieve. Just to the extent that they are designed to illustrate a dogma which the author has already consciously accepted as all-inclusive and final, there is an element of sham in the investigations which they appear to be making, but at least they maintain that pretense of actually exploring anew which was, in the case of the Ibsenites also, sometimes not much more than pretense. Many of the recent "revolutionary" plays have, on the other hand, adopted much more elementary and much less intellectual dramatic methods. Some have been simple melodramas in which the dramatic formula is as familiar as the plays themselves are supposed to be novel; others hortatory discourses hastily and imperfectly cast into dialogue form.

Mr. Rice's *We the People* (1933) belongs in the last of these groups. It summarizes vividly the case against contemporary society and it manages to include in one or another of the twenty scenes nearly every item of indictment which has occurred to Mr. Rice in the course of a life devoted largely to dissent of one sort or another. Here also, it must be admitted, are logic, clarity and a sincere intensity which could hardly fail to make even the most convinced defender of the status quo feel the force of the onslaught. Yet the play was a failure for reasons which it was not difficult for anyone except the enraged author to understand. In the first place it stands out chiefly because it is ambitious, elaborate, and complete, not because it is new, original, or inventive, even in substance. In the second place, it fails signally in such attempt as it makes to discover a form capable of rendering effective as drama discourses which in his play are interesting precisely to the same degree and precisely in the same manner that they would have been if delivered in the author's own person. The last scene represents the platform at a public meeting and the audience in the theater is supposed to constitute the audience at that particular meeting. But the device is not really a device at all. It is merely a confession of failure frankly recognizing at last a situation which had existed from the beginning.

Mr. Rice's next play, *Judgment Day* (1934), was a violent fantasy concerned with certain events which might have taken place if the judge at the Reichstag fire trial had been a survivor of pre-war German liberalism and finally decided to cut all knots by a bullet sent into the dictator's heart. Obviously the intention was to substitute melodramatic action for discourse and to achieve dramatic effect by the sheer violence of the action, which is, indeed, frenetic to a degree hardly equaled before or since except in some of Mr. Abbott's least restrained

farces. Here again, however, Mr. Rice failed either
to win popular success or to impress critics of the
drama and he failed, this time, because the rapidity
of the action precluded the possibility of any intellectual subtlety while it failed at the same time to
provide the simple emotional satisfactions which
successful melodrama must afford. From this standpoint it was, as a matter of fact, less satisfactory
than either *Gods of the Lightning* or *They Shall
Not Die* of which it may be said that while neither
actually adds much to what had previously been said
concerning the Sacco-Vanzetti and the Scottsboro
cases or wholly solves the problem of treating sensational news stories as melodramatic chronicle
plays, both succeed better than Mr. Rice had been
able to succeed in devising an action which neither
stagnated on the one hand nor, on the other, de-
scended into mere sound and fury. Both these plays
were highly praised for the service they were said to
be capable of performing in arousing public opinion, but their actual effect in accomplishing that
purpose would be hard to demonstrate and from the
standpoint of dramatic criticism neither is fully satisfactory either as "problem play" melodrama on
the one hand or as simple melodrama on the other.
What was needed if the full possibilities of the latter
form were to be explored was a politically minded
playwright willing and able to disregard entirely
the current tendency to intellectualize drama and to

compose a left-wing melodrama conceived in terms as elementary as those which purely popular authors were accustomed to employ. Such a playwright, or rather two such playwrights, appeared when the Messrs. Paul Peters and George Sklar composed *Stevedore*, presented by the Theatre Union in 1934 as the second of its offerings.

The distinguishing characteristics of melodrama have always been two: first, the absence of all shading in characterization and the resolute simplification of all moral distinctions until nothing remains except simple virtue on the one hand and a creature of hideous mien on the other; second, the tendency to rely for suspense upon a conflict which can be presented in visual terms and which usually ends in some form of physical contest. For obvious reasons such a play can succeed only if its moral and intellectual assumptions constitute a sort of largest common denominator for the audience and ordinarily, therefore, melodramas are the least critical of plays for the simple reason that they usually reflect the judgments, sympathies, and prejudices most widely prevalent. But if a melodrama is written for a special homogeneous audience the members of which not only hold the same opinions but adopt toward those opinions the same emotional attitude which the vulgar audience adopts toward its own most deeply rooted prejudices; if, in other words, it is addressed to a particular public which responds to words like "capitalist" and "worker" or "fascism" and "revolution" in the same automatic manner that the audience for Owen Davis's once popular plays responded to "honest poverty" and "ill-gotten gains" or even merely "vice" and "virtue," then a play about social conditions can be conceived and executed in precisely the spirit of all standard melodrama. No exposition or defense of "revolutionary" ideas is necessary; the hero and villain can be drawn in pure black and white; there is no reason why re-enforcement for the picket line may not arrive in the nick of time to be greeted by cheers from the audience precisely like those which on many occasions have greeted the opportune arrival of a select company headed by Captain Blake, U.S.N., at the very moment when all seemed lost. Such a play may be good or bad, exciting or feeble—as melodrama. But it cannot rise above the intellectual or artistic level of melodrama, and it is always upon that level—good though it is in its own way—that *Stevedore* remains.

It is, however, not only effective as melodrama but also effective as propaganda; or rather, more accurately, as agitation. Though it is not calculated to change anyone's opinions, it is successful in the attempt to arouse to fever heat the passions of an audience already convinced of the truth of its fundamental assumptions and whole-heartedly in sympathy with one side in the conflict which it undertakes to present. There are, to be sure, occasional and slightly intrusive efforts to expound the Marxian interpretation of events, a few moments when the action is slowed up while some *raisonneur* explains its ideological significance to an audience which, while the play was being performed in the Theatre Union's playhouse, was obviously the last in the world to need such explanation. But on the whole *Stevedore* is remarkably free from such defects and for the most part proceeds with steadily growing tension on its exciting way.

The subject is a race riot in Louisiana; the method frank but skillfully cumulative melodrama, and the whole reaches a really smashing climax in a thunderous scene "on the barricades." If *Stevedore* is uncommonly effective both as melodrama and as propaganda, the reason probably is that it sticks with uncommon persistence to a single purpose—which is to inflame the passions of its audience and to sweep that audience forward on a wave of fighting hate. Most authors of such plays seem a little uncertain just what it is that they are trying to do. They explain a little, they debate a little, and they plead a little. The result is usually as dispiriting as a protest meeting and gets just as far. But those responsible for *Stevedore* adopted a different method. They assumed—safely enough—that their audience knew the arguments already and that its sympathy was with them. Their business, like the business of any mob leaders, is to get the crowd going somewhere, and *Stevedore* becomes an incitement to riot of the very first order.

The spectator at *Peace on Earth*, the play which preceded it at the same theater, might reasonably be expected to emerge from the auditorium and join an organization for the promotion of something or other. The spectator at *They Shall Not Die* probably felt like writing a letter to the *Times* about conditions in Georgia. But a goodly percentage of those who saw *Stevedore* were probably ready to seize the nearest club and crack someone over the head. Most books and plays offered as proof that "art is a weapon" remind one of wooden swords, but this particular work is really a bomb—homemade, perhaps, but full of power and quite capable of going off. Such a contraption may have seemed a bit odd in the hands of an organization which was so recently pleading for peace on earth, but that organization was not the first to conclude that a good deal ought to be blown up before we settle down to living in brotherly love with the survivors —if any.

Another reason why *Stevedore* succeeds in generating a fighting mood is that its victims of white injustice are not, like those in most such plays, merely victims. The central character is a huge Negro with firm ideas about the necessity of the class struggle and a gift for converting his more timorous fellows. When the mob bent on burning the settlement and hanging its inhabitants finally arrives, it finds a barricade erected and the preacher who had talked submission put in his place. Moreover, and when things look their worst, who should arrive, throwing bricks and demonstrating class solidarity, but a group of white workers from the union headquarters. Those brought up on melodrama may be reminded faintly of the old days when the marines used to get there at the last moment, but the device has its uses, and it was doubtless something of a relief for the audience at a radical play to find one in which the innocent did not get the worst of it—at least until after the curtain had fallen.

If "art is a weapon" then the best weapon is the best art. To employ a scalpel where a bludgeon would be more efficient is, in the simplest meaning of the word, "inartistic"; and if a play is to be judged by its effect upon social action we are brought face to face again with the same problem presented by Mr. Robert Sherwood's didactic farce *Idiot's Delight*. No Marxian aesthetician seems to have discussed the ultimate implications of a theory which suggests that any work of literature that converts two hundred persons to Communism or enrolls two hundred in a battalion of shock troops is, *ipso facto*, aesthetically superior to another that produces a similar effect upon only one hundred and ninety nine. Neither have other left-wing playwrights followed the pattern of simple melodrama either as closely or with such telling theatrical effect as did the authors of *Stevedore*. For example, both Mr. Albert Maltz in his story of a miners' strike called *Black Pit* (1935) and Mr. Albert Bein in *Let Freedom Ring* (1935) yielded to a tendency to preach which impeded the action and both failed to solve as ingeniously as it was solved in *Stevedore* the problem of reconciling melodrama's need for a triumphant conclusion with the actual status of the revolutionary movement in the United States.

Even the most ardently revolutionary of dramatists are more likely than not to be intellectuals and the intellectual finds it very difficult not to be concerned with means almost as much as with ends, not to prefer the scalpel to the bludgeon. For that reason as well, perhaps, as for others, such established playwrights as Mr. Rice, Mr. Lawson, and the more recently emerged Mr. Clifford Odets have tended on the whole less to cultivate frank melodrama than to attempt some adaptation of the methods of "the problem play" to the needs of their newer and more explicit creed.

Mr. Lawson is the author of a long and laborious work entitled *The Theory and Technique of Playwriting* (1936) in the course of which he ranges widely through dramatic literature, standard expositions of critical theory, and the writings of social philosophers in an effort to explain in terms acceptable to Marxians the relations supposed to exist between the formal excellence of a dramatist and the political or social doctrines he accepts. Unfortunately, however, Mr. Lawson's own plays have become progressively less interesting and the first written after he abandoned the expressionistic technique was the best of the new series. This apparent decline in his powers might, of course, be accounted for in various ways, but it may possibly be connected with the fact that as his political convictions have come to be more and more completely identical with the doctrines of the Communist Party, he has found it more and more difficult to preserve in his plays the illusion that answers already dogmatically formulated are being earnestly sought for.

Success Story (1932) marked his return to a conventional and coherent dramatic form. Its hero is an East Side Jew who begins as a radical but who ends as the head of a rich corporation. To Mr. Lawson, of course, this means that his hero has lost his way amidst the corruptions of contemporary society but to the hero himself it means only that he has outgrown the green sickness of his early ambition and learned that what he mistook in youth for idealism was only a disguise for the natural desire to get for himself what the more fortunate already had. The presence of these two alternate interpretations

of the meaning of events gives the play a certain
solidity and it is interesting despite the fact that it
moves without grace and is marred by the heavy
vehemence which always characterizes Mr. Lawson's writing. Unfortunately, however, all its defects are present and most of its virtues absent in
both *The Pure in Heart* and *Gentlewoman* which
were produced almost simultaneously in 1934.

The first is Mr. Lawson's version of a story long
dear to sentimentalists—that of the chorus girl who
remains pure in heart despite her physical inconti-
nence; the second is a very cloudy series of discourses the point of which seems to be that we mod-
erns can find salvation only by identifying ourselves
with the revolutionary struggles of the working
class. This thesis might no doubt furnish the basis
for an acceptable "problem play" and there is nothing fundamentally wrong with the plan to develop
it through a story of the influence of a personable
young radical upon the life of a spoiled, neurotic
woman of the upper class. Unfortunately, however,
a kind of adolescent romanticism closely akin to that
of *The Pure in Heart* dominates the conception of
the characters so that the heroine seems to have
been borrowed without acknowledgment from one
of those novels which teach nursemaids to pity
broken-hearted members of the aristocracy, and the
hero from any one of a dozen modern tales in which
the central character keeps himself drunk most of

the time because the world is not good enough for him. It is difficult to believe that anyone of Mr. Lawson's age and experience really wants to write lush fustian of the sort he so easily falls into and one cannot blame wholly upon his experience as a Hollywood writer a weakness for Elinor Glyn prose, Ella Wheeler Wilcox poetry, and undergraduate yearnings. One can only assume that he falls back upon such things when his original intention eludes him, as it seems so often to have done, and that it has always been easier for him to compose passages of dubious purple than to find the road again.

According to Mr. Harold Clurman who wrote a foreword to the volume in which the two plays under discussion were published, *The Pure in Heart* is Lawson's "swan-song for the jazz-and-racket age." "Annabel," he continues, "looks out at the lights of the city : 'I think those lights are the prettiest things I ever saw'; and Dr. Goshen replies : 'The lights are pretty enough, but what's behind 'em? Crazy people all hopped up with crazy ideas, selling bad stocks, passing bad checks, chasing money, chasing glory—a crazy show on a glaring stage. Every time I look at that skyline I want to die.' When he wrote *[The Pure in Heart]*, Lawson was caught between the two sentiments . . . For the greater part of his career, Lawson has been the singer of this divided conscience."

The evidence of the earlier plays would seem to indicate that Mr. Lawson had actually made up his mind rather earlier than this and that he schooled himself to feel nothing to which his political philosophy could not give its approval. But it is certainly true that a sincere emotional perplexity was responsible for the effectiveness of *Processional* which managed to articulate as clearly as, in the nature of things, it could be articulated the ambiguous judgment he felt compelled to pass upon the grotesque vitality of certain aspects of the American scene. Just how much more simple and dogmatic that judgment later became was made evident by a recent revival of *Processional* in which certain cuts and certain interpolations rendered the text acceptable to orthodox Communism and at the same time deprived of all justification the "jazz" method which had had meaning so long as it corresponded to the syncopated disorder of the author's mental attitude but which serves no purpose when a series of events is to be interpreted in terms of rigid dogma.

One might have expected that Mr. Lawson's conversion to the religion of revolution would result in the clarification of his plays. Actually, however, it seems rather to have deprived him of his theme and reduced him to the necessity of falling back upon mere fustian in the effort to maintain an appearance of interest in a conflict whose meaning he now believes to have been completely exposed, and whose ultimate resolution has, he is convinced, been infallibly predicted by Marxian analysis. For that reason, perhaps, his most recent play, *Marching Song* (1937), is, as its title suggests, offered not as a contribution to discussion but as a sort of revolutionary "pep talk" to rebellious workers. Unfortunately, however, it is deficient in both the originality which it perhaps does not need and the eloquence which it certainly does. By long experience at least and perhaps by native temper also, Mr. Lawson belongs with those who search their own souls, and for all his steadfastness in reiterating his loyalty to official Communist doctrine he finds it difficult to employ his imagination after soul searching has been foresworn.

Presumably his conversion is permanent, but it is impossible not to remember that his past is a series of discoveries concerning the nature or the cause of his inward dissatisfaction and that he has been vehement in announcing each. Once, in *Roger Bloomer*, his hero's suffering was the result of a lack of "sensitiveness" in the American temperament. Once in *Processional*, the difficulty lay in our failure to penetrate the real meaning of that spirit of jazz which reconciles vitality with confusion, and once, in *Nirvana*, it was the result of our need for a mystical faith. Then in *Gentlewoman*, Mr. Lawson announced definitively that the cause of all spiritual ills had been discovered in economic disorder and he seems to have rested in that conviction. The striking fact, however, is that he was all for sensitiveness in the day when everyone was discovering the crassness of American life and is now all for economics when that has become, in its turn, the fashion. To point these facts out is not to doubt his sincerity or to accuse him of deliberately following the mode of the moment. But it does suggest the possibility that he has exhibited a certain tendency to attribute his own spiritual dissatisfactions to whatever defect in society happens to be most under discussion at the moment and that he is, in a word, much like the medical student who is said to discover in himself the symptoms of each disease as his text book describes it. Mr. Lawson's distresses have been genuine enough, at least to himself, and if he has interpreted them in terms borrowed from the discussions taking place around him he is not the only dramatist who has been similarly misled. Even O'Neill has often exhibited a similar tendency and only late in his career discovered how to free himself completely from the influence of mere intellectual fashion.

In December, 1938, Elmer Rice, who had followed the unsuccessful *Judgment Day* with the equally unsuccessful *Between Two Worlds* (1934), returned in a quieter mood to the theater which he had publicly renounced and produced *American Landscape*. Never orthodox in his radicalism, Mr.

Rice seems to have veered more and more definitely toward the position of those who have renounced the revolutionary attitude of Marx and Lenin in favor of one which they hold to be more moderate as well as more in accord with our native tradition, but his new play, though far less intemperate and confused than his other most recent work, seems prosy and dull because its personages so obviously have little life of their own. It is hard to believe that a writer who, even in such minor plays as *Counsellor-at-Law* and *The Left Bank,* revealed an almost uncanny gift for catching the rhythm of everyday speech and imitating the gestures of men and women, could write dialogue as lifeless as most of that in the play. The fact that he can do so may stand as an awful warning to the artist who confuses artistic seriousness with seriousness of any other kind.

Mr. Rice's failure to re-establish himself in the favor of any public leaves the much-younger dramatist Clifford Odets in very nearly undisputed first place among the playwrights whose professed aim it is to interpret contemporary society in the light of a specific political doctrine. Mr. Odets had appeared as an actor with the Group Theatre before his first play was produced and, like Mr. Lawson, he seems to have identified himself with the Communist Party only after he had begun to write. Unlike Mr. Lawson, however, his conversion did not deprive him of a subject and one of the most interesting things about his plays is the fact that he has managed to avoid rather more successfully than any of his fellows the tendency to assume almost automatically that a Communist play must treat directly one or another of the two or three situations which have come to be taken for granted as inevitable. In none of his three best pieces does the action center about either war or a strike, and this simple avoidance of the obvious is in itself sufficient to account in some part for the air of originality by which his plays are distinguished.

Mr. Odets first attracted attention as a playwright with a short and ingenious sketch called *Waiting for Lefty* which was first given at a special performance and later (1935) revived as part of one of the Group Theatre's regular offerings. His next produced play is said to have been written, in rough draft at least, some three years before *Waiting for Lefty* and to antedate his definite conversion to Communism, but since he was first introduced to the public through the short sketch it will be best perhaps to consider *Waiting for Lefty* first.

This sketch was suggested by a strike of taxicab drivers, and though it is hardly more than a *tour de force* there is no denying its effectiveness in achieving all it sets out to achieve. It begins *in media res* on the platform at a strikers' meeting and "plants" interrupt from the audience to create the illusion that the meeting is actually taking place at the very moment of representation. Brief flashbacks reveal crucial moments in the lives of the drivers, but the scene really remains in the hall itself, and the piece ends when the strike is voted. The pace is swift, the characterization is for the most part crisp, and the points are made, one after another, with bold simplicity.

Cold analysis, to be sure, clearly reveals the fact that such simplicity must be paid for at a certain price. The villains are mere caricatures and even the very human heroes occasionally freeze into stained-glass attitudes, as, for example, a certain lady secretary in one of the flashbacks does when she suddenly stops in her tracks to pay a glowing tribute to *The Communist Manifesto* and to urge its perusal upon all and sundry. No one, however, expects subtleties from a soap-box, and the interesting fact is that Mr. Odets invented a form which turns out to be a very effective dramatic equivalent of soap-box oratory.

Innumerable other "proletarian" dramatists have tired to do the same thing with far less success. Some of them got bogged down in futuristic symbolism which could not conceivably do more than bewilder "the worker"; others stuck close to the usual form of the drama without realizing that this form was developed for other uses and that their attempt to employ it for directly hortatory purposes can only end in what appears to be no more than

exceedingly crude dramaturgy. Mr. Odets, on the
other hand, here made a clean sweep of the conventional form along with the conventional intentions.
He bóldly accepts as his scene the very platform he
intends to use, and from it permits his characters
to deliver speeches which are far more convincing
there than they would be if elaborately worked into
a conventional dramatic story. Like many of his
fellows he had evidently decided that art is a weapon,
but unlike many who proclaim the doctrine, he had
the full courage of his conviction. To others he left
the somewhat nervous determination to prove that
direct exhortation can somehow be made compatible
with "art" and that "revolutionary" plays can be
two things at once. The result of his downrightness
was success where most of the others had failed. He
did not ask to be judged by any standards except
those which one would apply to the agitator, but by
those standards his success was very nearly complete.

Waiting for Lefty was played upon what is prac-
tically a bare stage. It could be acted in any union
hall by amateur actors, and the fact accords well
with the intention of a play which would be wholly
in place as part of the campaign laid out by any
strike committee. Indeed, it is somewhat out of
place anywhere else for the simple reason that its
appeal to action is too direct not to seem almost absurd when addressed to an audience most of whose
members are not, after all, actually faced with the

problem which is put up to them in so completely concrete a form. The play might, on the other hand, actually turn the tide at a strikers' meeting, and that is more than can be said of most plays whose avowed intention is to promote the class war.

It was doubtless the attention attracted by *Waiting for Lefty* when it was first given before a special audience which led to the production of *Awake and Sing* (1935), a full length play by no means so perfect but much more ambitious, and also revealing dramatic talents of a kind which had not been demonstrated in the shorter piece. The conclusion of the play in which one of the principal characters announces his intention to devote the rest of his life to promoting the cause of the working class is obviously tacked on, but it was not only because most of the play was written before his conversion to Communism that the characterization is richer than that found in any other of our "revolutionary" plays. In his most recent work also Mr. Odets demonstrates his ability to create vivid and passionate individuals and he does not seem to have lost that interest in the study of human character which most radical playwrights, not unnaturally perhaps, lose as soon as they become convinced that what is traditionally called "personality" is only an epiphenomenon accompanying the true phenomena of the economic processes.

In *Awake and Sing* a new poignancy is given to

a picture of life in a milieu not unfamiliar on the stage. To say that the play deals with the humor and the tragedy of a Jewish family domiciled in the Bronx, that it recreates from shrewd observation the minds and manners of a stubborn and struggling family, is by no means to say enough. Realistic plays of Jewish life are sufficiently common to be almost standardized, but one of the most important things about *Awake and Sing* is an extraordinary freshness. Observation is there in full measure but so, too, is something else—enthusiasm, passion, and the same almost painful intensity of feeling that distinguishes the characters. What Mr. Odets has done is to achieve a paradoxical combination of detachment and participation. He observes like an outsider, reproducing with vivid and humorous truth manners and habits which only an outsider could thus set down. Yet at the same time it is plain enough that his detachment is purely intellectual and artistic. Emotionally he is still close to the people he is writing about and he understands them from the inside out. His is another generation and it has formulated a new philosophy, but he holds his convictions and pursues his aims with the intensity of his fathers.

Ostensibly the moral of the play is a revolutionist's moral. It ends when the young son of the family frees himself from his obsession with a purely personal rebellion against the poverty which separates him from his girl and determines to throw himself with enthusiasm into the class struggle. But this conclusion, which comes very suddenly and without having been adequately prepared for, is obviously an afterthought. Actually, the subject of the play is not this one specific protest and rebellion but the persistent and many-sided rebellion of human nature against everything which thwarts it. No member of the family really understands what the others want. The competent, managing mother no more understands the passion of the grandfather for Marx and music than she understands her daughter's desire for something more than a safe marriage. And yet, to a certain degree, each can understand the other because each knows what it is to want something with agonizing intensity and to nurse that want day in and day out without a moment's remission. The young son who turns revolutionist is directing his determination into one channel, but, as the play so vividly illustrates, the same sort of determination may be directed into any one of many. Perhaps his aim is, for the moment at least, the most intelligent and useful; but the real secret of mankind's success, the real hope for its future, does not lie in anything so specific as any one crusade or any one determination. It lies in the persistence of its passion, its unwillingness to accept defeat for its desires. It can go on indefinitely insisting that it will be happy and free, tirelessly protesting against the fact that it is not; and if perchance one generation does surrender, there is always another wanting the old things with a young determination to have them. Mr. Odets's characters are ignorant and often crude, but his play, despite its tragedies, is exhilarating just because he makes it so clear that people like this are going to go right on demanding of life more than it will ever give them.

Mr. Odets probably learned something of his manner from Hemingway and the other members of the hard-boiled school. He has something of their clipped utterance and of their brutal and shattering irrelevancies. But he is not really a member of their school because he has none of their despairing sadism; because, in a word, he constitutes in himself a specific literary illustration of the thesis of his play: as soon as one generation of writers has demonstrated to its own satisfaction that it is no longer possible to admire anything in human nature or to hope for anything in it, another comes along and does both.

As a playwright the author of *Awake and Sing* was obviously at a crossroads, and it might have been difficult to predict whether he would go off in the direction of the definitely "revolutionary" drama or follow the more broadly humanistic tradition from which *Awake and Sing* does not really depart. Even *Waiting for Lefty* was hardly sufficient to answer the implied question because it was too obviously a stunt to be taken as announcing a program of dramatic writing, but Mr. Odets did finally proclaim his definite commitment to the Communist cause though the results were, as it turned out, not quite those which were feared by admirers outside the Communist Party.

Little need be said of his next two plays, *Till the Day I Die* (1935) and *Paradise Lost* (1935). The first is a crude melodrama about a young German Communist who survives the tortures of the Nazi storm troopers and it may owe its air of unreality in part to the fact that the author had no first-hand knowledge of Germany. The second, a much more complicated work, undertakes to exhibit the decadence of a family which is presented as a symbol of social collapse, but it carries exaggeration almost to the point of burlesque and seemed to suggest that its author had completely lost his grip upon reality. In *Golden Boy* (1937), however, he regained his equilibrium and produced a play which re-established his claim to consideration as the most able of all recently emerged playwrights. It was certainly his best play since *Awake and Sing* and to say this is to say that the piece exhibits unmistakable power and genuine originality, even though it is not, unfortunately, to deny that there is still in his work something which suggests imperfect mastery of a form he will probably have to invent for himself if he is ever to become completely articulate. There are moments when *Golden Boy* seems near to greatness; there are others when it trembles on the edge of merely strident melodrama.

Ostensibly the play deals with the career of a young Italian boy who abandons the fiddle for the prize ring because "you can't pay people back with music," and because he wants the money which will make him forget an embittered youth. Actually the theme is the same as the theme of *Awake and Sing*, and the power which Odets exhibits is again the power to suggest the lonely agony of souls imprisoned in their own private hells of frustrated desire and inarticulate hate. No one that I know can more powerfully suggest the essential loneliness of men and women, their inability to explain the varied forms assumed by the symbols of their desire, and the powerlessness of any one of them to help the other. His dialogue is often brilliantly suggestive, especially when he puts it into the mouths of ignorant or uncultivated people; even the most vulgar of his villains rises to the dignity of the tortured; and he involves the spectator in the agonies of his characters until the palms sweat and one goes out of the theater tense with an emotion which the author has been unwilling or unable to resolve.

The interpretation which Mr. Odets puts upon his own play is obvious enough. It is, I assume, that suffering like this "is inevitable under capitalism," and that the fiddler turned prize fighter is the type of those in whom rebellion assumes a merely symbolic instead of an effective form. But this time, at least, Mr. Odets keeps his political theories in the background where they belong and writes a play which does not depend for its appeal upon a concern with his economic opinions. The agonies of his characters are real and affecting, whatever one may think of the reasons for their existence.

Golden Boy is remarkable for the extent to which it manages to exemplify the traditional virtues of the drama. Presumably it is orthodox enough and didactic enough to satisfy the Marxian conscience of the author but it is, at the same time, capable of engaging the interest of a spectator little concerned with either political agitation or the attempt to interpret human nature in Marxian terms. The action would, as a matter of fact, remain meaningful even to those who had never heard of the economic interpretation of character, and to that extent it belongs to dramatic literature as a whole rather than merely to the political party of which its author happens to be a member.

To what extent Marxism as an inclusive philosophy will gain adherents among writers in the decade to come is, of course, impossible to say, but the evolution of Mr. Odets' talent leads one to wonder whether the "Marxian playwrights" of the immediate future may not tend to become less and less a class wholly apart as they come more and more to take their creed for granted. The greater the imagination of a writer, the less the validity of his work depends upon the validity of his formal creed, and a Marxian dramatist of real genius would probably write plays quite as acceptable to non-Marxians as the novels of Tolstoi are to those unable to follow the author through his successive changes of faith.

Certainly Mr. Odets' most recent—and in many respects best—play, *Rocket to the Moon*, seems to support the theory that the more talented the Marxian dramatist the less sharply his plays are set off from the best work of writers holding different political opinions, and it would be a pity if Mr. Odets's plays should be made political issues. Whatever his opinions may be, those opinions are shared by many, while he reveals a gift for characterization and a gift for incisive dialogue unapproached by any of his Marxian fellows and hardly equaled by any other American playwright.

Rocket to the Moon carried him at least one step further along the road he is traveling, and makes most other recent plays seem pallid indeed. Certain crudities, though they are less conspicuous than those in any of his previous works, do remain. Moreover, the fable of *Rocket to the Moon*, like that of *Awake and Sing* and *Golden Boy*, seems more powerful in conception than in development; so that as the story approaches its end the manipula-

tion of events tends to become more clearly mechanical. Perhaps the play as a whole never rises
above the level of its first act. But the personages
are endowed with a life almost painfully intense,
and the incisive thrusts of the dialogue follow one
another relentlessly from the beginning to the end.

Reduced to an outline, the story may seem almost
commonplace. The action takes place in the dingy
office of an unsuccessful dentist who is married to a
nagging wife and who finds himself at forty in the
arms of the eager but pathetic child engaged to keep
his books and clean his instruments. In the end he
is compelled to bid for her favors against his own
father-in-law, a man of wealth and power, and in
the end also both lose to the girl, just intelligent
enough to know that neither the love of a timid
failure whom his wife will always rule, nor the
love of a man who will soon be old, is quite good
enough. But no such outline can suggest either the
solid reality of the characters or the insight exhibited into the workings of their minds. Not one of
the personages is a story-book cliché; not one of
the situations seems other than freshly imagined;
and Mr. Odets exhibits, among other things, two
gifts not often combined—the gift for a kind of
literal realism which makes his characters recognizable fragments of reality, and the gift for endowing
these same characters with an intensity of life which
lifts them into another realm. They are immedi-

ately recognized and accepted, but the sense that one has met them before is soon succeeded by the realization that the full force of what they are and what they imply is here thrust for the first time upon an awakened awareness.

Like the best of the author's previous work, *Rocket to the Moon* is in one sense not a "pleasant" play. The spectator is spared no ugliness and, except perhaps at the very end, permitted no romantic or sentimental evasion of the situation. The broken spirit of the middle-aged failure, the desperate gallantry of the old man trying to pretend that he can accept the emptiness of his own life, and the unconscious cruelty of the girl who cannot even imagine what it is like not to have a whole lifetime before one, are realities which nothing can explain away and nothing make other than painful in themselves. Yet the intensity which makes the play at moments almost unbearable is responsible also for the fact that it is more than a tale of frustration and rises above mere realism toward the tragic level. No desires so agonizingly intense as those which possess these people can be really trivial, and even the defeated become heroes when they fight with such desperation.

The political implications of the play, if they exist at all, are even less intrusive and less explicit than they were in *Golden Boy* and seem to come down to no more than the suggestion that money or the

lack of it plays some part in determining the course
which our lives must take. It needs no ghost come
from the grave to tell us that, and the fact is often
enough recognized by writers without party affilia-
tions. Whatever further private meanings the play
may have for the author need be no concern of
either the general public or the critic. Mr. Odets
is welcome to any opinions he may care to hold so
long as he can write as impressive a play as *Rocket
to the Moon.*

Since it is the intention of this volume to deal
primarily with what the drama has been rather
than with what it might or should be, less stress has
been laid on the so-called experimental play than
is usual in current discussions of the theater. In
ethics the status of good intentions is debatable but
they count for nothing in art. Literary "experiments" deserve scant praise unless they are successful and to say of a writer only that he "means well"
is to damn him utterly as an artist whatever com-
pliment to him as a man may be implied. For this
reason little attention has been paid to several playwrights who have been enthusiastically hailed
chiefly because of their intention to treat current
problems in the theater. At least one other writer
who resembles Odets to the extent that he also has
attempted with some success to find a genuinely artistic form for plays of "social significance" does,
however, deserve mention. Irwin Shaw attracted

genuine interest with his long one-act play *Bury the Dead* (1936), and then—after *Siege*, which was a failure in 1937, and after some work in Hollywood —achieved his first long run with *The Gentle People*, produced by the Group Theatre in 1939.

Bury the Dead is an anti-war play based upon a conceit of originality and power. Six men just laid in their graves by a weary detachment of soldiers rise slowly to their feet and quietly refuse to submit to the final indignity—dirt in their faces. They do not deny that they are dead but they won't be buried and they won't lie still, no matter how anxious the living may be to have them covered and forgotten at last. A certain resemblance (possibly merely the result of coincidence) to Hans Chlumberg's *Miracle at Verdun* was commented upon but a more serious impediment to the success of the play was the fact that the first twenty minutes present by far the most interesting portion of the whole so that the rest of the play seems like a not particularly inspired attempt to elaborate an idea more suited to very brief treatment. *Bury the Dead* remains, nevertheless, one of the most interesting of recent left-wing dramas.

The Gentle People resembles *Bury the Dead* in only two respects: it also has a social theme and this theme is again treated fancifully rather than either literally or imaginatively. It tells, almost whimsically, the story of two men who live for the sake of

the evenings they can spend alone on their little
fishing boat and who are happy in this escape from
the drabness of their lives until they are preyed
upon by a minor racketeer who gets them into his
clutches. Finally they kill him, escape detection,
and, presumably, live happily ever after. Obviously
this little tale is an allegory intended to suggest that
there comes a moment when the meek must stand
up to the bullies if they hope to inherit the earth.
But the theme is nowhere explicitly stated and the
story is told humorously in a style whose superficial realism is not intended to conceal the fact that
the mood is half that of the fairy story and the two
heroes not too remotely related to Jack the Giant
Killer. Certain dangers are inherent in the predilection for fancy which is revealed in both *The Gentle
People* and *Bury the Dead*, but Mr. Shaw is one of
the very few left-wing dramatists who has discovered a manner which permits an escape from
pedestrian didacticism.

Meanwhile the distinction is growing clearer between such relatively subtle and complex plays as
Golden Boy and *Rocket to the Moon* and simple
didactic fables or inflammatory melodramas. While
Mr. Odets was developing a "Marxist drama" whose
most significant virtues are traditional ones, the
Federal Theater Project was inventing a new form
of theatrical exhibition appropriately named the

"Living Newspaper." Several "issues" have appeared and at least two of them have been admirable in themselves, though perhaps the most significant thing about the whole enterprise is the fact that it recognizes more clearly than such dramatists as the Messrs. Rice, Lawson, Maltz and the rest have ever been willing to recognize the distinction between dramatic imagination and the merely journalistic presentation of facts and arguments of the sort which journalism is entirely competent to handle.

So far the most successful of the "Living Newspaper" performances have been *Power* (1937) and *One-Third of a Nation* (1938), of which the second will serve to illustrate the aims and accomplishments of the method. The subject is slum housing in New York and the performance opened and closed with a brief scene, brilliantly staged, of a fire in a three-story tenement. The major part of the evening was, however, devoted to frank journalism of an ingenious kind.

Many of the devices used have been made more or less familiar by various *avant-garde* experiments; there are, for example, the off-stage voice, the interpolated moving-picture film, the "plant" in the audience, and the tendency to move on different levels of abstraction in dramatizing the various scenes. But for a reason to be mentioned presently, none of them seems ever to have justified itself so completely as in the "Living Newspaper." Each of them serves here a genuine purpose, and that fact removes from all the curse of preciosity.

If one insists that *One-Third of a Nation* is journalism and not art, the distinction need not be either invidious or based upon any considerations either esoteric or academic. It may imply merely something which is perfectly obvious—namely, that the purpose of the performance is to convey certain bits of specific, documented information and to enforce certain simple definite convictions; that it is, in a word, not a piece of fiction but a "feature article," whose primary concern is the effective presentation of fact. To say that is of course to say that the substance of the piece should be reviewed by an economist rather than by a dramatic critic, who, as a layman, can say no more than that the exposition carries intellectual conviction. But it does leave the critic the right to deal with the method of presentation, and it tempts one to say that it is by far the most successful effort to use the stage for the purpose of propaganda made here during this generation.

One-Third of a Nation is as good as it is partly because Arthur Arent, the author, Philip Barber, the producer, and the others concerned in the production are obviously men of talent. But perhaps even more credit belongs to whoever it was who realized that the proper way to go about doing what they wanted to do was to do just that without

trying to do anything else. Indeed, unless one has
seen a play like, let us say, John Howard Lawson's
Marching Song, it is impossible to realize how much
is accomplished by the simple expedient of presenting information and a few concrete illustrations of
what that information means instead of trying to
slip the information and the argument with which
one is really concerned between the lines of a conventional play in which one is not interested at all.
It has long been my conviction that to talk of "fic-
tionizing" biography, or history, or economics, or
politics is to talk nonsense. Nothing can be "fiction-
ized" because a subject is either fiction to begin with
or it never will be. But that does not mean that
biography and politics and all the rest are not interesting in themselves or that they cannot be presented
vividly through exposition which includes concrete
illustrations. The "Living Newspaper" does just
that. It is interesting in itself, and it may teach
others to present effectively what they have to say.
It may also help prevent the writing of a good many
bad plays.

Some mention should also be made of the sensation created by Marc Blitzstein's musical cartoon
The Cradle Will Rock (1938), which was orig-
inally intended as a Federal Theater production and
then, when that production was canceled for reasons generally assumed to be connected with the

violence of its partisanship, given without costumes before a special audience. At this protest performance it was so vigorously applauded that it was later presented to the general public in the form of the original impromptu rehearsal with the composer at the piano and with an uncostumed company, the various members of which simply rose from chairs at the back of the stage to act or sing their sketchy roles.

Charles Lamb once denounced the cantata as a corruption of the cheerful uses of the playhouse. What he would think of *The Cradle Will Rock* it is difficult to say, for if that work is something like a cantata, it is not a bit like Handel. It is only intermittently "cheerful," but it is by no means solemn; and if the author is aware that Robert Burns once wrote *The Jolly Beggars* in a similar form, even Burns cannot have helped him much. Mr. Blitzstein's unjolly proletarians are not beggars but demanders, and are much more interested in the steel strike than in warbling the delights of rolling in the hay.

So many superlatives were used by so many critics that there was some danger that the spectator would expect too much, for the piece has no more shading than a political cartoon and the writing and the singing were as casual as the staging. Its success depended upon two things—a certain dash in

the performance and also a certain hearty partisanship on the part of most of the spectators by virtue
of which they were ready, when necessary, to assume that whenever malefactors of great wealth
are being denounced violently they are necessarily
being denounced effectively as well. Mr. Blitzstein's
vehemence is continuous but his wit is intermittent.
The very ferocity of the satire is, however, remarkable, some of the lyrics are raffishly amusing, and
there is a savage cumulative absurdity hard to describe even in such minor matters as the successive
introduction of the mill-owner and his family—Mr.
Mister, Mrs. Mister, Junior Mister, and Sister
Mister.

The method of *The Cradle Will Rock* is as far
from that of such simple didactic fables as *Peace
on Earth* as it is from the esoteric symbolism
of the plays formerly written under the influence
of Russian expressionists. It illustrates both the fact
that "revolutionary" playwrights have not come to
the end of their experiments and the fact that the
political sympathies of an audience still play a very
large part in determining whether it will regard the
experiment as successful or unsuccessful. There is,
however, something worth noting in the fact that
the tendency to depart from the methods of strict
realism is equally conspicuous in the political and
non-political theater. It is no mere accident that the
same season should have witnessed two plays as

different in intention as *The Cradle Will Rock* and Mr. Thornton Wilder's nostalgic *Our Town*, in both of which characters generalized almost into abstractions were presented upon a stage as bare as that of a Chinese theater.

CHAPTER VI

THE POETIC DRAMA:
MAXWELL ANDERSON

THROUGHOUT most of the period which this discussion covers it was commonly assumed that realism and prose constitute the inevitable norm of "modern" drama. That drama had been born when Ibsen turned away from verse and when, in so doing, he symbolized his intention to turn also from the traditional themes as well as the traditional methods of the drama. Nothing was more characteristic of him than his insistence upon the contrast between fact on the one hand and pseudo-truths on the other, nothing firmer than his conviction that the ghosts of dead ideas could be laid only by an appeal to the specific instance. And prose is, or at least then seemed to be, the natural language of realism just as realism is, or at least seemed to be, essentially an appeal from the accepted generalizations of romance or poetry to the specific and recognizable fact.

Probably the methods which the dramatists of the late nineteenth and early twentieth centuries employed were the best for their purpose. If any one of them had been born a supreme poetic genius he might, of course, have created for himself a new language to express his revolutionary attitudes but no such supreme poetic genius appeared and, under the circumstances, it was almost inevitable that the best work of each should consist, partly at least, in a sort of prose protest against the emotional and intellectual convictions associated with conventional poetry. To write rhythmically or even with an eloquence too obviously not that of everyday speech seemed to be to run the risk of falling into patterns of thought or feeling which it was an important part of their intention to break.

In discussing the emergence of the new American drama it was suggested that by 1924 the gap between the convictions of the playwright and the convictions of his audience had been nearly closed. From that moment on the difficulties in the way of a drama which might conceivably employ verse as well as other methods of heightening its purely dramatic effects were very sensibly diminished, but though our theater has actually tended to interpret its realistic creed more and more liberally, this process of liberalization has taken place almost unconsciously and at least up until only a year or two ago it was still pretty generally assumed that fidelity to literal fact furnished one of the universally accepted criteria of excellence.

To say this is not to say that fantasy of one kind

or another—especially satiric fantasy—had not appeared from time to time and found acceptance. It
does not mean even that verse was never spoken on
the stage, for as far back as 1919 so determinedly
modern a group as that at the Provincetown
Theater had presented Miss Edna St. Vincent Millay's *Aria Da Capo*. It does mean, however, that
anything admittedly non-realistic in conception or
language was regarded, not only as an exception,
but as obviously outside the main stream and aside
from the main business of the theater. So strong
was the tendency to associate the idea of the serious
or the substantial with that of the actual that even
O'Neill was commonly called a "realist" and explanation of the power of such a play as *Desire
Under the Elms* was sought in its validity as a picture of puritan manners.

In recent years two plays by established American
poets have been produced on Broadway—Mr. Archi-
bald MacLeish's *Panic* (1935) and Mr. T. S. Eliot's
Murder in the Cathedral (1936). The second attracted a considerable audience when performed
by one of the Federal Theater companies and was
produced commercially a little later; both will be
referred to again; but neither was written by a man
interested primarily in the theater and neither seems
likely to exercise any profound influence on the
course of contemporary playwriting. Only Mr.
Maxwell Anderson has written plays in verse which

seemed to fit easily into the pattern of the contemporary stage, which attract in large numbers the regular patrons of the theater and which seem natural outgrowths of contemporary dramatic writing rather than protests against it.

For that reason if for no other, Mr. Anderson's career would require examination and he is, as a matter of fact, cited more often than any other writer except O'Neill in current discussions of the worth of contemporary American playwriting. Like O'Neill he aspires with some measure of success to reach beyond realism into tragedy, but except in this obvious respect the two playwrights could hardly differ more widely or exhibit characteristic virtues and defects more antithetical. Before any contrast is drawn it would, however, be better to examine briefly some of the facts of Mr. Anderson's career.

Now in his late forties, Mr. Anderson is the author of nearly a score of plays, many of them outstanding financial successes. His second produced work, written in collaboration with Laurence Stallings, was *What Price Glory* (1924) which was discussed at length in an earlier chapter. It was followed by two unsuccessful collaborations with Mr. Stallings, also previously mentioned, and later by a series of more conventional comedies and dramas of which the most successful was *Saturday's Chil-*

dren (1927) —a sentimental comedy of love in the modern urban equivalent of a cottage. Then turning suddenly bolder, Mr. Anderson produced in 1930 *Elizabeth the Queen,* the first of a series of romantic tragedies written partly at least in loose blank verse. Since that time Mr. Anderson has continued with what appears an astonishing facility to turn out play after play and to succeed with equally astonishing frequency in pleasing both the reviewers and the public. His work is varied as well as uneven but *Mary of Scotland* (1933), *Valley Forge* (1934) and *The Masque of Kings* (1937) follow more or less in the style set by *Elizabeth the Queen* while his two best pieces *Winterset* (1935) and *High Tor* (1937), are plainly less facile but more deeply felt expressions of a romantic imagination which, in the other plays, finds almost too readily the words and situations in which to body itself forth.

It is obvious that success was far easier for Mr. Anderson than for Mr. O'Neill. Either instinctively or through conscious design he adapted himself to the requirements of the current stage instead of demanding that the current stage should adapt itself to him. Since his originality is far less absolute than that of O'Neill he seemed less eccentric to ordinary audiences and imposed less strain upon their capacity to adjust their imaginations to an unfamiliar vision of human life. At the same time he

had the verbal facility which O'Neill so conspicuously lacks. The latter seems often strangely inarticulate, unable to put his ideas into words with
even ordinary fluency; Mr. Anderson, on the contrary, seems at times to suffer under the even more
painful inability to find ideas for the words which
flow almost unbidden. The one has a poet's imagination without his power of expression, the other falls
easily into verse which critics (especially when they
come to examine it in cold type) often find is not
so much poetry as something which sounds rather
like it.

Moreover—and to say the most damning things
first—Mr. Anderson's facility often betrays him
into a willingness to accept emotional clichés as well
as verbal ones. *Elizabeth the Queen* was hailed as
something new in our theater because it was a romantic tragedy in verse, but except upon the surface its novelty is far from absolute. There is little
in it more unexpected to us than it would have been
to our grandfathers, and this is true whether one
thinks of the form or the substance. Mr. Anderson
did not invent a tragedy or a tragic view of any
series of events; he revived one. He did not, as
O'Neill did in *Desire Under the Elms*, discover the
tragic core of meaning never before discovered in
events taking place in a certain milieu. Instead he
told a tale which is unmistakably tragic because it
has long been so, because other imaginations have

long ago given it the tragic form. And what is true
of *Elizabeth the Queen* is equally true of *Mary of
Scotland* and *Valley Forge*. However agreeable any
one of them may be as a stage spectacle, none actually creates a new tragic pattern or reveals in the
story it tells a tragic meaning hitherto unperceived.

Mr. Anderson is—as we shall see—capable of
work much profounder than this but he is also
capable of relapsing into easily followed grooves
and of producing something as dangerously near to
pastiche as the most recent of his romantic tragedies,
The Masque of Kings (1937).

Perhaps this last is the best of his plays in this
particular manner. Certainly it is extraordinarily
effective as theater and it is difficult to think of any
other living playwright who could refurbish the
familiar romance of splendid courts and sinister in-
trigues as Mr. Anderson does in this possible version
of the events which led up to the finding of Prince
Rudolph of Austria dead in the hunting lodge at
Mayerling. That he has thoroughly mastered the
grand romantic manner in so far as its purely theatrical aspects are concerned seems beyond dispute.
Moreover, he has an important theme which he has
developed in eloquent language. Prince Rudolph,
having dreamed of a just government established
upon revolution, abdicates before he has been
crowned :

> To the old and dying
> I leave their dying kingdoms to be plowed
> By the new sowers of death—fools like myself
> Who rush themselves to power to set men free
> And hold themselves in power by killing men,
> As time was, as time will be, time out of mind
> Unto this last, forever.

And yet the feeling that one has heard or seen it all before, the absence of any sense that one's thought or feeling is being anywhere enlarged, persists, and one is less sure of anything else than of the fact that Mr. Anderson can write plays capable of holding an audience.

It has been shrewdly said that a really great and successful writer must have a good deal of talent as well as a good deal of genius. That means, no doubt, that the ease and facility which may seem so little important when they constitute the whole of an artistic equipment are nevertheless indispensable if genius is to be rendered fully effective, and that Shakespeare, for example, would not be universally recognized as the supreme example of greatness in literature if he had not been, incidentally, a master of all the minor ingeniosities which, taken by themselves, are no adequate measure of his stature as a writer.

But it has not, so far as I know, ever been pointed out that this fact also supplies the reason why these really great writers are often misjudged in their own time and put on the same level as lesser men who approach them in talent without having any genius at all. Time was necessary before it could be universally agreed that Shakespeare was more than a popular entertainer, just as, to take a more recent example, Dickens was conventionally placed below Thackeray largely because the exuberance of his talent aroused doubt about his solider virtues even in minds which perceived them without quite daring to trust their perceptions. Genius which comes rough and without the art to recommend itself we recognize easily if we are able to recognize it at all, because, if we are pleased, we know that it can be for the one reason alone. But art which is wholly amiable is often, like men or women who are the same, unjustly suspect, for the simple reason that we are so often not quite sure whether we are being legitimately charmed or only seduced. And even this, alas, is not the only difficulty, for the danger is double-edged, and the writer whose talents are so conspicuous that we tend to overlook his genius is rather less common than his false twin whose talents win a reputation which only time can reduce to its proper proportions.

In any event many spectators have professed to see in such plays as *The Masque of Kings* none of the defects which have here been alleged and base chiefly upon such work the claim which they make for Mr. Anderson as a genuinely important playwright. I myself should prefer to base it principally upon the tragedy *Winterset* (1935) and the romantic comedy *High Tor* (1937) which were awarded the Critics Prize for successive seasons though neither proved as popular with the public as other of the author's plays.

Winterset like many of Mr. Anderson's other works, enjoyed the advantages of an excellent cast and superb staging. The curtain rose on a stage of somber but breathtaking beauty. To the right the huge concrete pier of a bridge lifted itself sheer into the darkness above, and to the left a sullen block of tenements balanced the opposing mass. In the remote gloom of these lower depths the solid foundation of the proud bridge seemed a fitting monument to the dismal despair of the tenements, and the fact added meaning to the pure plastic beauty of the forms. Physically and spiritually the foundations upon which the city rests are seen from the perspective of those who crawl about their bases, and it is not often that the creative possibilities of stage design have been so convincingly demonstrated.

During the three or four seconds which immediately succeed the rising of the curtain, many spectators must have had time to reflect that if the author's play could live up to the promise of Jo Mielziner's set it would win for itself a very high place in our dramatic literature. Long before the final curtain went down, the audience had divided itself into two camps, but *Winterset* seems to me bold, original, and engrossing. In its most general aspect the play might be described as an attempt to treat some of the material of contemporary life in a manner more richly imaginative than the method of realism permits. Thus, while the time is the present and the plot one which might serve for a tragic melodrama, the whole emphasis of the treatment is such as to stress the eternal rather than the local aspects of the passions involved and to lay the emphasis less upon the action itself than upon its reverberations in the souls of the protagonists.

Long before the play begins, a radical agitator (vaguely reminiscent of Vanzetti) has been railroaded to death by a court which shared the popular determination to fix the guilt of murder upon a man whom it had other reasons to hate. More recently, a college professor, reopening the case, has pointed the finger of suspicion at a gangster just released from prison, and thus a ghost has been raised to plague those who had had a part in the now almost forgotten events. The key to the mystery is held by a young witness lost in the obscurity of the lower depths, and upon him converge all those most deeply concerned—the actual murderer, determined at all costs to prevent the truth from coming to light, the outcast son of the man who paid the penalty for the crime he did not commit, and, finally, the

presiding judge, now driven out of his wits by the
unsuccessful effort to convince himself that he had
done only what duty compelled him to do. Obviously there is in all this no lack of exciting action
or of opportunities for direct socio-political argument. But both are subordinated as they would be
in a classic tragedy to a brooding and poetic treatment of the themes which the action suggests—
namely, the nature of guilt and of justice and the
meaning of revenge.

Much of the dialogue is cast in the form of blank
verse, and the fact is of course significant chiefly
for what it implies. It means that the author, in
claiming the right to make his characters speak
more pointedly and more richly than ordinary people do, claims at the same time the right to make
them think and feel more richly too. It means that
even the lowest of his characters is, like the characters in Shakespeare, permitted to be both a poet and
a philosopher, limited in certain ways no doubt by
the limitations of his soul, but by virtue of poetic
and philosophical gifts, capable of defining and expressing that soul with the clarity and intensity of
the poet and the philosopher. It means, in other
words, that the play is at least capable of being
more interesting than any other kind of play just
because only poets and philosophers are capable of
realizing and feeling to its full depth the meaning
of the experiences through which they pass.

Mr. Anderson had written in conjunction with Harold Hickerson a play, *Gods of the Lightning* (1928), previously referred to and based directly upon the Sacco-Vanzetti case. It had dealt with the events journalistically in the mood of direct social protest and some have argued that that play is better or at least "more useful" than *Winterset*. But to make any such judgment is to reveal a fantastic misconception of the whole nature of drama and literature. Probably *Winterset* would never have been written if Mr. Anderson had not concerned himself with the famous case. But if the earlier play represents the immediate reaction of the citizen, *Winterset* is the product of a poet's brooding. It represents no change of opinion; the social protest is still here if one cares to look for it. But here also is that deeper penetration into thoughts and passions and souls which it is the dramatist's business to achieve.

The objection—actually raised against the play —that "gangsters don't speak verse" is, of course, frivolous. Neither do fourteen-year-old Italian girls, early Danish princes or, for that matter, any other persons whatsoever, and the appropriateness or inappropriateness of elevated speech to any character depends, not upon his social or intellectual status, but upon the success of his creator in endowing him with an intensity of feeling for the expression of which the best of utterance is none too good.

If, in the present instance, rhythmical utterance seems not absurd but almost inevitable—far more so indeed than it does in the mouth of the author's Mary of Scotland or his Rudolph of Austria—it means that Mr. Anderson has endowed the characters of this play with more life than he had been able to borrow from the romance of the past for the ready-made figures of his historical romances.

These latter had, to be sure, been hailed by some as exhilarating proof that tragedy in verse was still possible. But the very fact that Mr. Anderson, who had collaborated on *What Price Glory* and independently written at least one excellent comedy, turned to a historical subject when he wished to write a verse play ought to have been, on the contrary, distinctly dispiriting. It seemed to confirm the almost universal if tacit assumption that only the past can be conceived in poetic terms, that the poetic drama had ceased to exist, not because we had left poetry, but because poetry had left us— because modern life and our conception of it were radically unsuited to that degree of elevation which makes verse a natural medium of expression. In so far as *Mary of Scotland* and *The Masque of Kings* partake of the nature of a pastiche they are not only not works of art but also confessions on the part of their maker that he was compelled to use fragments of other men's art because he had found it impossible to transmute his own experience into art of his own creation.

The business of poetic tragedy is to reveal what the ordinary experiences of life leave hidden, to bring within the charmed circle of poetry and tragedy aspects of human existence which had remained mere prose until the poet had treated them. To stress the fact that the scene of *Winterset* is contemporary is not of course to imply that only in connection with contemporary events can anything significant be said. But the choice of a contemporary scene is an outward sign of the fact that the poet proposes to attack in the directest possible manner the problem of demonstrating that the process of transforming into poetry and tragedy what was never poetry or tragedy before is still possible, that if life is no longer poetic or tragic that is only because we no longer have the power to see it as such.

To make *Winterset* the occasion of such reflections as this, one does not need to remain blind to certain of its weaknesses. There is a high degree of fortuitousness in the final catastrophe and the story of the young lovers is marred by the too easy lyricism to which Mr. Anderson is prone. Moreover, the main *action* of the play is at times not very closely integrated with the main *theme*, so that the thought and the movement seem less one than two separate things, the second of which serves only to create an action, not always necessary for the development of the first. The fact remains, however, that *Winterset* is more than merely Mr. Anderson's best play. In it he seems to have come closer than any other recent American dramatist except O'Neill to the achievement of a form conveying a tragic view of life at once valid and unmistakably of our own time. The possible tone, and manner, and matter of a great modern tragedy seem more clearly conceivable now than they did before the play had been written.

Since *Winterset*, Mr. Anderson has produced both *The Masque of Kings* and, still more recently, the highly successful but pretentious and derivative comedy *The Star Wagon* (1937) in which a clumsily conceived "time machine" provides the occasion for some highly unoriginal speculations on the theme of Barrie's *Dear Brutus* and for some pleasantly executed but not very novel scenes poking gentle fun at the manners prevalent during the American Age of Innocence. Both plays—especially the last—are discouraging enough to those who had hoped that Mr. Anderson would waste no more time writing the kind of easy successes he has already so abundantly demonstrated his ability to turn out. Both would, however, be more discouraging than they are were it not for the fact that since *Winterset* he has also written *High Tor*, the best of his comedies and one which has at least a certain relation to what seems the most important part of his potential

contribution to contemporary dramatic writing. It
is light and insubstantial, but it is also an attempt
to find a place on the modern stage for a kind of
comedy which seems to have died almost three centuries ago. And to that extent it is, like *Winterset*,
an effort to reclaim for our own use a source of
delight which our ancestors took for granted but
of which we have lost the secret.

Anyone who came in near the middle of a performance of *High Tor* might have been pardonably
bewildered. High in the air he would have seen
two substantial but sinister citizens imprisoned in
the bucket of an idle steam shovel, while upon a
crag just beneath, the robustious shade of one of
Henry Hudson's men was holding converse with a
stenographer from a twentieth-century office. Other
things just as odd as that happen quite regularly
throughout the play, and yet they can seem quite
reasonable to one who has followed from the beginning the airy and delightful fantasy. Versatility is
one of the most conspicuous though not the most
important of Mr. Anderson's many virtues, and in
High Tor he wrote a playfully imaginative comedy agreeably unlike anything our theaters are
accustomed to house.

Some spectators, to be sure, did seem to have
fretted themselves into believing that they did not
understand everything as precisely as they should;
but that is only because they were looking for a

more solemnly detailed symbolism than the author
had any intention of providing, and the outline of
the story is simple enough. A romantic young man
owns a bit of mountain overlooking the Hudson.
Living there in a refuge from the modern world
which he hates, he refuses to sell out to the indus-
trialists who are gradually taking over the region;
and during the course of one wild night, while the
emissaries of the enemy are imprisoned in the
bucket, he holds converse with those same Dutchmen who put Rip Van Winkle to sleep. They are
embodiments of his romanticism as well as representatives of a race displaced by his forefathers exactly as he is about to be displaced by new aliens,
and they convince him that it is folly to resist new
civilizations—partly because they will win anyway
and partly because, as an Indian surviving in flesh
and blood explains, even the new turns into the
quaint if you give it years enough; there is nothing
man can build which does not make a very romantic
ruin in time.

No one is likely to misunderstand that much of
the plot and meaning, but to hunt for precise symbolism in all the fantastic details which embellish or
enliven the play is to assume a tight allegory when
what one has is a freely playful fantasy instead.
What one needs is not profundity but liveliness of
imagination, and the curtain of the first act will
illustrate as well as anything else the spirit of the

piece. There has been some talk of the legendary Dutchmen, whose existence our hero will neither affirm nor deny, but who are said to appear in stormy weather. As dusk falls, he is facing the audience when suddenly one sees their silhouettes, schnapps keg and all, advancing across the crest. As the young man turns, we wait for the cry of astonishment. Nothing happens for an instant, and then he remarks calmly, "Well, it's going to rain all right." Now that, of course, doesn't mean anything except that the Dutchmen are a familiar sight to the hero. But at the moment when it comes, it is surprising and funny and delightful.

Using the word merely to define and not to evaluate, *High Tor* is surprisingly Shakespearean —or Beaumont and Fletcherish—in the sense that its immediate ancestors seem to be not any of the symbolic plays of recent years but the freer romantic fantasies of the Elizabethans, dominated by poetry and playfulness rather than by allegory. Nor could I help feeling that one of the most striking things about the performance was the happily receptive attitude of an audience which, I feel perfectly sure, would have felt it a duty, even five years ago, to resent anything so devoid of "sophistication." Perhaps the scene in which one of the Dutchmen mistakes two men under a blanket for a double-headed monster is a bit too directly Shakespearean *(vide The Tempest)*, but Mr. Anderson modernizes the incident very amusingly, and his whole play may help accomplish something which the modern drama needs as badly as it needs anything else. It may help limber up the imagination.

Mr. Anderson's plays have frequently done just that. Many persons who do not count themselves among his most enthusiastic admirers would probably be willing to admit that he has succeeded more fully than any of our other dramatists in persuading a large popular audience to follow him gladly beyond the rather narrow circle of subjects, attitudes and methods within which it had grown accustomed to remain confined. That audience has not usually found him difficult. It has, on the contrary, responded easily to the appeals which he has made even when they were not those to which it was most accustomed in the theater, and something of the same sort may be said in favor of his verse which found ready comprehension in part because it did not, like so much modern poetry, require for its comprehension a familiarity with a modern tradition of which four-fifths of the theater-going public is completely ignorant. It has at least the primary virtue of dramatic verse inasmuch as it is easily speakable and easily understood when spoken. That virtue is not only the one without which the profoundest and subtlest poetry is useless in the theater, but also the one which our best poets seem least capable of exemplifying.

All these facts help to explain why it is useless to compare Mr. Anderson's work and, especially, his verse plays, with Mr. MacLeish's *Panic* or even Mr. Eliot's *Murder in the Cathedral*. The latter is impressive on the stage but perhaps even more so in the study where the meaning and the beauty of certain passages too subtle and too compact to be understood in declamation are fully appreciated. It exhibits the same virtues of feeling and expression present in Mr. Eliot's other poetry, but a discussion of it seems to belong rather in a discussion of contemporary literature than in any essay upon the contemporary theater to which it hardly seemed to belong. *Panic*—though its author doubtless has a livelier interest than Mr. Eliot in the possibilities of performed poetry and has, indeed, written for the radio—is even further from the familiar form of the drama. It was a deliberately radical experiment in choral and chant which was given only a few performances interesting to a small group but without immediate or apparent significance in connection with the course of current writing for the stage.

Mr. Eliot and Mr. MacLeish may be thought of as poets each of whom is the author of one play written from without (and perhaps from above) the tradition of the current drama. Mr. Anderson, on the other hand, works from within, and when something in one of his plays rises above the familiar level or when he strikes a phrase more elevated in tone than those we are accustomed to hear spoken on the stage, the imaginative scene or the elevated phrase emerge from the current tradition which they seem thus to enlarge while the plays which contain them remain *of* the contemporary theater and, not as Mr. Eliot's or Mr. MacLeish's plays are, something imposed upon it.

Nor is it necessary, in recognizing this distinction, to take sides, or to proclaim dogmatically either that any possible future for the poetic or literary drama in America lies with the popular and practical playwright in touch with real audiences or that, on the contrary, the theater is damned to eternal vulgarity unless, as the result of some *coup d'état*, it is captured by poets and artists of a race which at the present moment finds little welcome there. Indeed, if some future more glorious than its past is really in store for the American theater, then it may possibly be that its coming will be preceded by an obliteration of the distinction between the two classes, just as the perhaps less sharp distinction between the man of letters and the playwright was to some extent obliterated in both England and America during the late nineteenth and early twentieth centuries. Popular playwriting may increase in subtlety and elevation until its normal level is at least as high as that of the most esoteric of contemporary writing and the dramatist finds it mean-

ingless to ask whether he has risen from playwright
to poet or condescended from poetry to playwriting.
And it is well to remember that there is nothing
too highly improbable, either *a priori* or in the light
of history, in the hope that a popular art, or even
merely a form of popular art, may rise above its
own apparent level as the popular drama of England
once did.

Any such hope as this is, to be sure, resisted by
certain prejudices which happen to be very widely
current at the moment. The contemporary theater
belongs primarily to the upper middle class and that
class is commonly assumed by the intellectual to be
damned below all others. In any vision of the future
of art which he contemplates he is almost certain to
see it as something created either by the practition-
ers of the more esoteric forms on the one hand or
by "the people" on the other. And when he says
"the people" he certainly does not usually mean
the middle class nor does he, indeed, even include
the members of that class. When he speaks of the
possibilities of a popular art, he is not thinking of
any art which is actually at the present moment
popular, but rather of some style which he thinks
ought to be popular and which, he is sure, actually
will become so when "the people" have had adequately explained to them what they really like.

And yet the contemporary drama is a popular
art in the sense that it genuinely appeals to a con-

siderable number of people. Moreover, it is far closer to what even the radical propagandist would like it to be than is the moving picture which makes its appeal to a wider public and is much more a popular art in the broadest sense of that term. To assume that the future of a living and growing institution is less hopeful than the future of an institution not yet founded is to give an absurd weight to purely *a priori* dogmas the validity of which has never been tested.

At the very beginning of this volume it was admitted that the modern American drama could neither be assigned a definite beginning nor defined in any way which would set it off absolutely from the work of playwrights who were excluded, if not merely for convenience at least on the basis of very general considerations. It is hardly to be expected that this modern American drama should obligingly come to an obvious end or even reach a definite stage in its development at the precise moment when the present writer was moved to discuss it in a volume. Accordingly, if his discussion was compelled to begin somewhere within an area rather than definitely at a point, it runs the risk of trailing off as it leaves hanging in the air not only the story of the contemporary drama but also the careers of most of the major playwrights considered. Since there is no "finis" to be written it may be well first to reconsider the immediate past in the light of such analysis as has been made of it and then to note whatever tendencies seem to have been observable during the last two or three years.

The first claim made for the recent drama was, it may be remembered, that this drama reflected rather more accurately than any previous American drama ever had the interests, attitudes, and convictions of the literate public. To say this is to say that it possessed certain virtues, but certain defects also are likely to follow from too exclusive an emphasis on contemporaneity, and these defects have certainly been very often apparent. Our drama has actually tended to reflect current interests so successfully and so directly as to seem at times prevailingly reportorial and journalistic.

The contemporary theater seems, on the whole, to have found a place for the best our playwrights could produce, and that best was not only good enough to challenge comparison with the best of contemporary American literature in other forms, but also good enough to win for the first time wide European acceptance of the American play. Yet the fact remains that no playwright who has emerged since 1918, not even O'Neill, has produced an impact even remotely comparable to that produced by Ibsen or Shaw. Nor does the surviving corpus of dramatic writing seem to justify entirely the sense which one has had from year to year that excellent plays were being produced in considerable number. Too many of these plays seem to have fulfilled their function of keeping alive a vital and interesting theater without actually achieving any permanent place in dramatic literature. The "best play of the year" has very often owed its popularity to some novelty of theme or dramatic method which seemed exceptionally interesting at the moment but which failed to remain so for very long, and some of these "best plays" have already been almost completely forgotten.

On the other hand, it is worthy of remark that the playwrights whose names most persistently reappear in any discussion of the possibly permanent achievements of the contemporary drama are those in whose work the formal element is conspicuous. It is true that Eugene O'Neill, Maxwell Anderson and S. N. Behrman have all dealt sometimes with current topics. It is also true that they could not have been so important as they are had they not been unmistakably of our day. But it is not primarily of their timeliness that one thinks; they are, first of all, a writer of tragedies, a poetic dramatist and a creator of comedies, respectively. That means that each has thought his way through his material with such thoroughness that he has been able to give it one of the forms eternally appropriate to the drama. It also suggests that such a process is necessary before any play can achieve permanent interest and that we have, perhaps, been too ready to assume that intellectual honesty in the presentation of contemporary themes is in itself all-sufficient.

Perhaps, in other words, the modern drama did not actually come of age when it succeeded in achieving that relevance to contemporary life of which it may truthfully boast. Perhaps the adoption of contemporary themes and the re-orientation of its thought were only necessary first steps and perhaps it will not reach true artistic maturity until it has gone on to rediscover how it may give classic form to materials which have never been given such form before. Such form in the drama is not something artificially imposed from without. It is the shape which material inevitably takes when it has been thought through to the end and its pattern revealed. Mr. O'Neill's tragedies are genuine tragedies, and Mr. Behrman's comedies genuine comedies because, despite the fact neither could have been written in any age except this, they achieve the formal perfection of one of the classic patterns and produce an effect of completeness and finality possible only when such a pattern has been evolved.

The re-emergence of these forms is one of the most hopeful signs in contemporary dramatic literature. Another is the increasing realization of the importance of truly expressive speech, whether that speech be frankly poetic or merely prose of more than ordinary richness and precision. One of the boasts of the journalistic playwright had commonly been that his dialogue was realistic and that his personages talked as real people do. Even the boast is, of course, an exaggeration at best since the most realistic dialogue which can be tolerated on the stage is more economical and more vigorous than actual conversation commonly is. But that is not all, for the virtue claimed is a mediocre one at best. In so far as it implies that conventional rhetoric and the clichés of a dead tradition have to be discarded, it may mean that the playwright has achieved a freshness which befits the journalistic fidelity of his plays; but in so far as it means that he has been unable to make his characters talk very much better than their immediate prototypes would talk it indicates a failure analogous to the failure to achieve finality of form in the structure of the play. The prose dialogue of Behrman and O'Neill is, at its best, hardly more realistic than the verse of Maxwell Anderson. The characters of Mr. Behrman speak with a precision which suggests less the way wits actually talk than the way we wish that they would. The characters of Mr. O'Neill speak a language appropriate to the passions they feel rather than to the milieu from which they come.

There is no doubt that the emphasis on new themes and new attitudes insisted upon by the Marxian dramatist tended to distract attention from the work of the somewhat older playwrights less con-

cerned with new ideas than with the business of discovering how the classic dramatic virtues could be
achieved in plays which took for granted all that
had been, twenty years before, no less new than
what the Marxians now propose. But it is remarkable in how short a time Mr. Odets, by general consent the ablest of the younger group, has proceeded
from *Waiting for Lefty* to *Rocket to the Moon*, and
that progress suggests that even he and his fellows
may be coming to perceive that the most effective
drama is less likely to preach a doctrine than to in-
corporate that doctrine with the other fundamental
assumptions upon which the play in question rests.

It is, of course, possible that the immediate future
of the American drama may be less interesting than
its past. Certainly in England the present generation of playwrights is far from being as impressive
as that of Shaw and Barrie, and there is no guarantee that the growth and vitality which have recently
been evident here will continue to manifest themselves. But it does seem safe to assume that if the
American drama continues to develop it will develop in one of two directions. Either an increasing
interest in the Marxian doctrine in general and an
increasing sympathy with the dogma which proclaims that "art is a weapon" will result in a theater more directly didactic and more unmistakably
journalistic than that which arose here just after the
War, or the tendency already observable in the di-

rection of plays which aim more, rather than less, at the traditional virtues of the drama will continue and be accentuated.

I have doubtless already indicated my own belief that the second of these two possibilities seems the more probable, and I hold it to be so whether or not one assumes that the influence of the Marxian interpretation of society is likely to grow. There are plain signs that even the Marxians are dissatisfied with the results of assuming that their philosophy justifies no art except that which is simply didactic, and Mr. Odets has shown that the more Marxism is taken for granted the less it is incompatible with plays whose artistic virtues are of the same kind as those exhibited by imaginative works uninfluenced by Marxian doctrine.

A few years ago when the Theatre Union was founded, apparently upon the assumption that "art is a weapon," there were those who assumed that it was destined to lead the way to a new drama. Before very long it was, however, compelled to suspend operations and the Group Theatre, sponsor for Odets, has definitely disclaimed political allegiance. During the seasons of 1937–8 and 1938–9 the most popular plays included *Golden Boy* and *The Little Foxes*, both of which were to some extent influenced by the left-wing sympathies of their respective authors, but great popularity was also achieved by such fanciful and purely non-political works as

Maxwell Anderson's *The Star Wagon*, Thornton Wilder's *Our Town* and the dramatized novel *On Borrowed Time*. Perhaps, however, nothing was more indicative of popular taste than the furore created by the interpretations of Shakespeare offered by John Gielgud and Maurice Evans or the interest aroused by Orson Welles and his Mercury Theater productions of *Julius Caesar* and Dekker's *Shoemaker's Holiday*.

It is not easy to find a common denominator for these or the other most popular plays of the last two years, but if one exists it is certainly not either a specific political doctrine or even a conviction that social conflict furnishes the only acceptable material for drama. The Pulitzer Prize for the season 1938–39 was given to Robert Sherwood's *Abe Lincoln in Illinois* which, like a rather remarkable number of plays of that season, dealt with the past, but *Abe Lincoln in Illinois* was romantic as much as it was didactic and if there is anything which all the plays mentioned have in common it is a certain tendency toward the imaginative rather than the literal treatment of whatever themes they present. Even Marc Blitzstein's much-discussed satiric cantata *The Cradle Will Rock* was as remarkable for its free non-representational form as it was for the bitterness of its satire on contemporary society, and it might be argued that an audience which shows a renewed interest in Shakespeare as well as a renewed interest in contemporary plays which deal with historical and fanciful subjects in a manner certainly not realistic, is an audience beginning to rediscover the possibilities of a theater which is imaginative rather than realistic.

Probably the most serious general criticism which could be leveled against the American drama during the period with which this book has been concerned is the charge that, however sincere, intelligent, and technically competent, it has seldom if ever been intense enough. The classic patterns of comedy and tragedy toward which Behrman and O'Neill have worked owe their effectiveness to the fact that they make possible a maximum of intensity while at the same time they provide for orderly progress toward a clear conclusion. Heightened speech, whether in verse or prose, also exists for the purpose of achieving strength of utterance without violence, and it may be that the increased sympathy of present-day audiences for plays outside the tradition of that naturalism which seemed for a generation the normal method of the contemporary drama indicates an increasing need on the part of the audiences for experiences intenser than any which merely rational and merely realistic plays can provide.

That these audiences are actually aware of what they seek seems to me highly improbable. But they are certainly no longer, as they once tended to be, complacently superior to whatever is not prosy and

literal. Certain of the more fanciful of recent popular plays—including Maxwell Anderson's *The Star
Wagon*—seemed to me feeble or even silly; but fantasy is only imagination not powerful enough to
convince itself, and an audience which acclaimed
these plays was an audience which would have liked
to be convinced if it could. If the American drama
has an important future, I venture to suspect that it
lies in the direction of something more intense than
anything provided by any except a few of the new
works produced during the twenty years just passed.
Orson Welles with his non-realistic stagings of old
plays and Thornton Wilder with his equally frank
employment of non-representational methods have
discovered that the shortest distance between two
points may be by way of an artificial convention.
Mr. Anderson is trying to take advantage of the fact
that men may most truly reveal themselves in language better than any they have ever actually
spoken.

CHAPTER VII

POSTWAR

WITH the exception of O'Neill, no playwright who contributed to the modern American drama wrote any important work before the outbreak of the First World War. Apparently, however, that was merely an accident of time and certainly the Second War did not mark the beginning of any distinct epoch. Inevitably, a certain number of war plays appeared, notably Robert Sherwood's *There Shall Be No Night* and Lillian Hellman's *Watch on the Rhine*, but these introduced neither a new writer nor a new aspect of his talent. And it is significant that the most popular war play, *Mister Roberts* by Thomas Heggen and Joshua Logan, was a sort of sea-going *What Price Glory*, reaffirming its ribald disrespect for the pride, pomp, and circumstance of glorious war which had made the earlier play unlike anything previous in our dramatic history.

The lifting of the economic depression plus the new sense of loyalty to our government and nation had the negative effect of arresting the development of that school of left-wing propagandist drama, largely Marxian in atmosphere, which had the support of the Federal Theater and for a time was widely regarded as setting the pattern of things to come. In fact, the only playwright belonging to that school who is now very favorably remembered is Clifford Odets whose most significant plays have already been discussed.

A number of writers whose reputations were already established continued to produce, and a few of them contributed plays worthy to be compared with their previous work. Maxwell Anderson's *Anne of the Thousand Days* was a historical verse drama more or less in the manner of *Elizabeth the Queen* and his *Joan of Lorraine* also utilized a historical theme; Odets's *The Big Knife* and *The Country Girl* reflected the author's new life as a Hollywood scenarist and though they attracted renewed attention to a writer with great theatrical talent neither had the strong individuality which first distinguished him. This seemed to have disappeared with the waning of his commitment to left-wing social convictions. Sidney Howard's entertaining fantasy on the Faust theme, *Madam, Will You Walk*, was written shortly before his death but did not reach New York until 1954. O'Neill provided two major new tragedies and George Kaufman continued his success in the old line with, among others, *The Man Who Came to Dinner*, written again in collaboration with Moss Hart. But perhaps the most original new twist to smart farce comedy was given by a new writer,

Garson Kanin, whose enormously successful *Born Yesterday* tells the story of a seemingly "dumb blonde" who blossoms into social consciousness under the tutelage of a liberal journalist, turns the tables on her racketeer lover, and, reversing the old farce formula which traces the transformation of a Cinderella from glasses into glamor, traces her evolution from glamor to glasses.

In a more serious vein Thornton Wilder, previously known in the theater chiefly for *Our Town* which had been awarded the Pulitzer Prize in 1938, took that award again in 1943 for the very different *The Skin of Our Teeth* in which he uses what might be called the method of humorous surrealism to tell the whole history of civilization from the time of the cave man down to the present as though it had all happened to a certain Mr. Antrobus, his wife, and their siren-housemaid, Sabina (a veritable Lilith). Mr. Antrobus invents both the alphabet and the wheel and he survives "by the skin of his teeth" the Ice Age and a third world war—even though he is temperamentally incapable of seeing the calamities before they arrive and can never quite make up his mind how to choose between the mother of his children and the siren whose charms inspire him to conceive his happiest inventions. Some professed to find the play incomprehensible, but the allegory is transparent and to others, including the present writer, the whole was delightful.

As for the short-story writer William Saroyan, his skyrocket rose so suddenly into the theatrical firmament and then fell from it so suddenly that he seems to belong, not to a decade, but to the single year 1939 which saw the production of the only two of his several plays to win enthusiastic praise from either reviewers or the general public. But both of these pyrotechnic displays were so original and delightful that they inspired reasonable hopes which the future did not fulfill though their author has continued more successfully as a writer of short stories and sketches.

Mr. Saroyan seemed to be everything uncharacteristic of a year which was just emerging from the gloom, anger, and dismay of the depression decade which had turned the thoughts of so many of his generation toward pessimism or, more often, revolutionary proposals to shatter our world to bits in order that it might be rebuilded nearer to what they supposed to be their hearts' desire. Mr. Saroyan was gay, exuberant, romantically an individualist, and so convinced that the world was full of "beautiful people" as well as of all manner of other delightful things that we should all be happy as kings if we would only relax, "breathe in and breathe out," and, as he also put it, "believe everything." Quick fancy, exuberant humor, a real gift for words, and occasional flashes of what were almost—sometimes perhaps actually—profound insights, all combined to produce an impression of astonishing freshness. The short-length *My Heart's in the Highlands*, told—by a technique halfway to expressionism—the story of a happy-go-lucky family which is completely converted to the Saroyanism it seems to have practiced all along by the appearance of a mysterious stranger who teaches philosophy by blowing "My Heart's in the Highlands" on a bugle. *The Time of Your Life*, full length and somewhat more conventional in structure, had as its ambiguous central character a mysterious youngish man of great, unexplained wealth who spends most of his time in a raffish saloon brooding over the problems of his existence and in various seemingly minor ways playing God to the beautiful people with whom he comes in contact. Various often delightfully eccentric persons float in and out but the hero's chief miracle is bringing to self-respect and a decent way of life a sad young prostitute with no love for her profession. Here Saroyan comes closer than before to unmistakable sentimentality but is saved by bubbling humor and unexpected moments of charming fancy. That none of his subsequent plays have quite come off or achieved theatrical success may be due in part to a simple exhaustion of the vein but is probably due also to an increasing slackness in construction, and what seems to be the failure to move in any discernible direction. Mr. Saroyan's theory that one should write by simply letting oneself go may have been responsible for the spontaneity of the first two plays but is more certainly responsible for the diffuse meanderings of the others.

O'Neill was unquestionably the most discussed playwright of the twenties and Odets of the thirties. During the decade just past the distinction has been shared almost equally by two newcomers neither of whom had been heard in the New York theater before 1945: Tennessee Williams whose first Broadway production, *The Glass Menagerie*, was given the Critics Prize for the season 1944–45 and Arthur Miller whose first, *All My Sons*, received the same award for 1946–47.

Mr. Miller's work is obviously related to that produced by the "socially conscious" playwrights of the thirties and also, rather more directly than the latter were, to the explicitly "social" plays of Ibsen. *All My Sons* was concerned with a dishonest manufacturer of war materials whose own son was killed because of a defect in one of the father's products. The play exhibited a talent sufficient to cause critics to overestimate somewhat its actual merits, which are diminished by a certain stiffness and a certain irony too simple, too neat, and obviously contrived. It exhibited also what has proved to be a characteristic hesitation on the part of the author in this important respect: he seems to want to imply, without quite explicitly committing himself to the implication, that this is not merely the story of an individual guilty man but that of an evil inevitably characteristic of "our social system." *Death of a Salesman*, his most successful and best play to date, tells the story of the final dismal years of a pathetic traveling salesman who is the victim partly of his own vulgar idea of success, partly of a social system which encourages just such vulgar ideals. Despite a few expressionistic touches the method is predominantly that of a literal, Dreiseresque naturalism, and the atmosphere is that of lives unrelievedly drab while the moral is again slightly ambiguous.

Of his two subsequent full-length plays *An Enemy of the People* was a rewriting of Ibsen's play which seemed to some a perversion of the original in that it transformed the hero into a conventional modern liberal and thus rested the case for him rather upon the supposed correctness of his ideas than upon the abstract right of dissent even if it be a dissent from what passes among the intellectuals for right thinking. *The Crucible* laid its scene at the time of the Salem witchcraft trials with the obvious intention of drawing a parallel between them and the "security trials" of the present day. Its validity depends upon the validity of the parallel and those who find it invalid point out that, whereas witchcraft was pure delusion, subversion is a reality, no matter how unwisely or intemperately it may be combatted.

The plays of Tennessee Williams, like those of

Miller, are also what Shaw would have called "unpleasant plays." But in them the attention is centered persistently upon the inner life of the characters whose difficulties are presented as first of all
psychological rather than social or political—whatever the relation between these psychological problems and the society in which they live may be. The
stress is upon what is sometimes called "the irrational
element" in human life and the central personages
are neurotic rather than, as in Miller, the victims of
false convictions and an evil social system. Unfavorable critics are likely to call Miller "doctrinaire"
and "preachy"; Williams, "morbid."

He first attracted wide attention with *The Glass
Menagerie* in which an absurd and pathetic widow
who likes to think of herself as a member of the decayed Southern aristocracy, and hence the exponent
of "gracious living," is not only disappointed in her
efforts to find a husband for her shy, crippled daughter but is, in every other way, defeated by a crude
and pushing modernity which neither understands
nor respects her dream of gentility. *A Streetcar
Named Desire*, perhaps his best play, again has as its
theme a clash between an enfeebled tradition of gentility and a society which has never known what the
term means. But in this play everything is heightened and pushed further in the direction of a morbid intensity. The heroine, Blanche DuBois, has broken under the strain and is torn between her ideal of

gentility and a pathological impulse toward promiscuity, to the point where her sanity leaves her completely and she is led off to a madhouse.

Summer and Smoke seems to be essentially a more stylized version of a very similar situation. *Camino Real* and *Cat on a Hot Tin Roof* are concerned more directly, persistently, and almost exclusively with more or less outré manifestations of the sexual impulse and despite their powerful hold upon the attention (especially in the case of *Cat on a Hot Tin Roof*) they seem to the present writer less clear in their intention.

Inevitably comparisons are made between Miller and Williams on the one hand and O'Neill and Maxwell Anderson on the other. The two more recent writers are, like O'Neill and Anderson, men who achieved success with plays which can, loosely at least, be called "tragedies." In what sense are they all part of a continuing tradition? Can the works of Miller and Williams be called "true tragedies" or are they merely "unpleasant plays"?

Obviously neither Miller nor Williams plainly commits himself, as Anderson and O'Neill do, to either the form or content of classical tragedy. In his later short play, *A View from the Bridge*, Miller consciously seeks a link with classical tragedy. However, in their major plays neither he nor Williams exhibits as plainly as O'Neill a determination to seek persistently for something in the universe outside man to which he can appeal and "belong." Hence it is possible to interpret *Death of a Salesman* as brutal naturalism and *A Streetcar Named Desire* as a sort of semi-surrealist version of the Strindbergian submission to destructive obsessions. Alternately, both might perhaps be interpreted as, in a loose sense, "existentialist."

Possibly, however, there is something to be said on the opposite side and at the risk of being accused of over-interpretation I will say it. So far as *Death of a Salesman* is concerned, it is certainly intended as more than detached, "scientific" naturalism. Most spectators assume that Willy Loman is the victim of an unjust competitive society. He was first corrupted by false ideals and then exploited by those more ruthless than he. Society made him what he was and in a better society his fate would have been better.

But it is impossible thus to dismiss the play completely as no more than left-wing naturalism, because the author seems to be a sort of pluralist and his plays can be interpreted, not as a demonstration of the workings of a social determinism, but as a study of the effects of moral weakness and irresponsibility. Willy is a victim of society. But he is also a consenting victim, or a victim of himself. He accepted a vulgar, debased, and false system of values. He himself says, and the audience seems expected to believe him, that he might have led a happy life if he had followed his own bent and become, for example, a carpenter instead of submitting to the prejudice which makes a salesman more respectable than a man who works with his hands. His tragic guilt—and it then becomes his guilt rather than society's—is now a very oldfashioned one—he was not true to himself.

Seen in this light Miller is a moralist in very much the same sense that Ibsen was a moralist, and the play becomes a qualified reaffirmation of the individual's privilege of being, within certain limits, what he chooses to be.

The case of Williams is different but equally dubious. The most obvious interpretations put him among the despairing explorers of pathological states of mind just as the obvious interpretations put Miller among the sociological naturalists. In Williams's two most striking plays the central character is obsessed; and in *A Streetcar Named Desire* the obsession takes a sexual form. But in both these is another theme. Each of the heroines includes among her obsessions the fact that she is, or was, "a lady." In both the ideal of respectability, the sense that her parents and her remoter ancestors lived in accord with some code to which she herself would like to be loyal if she could, is so strong as to appear of crucial importance. In *The Glass Menagerie* the mother sees her family disintegrating because it no longer finds her dream of gentility more than annoying. In *A Streetcar Named Desire* the heroine seems to suc-

cumb to crude sexuality because she so fanatically
refused to accept a normal life among people who
appear to her as hopelessly unrefined.

Williams grew up in the South. The existence of
a decayed aristocracy was one of the inescapable
facts of the society with which he was most familiar.
Hence representatives of such decayed aristocracy
might be expected to turn up in his plays almost inevitably. But his persistent concern with them seems
to have some other significance. These helpless survivors from the past, these feeble and pathetic cling-
ers to a dead tradition, take on the importance of
symbols. They seem to mean something. Upon the
answer to the question, "What do they mean" depends the whole meaning of the plays in so far as it
is related to the question whether or not they are
tragedies in any traditional sense.

In *A Streetcar Named Desire* we see, as the curtain rises, a decayed aristocrat and fanatical "lady"
arriving to stay with her sister because she herself,
having become an obvious nymphomaniac, has lost
her job as school teacher. The sister has made what
some psychologists would call "a satisfactory adjustment." She has rejected and forgotten the tradition
of her past. She has accepted the frank squalor of
her surroundings and the ignorant brutality of her
husband. But Blanche, the nymphomaniac, is horrified by what some would call her sister's "normal-

ity." She makes a ridiculous attempt to instruct both the sister and her husband in the genteel tradition and she is violently repelled by their contented animality. And because she can lead neither their life nor the genteel life of which she dreams, the last defenses of her sanity crumble. The age has placed her in a dilemma. She looks about for a tradition according to which she may live and a civilization to which she can be loyal. She finds none. <u>Ours is a society which has lost its shape.</u>

Behind her lies a past which, at least in retrospect, seems to have been civilized. As she has good reason to know, the culture of the old South is dead. But it is the only culture she knows anything about. The world of Stella and her husband is a barbarism —some would say a vigorous barbarism, but a barbarism none the less. Blanche tries to choose the dead past and becomes the victim of an impossible choice. But she chooses this defeat rather than the "adjustment" of her sister. At least she has not succumbed to barbarism. It has been reported (whether truly or not I do not know) that when Williams himself was asked what the "lesson" of the play was he replied: "You had better look out or the apes will take over." If to say that suggests the true interpretation, then what we have is not morbidity but a choice made in the tradition of tragedy where man may be defeated but does not yield.

In any case the plays of Miller and Williams were major events in a decade of the American drama and would be the only major events had it not been for the appearance in 1956 of O'Neill's posthumous *Long Day's Journey Into Night* which unexpectedly reaffirmed his greatness.

None of the three works by O'Neill to appear after the war could be said to have done quite that. *The Iceman Cometh*, though impressive, seemed to surrender to a nihilistic pessimism which destroyed the tension of his best plays by abandoning the struggle against utter hopelessness. Neither *A Moon for the Misbegotten* nor *A Touch of the Poet* (neither of which reached Broadway) revealed any new aspect of his talent or achieved an expression of it equal to that in his best previous work. In fact, O'Neill threatened to retreat into the past. Critics were sometimes saying that he had been overestimated; the few revivals of his work were not very successful; and there was some tendency to regard him as only "historically important." But *Long Day's Journey Into Night* is certain to encourage reexamination and an upward reassessment.

Frankly autobiographical, the great length is justified by the effect of solidity which the length makes possible. The names given to the characters are not their real names but there is no attempt to disguise anything and the play frankly presents the real persons and the relationship between them as they appeared to O'Neill himself.

Nor is there any sparing of anyone. The actor-father is a congenital bohemian, talented but unstable and without self-knowledge or artistic integrity. He is lavish with his boon companions and reckless in making foolish investments, but niggardly with his family and incapable of understanding that wives and children need some kind of stability in their lives. The mother, after a long struggle to make the home that cannot be made under such conditions, has retired into a dream world sustained by the narcotics supplied by an unscrupulous physician. The two sons react similarly, but with a difference. One becomes a cynic and a wastrel. The other, who is of course the playwright himself, intellectualizes his own reactions and responds to his own tragic situation by the development of a tragic philosophy of life.

When the play opens the family is still precariously intact. Each member is still attempting to conceal the depths of his resentments. But during the day which the action covers the final debacle takes place. At the day's end there is a family no longer because things have been said and situations acknowledged which can never be retracted or again hidden. The author himself has learned beyond a doubt that he is tubercular and is about to depart for the sanitarium, perhaps to die. The dramatic irony consists, of course, in the fact that the audience knows something no character guesses : namely, that from this seemingly hopeless debacle a playwright will emerge.

With the minor exception of the comedy *Ah, Wilderness!*, none of O'Neill's other successful plays is so purely domestic or remains so consistently upon the level of the merely literal and rational without even a suggestion of symbolism. Yet the remarkable fact is that without transcending the limits of domestic drama it manages to involve by implication the large themes with which O'Neill has always been concerned.

Since the play is so frankly autobiographical it would have considerable interest if it were no more than a confession and even if it were inferior as drama. But it is so far from being inferior as drama that it would be powerful and absorbing if there were no known connection between it and the actual events of the author's life. It would still raise as it does those unanswerable questions which lie at the heart of drama.

Two such questions are here linked together and the first is the question of a human being's responsibility for his own character and fate. The family involved was as doomed as any generation of the house of Atreus. But to what extent is that doom self-imposed?

Each member is determined to exculpate himself,

to lay the blame elsewhere. The mother blames the
father for the parsimony and irresponsibility which
have driven her to drugs. The wastrel brother blames
both for having given him no example and no home.
The poet-to-be blames them for all this plus the
neglect of his illness which has driven him to despair. But is it or is it not still true that, despite this
welter of exculpation and blame, each is in his own
way guilty because he has used the character and the
actions of the others as an excuse for his own failures? Why does one son succumb to circumstances
and the other triumph over them? Is the fault in
the stars or in ourselves that we are thus and so?

The second fundamental question is posed in the
case of the hero alone. He is telling us very frankly
the outward and very special reasons which might
be said to account for the sombreness of his view of
human life. Does this mean, as some psychologists
would maintain, that this explains or explains away
his philosophy? It is, so they would say, only a rationalization and generalization of his own experience. To them what appears to be the tragic sense of
life expressed in his plays is "nothing but" the mal-
adjustment produced by a singularly unhappy childhood and youth. To them O'Neill was a man un-
derstandably but merely sick, one whose morbid
fancies may be easily dismissed by those who are
"normal" and "adjusted."

But thus we may attempt to explain away not

only O'Neill but all writers who have had a tragic view of life. Is the conclusion really justified? All men have had experiences of one sort or another which have influenced them. But are their thoughts, and feelings, and beliefs "nothing but" these influences? Are their conclusions "nothing but" a rationalization? Or are they instead general truths which individual experience has enabled them to discover? Do O'Neill's plays really mean nothing except that he happened to have an unhappy childhood and youth? Or is there really, as O'Neill believed, a heart of darkness within the human soul which some are led to discover and some are not?

These two great questions, the question of human responsibility for what is called Fate and the question of what general truth the tragic situation illustrates, are perhaps the questions which true tragedy always raises. A play which raises them so urgently, while at the same time telling a powerful, convincing, and absorbing story is a major contribution to our dramatic literature.

INDEX

340 *Index*